Media in the Middle East

Nele Lenze · Charlotte Schriwer
Zubaidah Abdul Jalil
Editors

Media in the Middle East

Activism, Politics, and Culture

Editors
Nele Lenze
Middle East Institute
National University of Singapore
Singapore, Singapore

Zubaidah Abdul Jalil
Middle East Institute
National University of Singapore
Singapore, Singapore

Charlotte Schriwer
Middle East Institute
National University of Singapore
Singapore, Singapore

ISBN 978-3-319-65770-7   ISBN 978-3-319-65771-4   (eBook)
DOI 10.1007/978-3-319-65771-4

Library of Congress Control Number: 2017951532

Cover image: © Oleksandr Rupeta/Alamy Stock Photo

Printed on acid-free paper

This Palgrave Macmillan imprint is published by Springer Nature
The registered company is Springer International Publishing AG
The registered company address is: Gewerbestrasse 11, 6330 Cham, Switzerland

CONTENTS

Part I   On Media Activism and Political Involvement

1   **Revisiting Cyberactivism Six Years after the Arab Spring:
    Potentials, Limitations and Future Prospects**   3
    Sahar Khamis

2   **Constructing an Alternative Public Sphere: The Cultural
    Significance of Social Media in Iran**   21
    Gi Yeon Koo

3   **You've Come A Long Way Baby: Women's New Media
    Practices, Empowerment, and Everyday Life in Kuwait
    and the Middle East**   45
    Deborah L. Wheeler

**Part II   On Governmental and Non-Governmental Media
             Organisations**

4   **Location, Regulation, and Media Production
    in the Arab World: A Case Study of Media Cities**   71
    Yushi Chiba

5 Preventing a Mobilization from Spreading:
   Assad and the Electronic War   89
   Matthieu Rey

6 Spectacles of Terror: Media and the Cultural Production
   of Terrorism   107
   Suzi Mirgani

Part III   Media, Culture and Language in the Middle East

7 Winning Hearts and Minds through Soft Power:
   The Case of Turkish Soap Operas in the Middle East   145
   Jana Jabbour

8 Locating Emirati Filmmaking within Globalizing
   Media Ecologies   165
   Dale Hudson

9 Protest Poetry On- and Offline: Trans-regional
   Interactions in the Arabian Gulf: An Example
   from Bahrain   203
   Nele Lenze

10 Arabic in a Time of Revolution: Sociolinguistic
   Notes from Egypt   223
   Ivan Panovic

Index   257

EDITORS AND CONTRIBUTORS

About the Editors

Nele Lenze is a Visiting Assistant Professor a GUST and a Senior Research Fellow at National University of Singapore. She holds a PhD in Middle East Studies and Media Studies from the University of Oslo where she lectured on the Arab online sphere. She obtained her master's in Arabic literature from Freie University Berlin. Lenze co-edited *Converging Regions: Global Perspectives on Asia and the Middle East* (2014) with Charlotte Schriwer as well as *The Arab Uprisings: Catalysts, Dynamics, and Trajectories* (2014) with Fahed Al-Sumait and Michael Hudson. Her first monograph *Politics and Digital Literature in the Middle East. Perspectives on Online Text and Context* is forthcoming in 2018.

Charlotte Schriwer is a researcher who has focused mainly on the history of the Levant, (Jordan, Syria, Lebanon), in particular on its agricultural history from the twelfth century to the 1800s. She has also explored the question of ethnic identity in the Ottoman architecture of the Levant. Since joining Middle East Institute in 2011, she has started a project documenting the history of protest art in the Arab world, with a focus on the Arab Uprisings. She holds a Ph.D. in History and an M.A. in Middle East Studies from the University of St Andrews, Scotland, and an M.A. in Islamic Art and Archaeology from the School of Oriental and African Studies in London. Charlotte Schriwer co-edited Converging

Regions: Global Perspectives on Asia and the Middle East (2014) with Nele Lenze.

Zubaidah Abdul Jalil graduated with a Bachelor's in Business Management (BBM) from Singapore Management University. She lived in the Middle East for an extended period of time, having studied in Amman, Jordan and at the Sultan Qaboos College in Oman. She currently works as Publications Executive at the NUS Middle East Institute.

Contributors

Lina Ben Mhenni is an activist, author of the popular blog "A Tunisian Girl," and a Teaching Assistant in Linguistics at the Faculty of Human and Social Sciences, Tunis University. After unrest began in Tunisia in December 2010, she travelled across the country to take photos and video footage of the protests and of people who were attacked in the ensuing government crackdowns. She also reported for many websites and news TV channels (Al Jazeera, Al Jazeera English, France24) when foreign journalists could not access the country. Her book, *Tunisian girl, la bloggeuse de la révolution*, has been translated into several languages.

Yushi Chiba is a Research Fellow of the Japan Society for the Promotion of Science. He holds a Ph.D. in Area Studies from Kyoto University. He is the author of *Contemporary Arab Media: From Transnational Radio to Satellite TV* (2014, Japanese); "The Geographical Transformation of Arab Media: The Decline of Offshore Media and the Rise of the Media City," *Asian and African Studies* Vol. 12 No. 1 (2012); and "A Comparative Study on the Pan-Arab Media Strategies: The Cases of Egypt and Saudi Arabia," *Kyoto Bulletin of Islamic Area Studies* Vol. 5 No. 1 (2012).

Dale Hudson is an Associate Teaching Professor of Film and New Media and Curator of Film and New Media at New York University Abu Dhabi (NYUAD). He has a M.A. from New York University, and earned his Ph.D. from the University of Massachusetts (Amherst). With Patricia R. Zimmermann, he co-authored *Thinking through Digital Media: Transnational Environments and Locative Places* (London: Palgrave, 2015). As a digital curator for the Finger Lakes Environmental Film Festival (FLEFF), he curated "Viral Dissonance" in 2014. Hudson was also a member of the pre-selection committee for the 2014 Abu Dhabi Film Festival (ADFF).

Jana Jabbour is a Ph.D. in Political Science and International Relations (Sciences Po Paris). She is a lecturer at Sciences Po Paris, and a research associate at Centre de Recherches Internationales (CERI) and Institut de Recherches sur le Moyen-Orient (IREMMO), where her research and publications mostly focus on the MENA region's political economy and international relations. She is also a co-founder of a research group on "Rising powers in the international system" whose aim is to examine the role of the BRICS and other rising middle powers in world governance.

Sahar Khamis is Associate Professor at the University of Maryland. She is an expert on Arab and Muslim media, and the former Head of the Mass Communication and Information Science Department in Qatar University. She is a former Mellon Islamic Studies Initiative Visiting Professor at the University of Chicago. She is the co-author of the books: *Islam Dot Com: Contemporary Islamic Discourses in Cyberspace* (London: Palgrave Macmillan, 2009) and *Egyptian Revolution 2.0: Political Blogging, Civic Engagement and Citizen Journalism* (London: Palgrave Macmillan, 2013). Additionally, she authored and co-authored numerous book chapters, journal articles and conference papers, regionally and internationally, in both English and Arabic. Khamis is a media commentator and analyst, a public speaker, a human rights commissioner, and a radio host.

Gi Yeon Koo is a researcher at the Institute of Cross Cultural Studies in Seoul National University and a post-doctoral fellow of Hanyang University in South Korea. She is also teaching at Yonsei University. She received her Ph.D. degree in Cultural Anthropology from Seoul National University. She recently published an article entitled, "Women as Subject of Defiance and Everyday Politics of Hijab as Dress Code in Modern Iran," *Asian Women*, Vol. 30 No. 4 (2014).

Suzi Mirgani is Manager and Editor for Publications at the Center for International and Regional Studies, Georgetown University School of Foreign Service in Qatar. She received a Ph.D. in Communication and Media Studies from Eastern Mediterranean University. She co-edited *Food Security in the Middle East* (2014), and *Bullets and Bulletins: Media and Politics in the Wake of the Arab Uprisings* (forthcoming). Mirgani is also an independent filmmaker, and writer and director of several short films, including "Hind's Dream," which was selected for the Short Film Corner at the 2015 Cannes Film Festival.

Ivan Panovic is an Assistant Professor in the Division of Linguistics and Multilingual Studies at Nanyang Technological University. He has an M.A. in Sociology & Anthropology from the American University in Cairo, and a D.Phil. in Oriental Studies from the University of Oxford. He co-authored Working with Written Discourse (2014) with Deborah Cameron. Panovic also presented "Fresh History, Stale Hopes: an Anthropological Reading of Early Literary Engagements with the Egyptian Revolution," and "Another Word on the Wall: Graffiti in Cairo in the Service of the Revolution," at the 2013 and 2012 Middle East Studies Association Annual Meetings, respectively.

Matthieu Rey is an Assistant Professor in Collège de France (Paris-France). He holds a Ph.D. in History from the École des hautes études en sciences sociales (EHESS, Paris). His recent publications are "'Fighting Colonialism' versus 'Non-Alignment': Two Arab Points of View on the Bandung Conference," in *The Non-Aligned Movement and the Cold War* eds. Natasa Miskovic et al. (2014) and "Une dècennie de silence: les Kurdes à l'heure de l'absence de rébellion (1946–1958)," (A Decade of Silence: the Kurds During the Absence of Rebellious Movements (1946–1958)), in *Enjeux identitaires en mutation: Europe et bassin méditerranéen* (Identity Issues in Transition: Europe and the Mediterranean Region), eds. John Tolan et al. (2014). He also intends to publish a book on the parliamentary system in Iraq and Syria between 1946 and 1963.

Deborah L. Wheeler is an Associate Professor of Political Science at the United States Naval Academy. She holds an M.A. and a Ph.D. in Political Science from the University of Chicago. Her Senior Fulbright research grant to Kuwait allowed her to publish *The Internet in the Middle East: Global Expectations and Local Imaginations in Kuwait* (2005) and also a series of articles. She co-authored a chapter with Lauren Mintz, entitled "Girls Just Want to Have Fun? Internet Leisure and Women's Empowerment in Jordan," in *Handbook on the Economics of Leisure*, ed. Samuel Cameron (2011). She also contributed a chapter, "Does the Internet Empower? A Look at the Internet and International Development," in *Handbook of Internet Studies* (2011).

LIST OF FIGURES

Fig. 2.1   Internet Users (Per 100 People)   26
Fig. 2.2   Mobile cellular subscriptions (per 100 people)   26
Fig. 2.3   Fixed Broadband Subscriptions (per 100 people)   27
Fig. 2.4   Some pictures used as Facebook profiles during the Green
            Movement   31
Fig. 2.5   Screenshot of forbidden website, taken by researcher in 2009   32
Fig. 2.6   Screenshot of forbidden websites, taken by researcher in 2014   33
Fig. 2.7   "My Stealthy Freedom" Facebook page ("My Stealthy
            Freedom," Facebook, accessed February 20, 2016,
            https://www.facebook.com/StealthyFreedom.)   33
Fig. 3.1   You've come a long way baby?   46
Fig. 3.2   Arab Woman, 1905–1906; John Singer Sargent. Metropolitan
            Museum of Art, New York   61
Fig. 8.1   A screening by Cinema Akil, Dubai   171
Fig. 8.2   An outdoor screening at Cinema Akil, Alserkal
            Avenue, Dubai   174
Fig. 8.3   Animated opening title for *The Gamboo3a Revolution* (2012)   195
Fig. 8.4   Scene from *The Gamboo3a Revolution* (2012)   196
Fig. 10.1   Shit happens (Arabic-scripted English)   247
Fig. 10.2   @آتِن الغضَبُ الساطعُ ('The glaring anger is arriving')   248

LIST OF TABLES

Table 3.1   Women's empowerment measurements   53
Table 5.1   Internet coverage in Syria since 2000   92
Table 10.1   Resources in contemporary writing practices in Egypt   238
Table 10.2   Egyptian tweets exemplifying the script-variety
             recombinations presented in Table 10.1   238
Table 10.3   Mixing of literary resources within single tweets   239

PROLOGUE

ONLINE ACTIVISM AND THE ARAB UPRISINGS: FOCUS ON THE TUNISIAN EXPERIENCE

In this chapter, Lina Ben Mhenni offers a first-hand activist's perspective of online activism in Tunisia during the Arab Uprisings.

Just after the ouster of the dictator Zine al Abidine Ben Ali from Tunisia on the 14th of January 2011, and with the beginning of the Arab Uprisings, experts, journalists, researchers, and people around the world highlighted the role of online activism in the Tunisian Revolution and during the tide of mass protests that swept through North Africa and the Middle East that followed.

People around the globe started talking about a "Facebook Revolution", an "Internet Revolution", a "Twitter Revolution", or a "2.0 Revolution". They shed light on the crucial role bloggers and cyberactivists played in the toppling of the despot. The domino effect that occurred subsequently in other parts of the Arab World further consolidated this idea, dealt with extensively in articles, books and media programs.

For months, we did nothing but thoroughly study social media networks and analyze their role in fulfilling the hopes and dreams of the Tunisian and Egyptian youths. It was said that these youth, who had longed for a total rupture from the old governance, which had marginalized and drove them away from public participation for several generations, had finally succeeded in toppling at least two regimes, by leveraging Information and Communication Technologies (ICT).

But how true are these claims? What was the role played by the Internet and online activists in the Arab Uprisings, and in the Tunisian revolution in particular? Can we really start and lead a revolution by just using the Internet?

Furthermore, what was the role of the Internet after the ouster of these dictators? Did cyberactivists succeed in using it to fulfill democratic transitions?

I will try to answer these questions in this, chapter focusing on the Tunisian context. I will start with the role of online activism prior to the revolutionary process in Tunisia on December 17, 2010, followed by its role during the Tunisian uprisings, from December 17, 2010 to January 14, 2011. After that I will deal with the role of social media and online activism after the ouster of the despot Ben Ali. To finish, I will tackle the issue of how successful online activism is.

Background and the role of online activism under the regime of Ben Ali

In order to understand the role of online activism under the regime of the dictator Ben Ali, we have to look at the context of that period.

Indeed, for more than half a century, my country did not experience more than two presidents. Both of those presidents were forced to leave office, the first following a coup hatched by his successor, and the second under popular demand for his departure from office. In January 2011, he cowardly fled the wrath of youth; youth who challenged his oppressive forces, his minions, and the omnipotence of his party-state.

When the events started, Tunisians did not only live in difficult economic and social situations caused by the spread of mafia-type practices and aggravated by corruption and nepotism, but they were also prevented from expressing themselves freely. They had to live both in fear and misery. The causes for the Tunisian revolt can be summarized by the slogan that was widely chanted from December 2010 to January 2011: "Employment, Freedom, Dignity". I find it necessary to start by contextualizing things in order to remind you that the online activism movement had started long before Mohamed Bouazizi's self-immolation, an event generally considered as the first spark of the Arab Uprisings.

Rather, the online fight for freedom of speech, freedom and dignity started years before. In fact, at the time, in a media landscape that was characterized by its lack of diversity and monopoly by state actors, blogs and social networks (mainly Facebook and Twitter) played two important roles: First, they gradually became the most reliable and well-fed sources of information; Second, they represented an essential and effective tool for online mobilization. The despotic regime underestimated what such tools could bring to the Tunisian youth as they defied censorship, the complicity of the Tunisian elite with the regime, and the shameful silence of the West. When the dictator and his regime were working to muzzle Tunisians its youth defied them using these new tools to break the wall of silence and unveil the truth.

Long before December the 17, 2010, online activists conducted online campaigns that deeply embarrassed the autocratic regime. Some of these campaigns were meant to support prisoners of conscience, and to advocate for freedom of speech prior to December 2010. These include inhabitants of the Gafsa Mining Basin and the social movement they started in 2008 to denounce the marginalization of their area, corruption and nepotism. At that time, online activism was mainly relegated to blogs. I personally started my blog in 2007. I mainly wanted to express myself and to share my passion for writing with an audience in the absence of other channels and platforms to do it. I was writing about different subjects, including cinema, literature, tourism, love, etc. The blog was some sort of a personal diary. Progressively, however, I found myself involved in human rights and political issues. Having no way to express myself politically, blogging on the Internet helped me to take an antagonistic stance against the regime.

I started to tackle some social and political problems in my country. And I think that it is worth mentioning here that I grew up in a family of dissidents and that my father was a political prisoner under the regime of Habib Bourguiba, the first Tunisian president. This allowed me to have an opinion different from the one disseminated by the unique party and its propaganda machine. I also had a plethora of opportunities to discover different parts of my country and to notice the gap between the official discourse promoting the image of a prosperous Tunisia and the sad reality that I saw on the ground. For years, we have been hearing about the Tunisian economic miracle, human rights respect, democracy, etc. But the reality was different. Each time I visited a small village in a remote area I saw poverty, absence of basic infrastructure, and marginalization.

I tried to write about all that. I tried to voice the pain and grief of voiceless people. I thus became a regular blogger, writing every day. I became addicted to blogging in general, and to reporting human rights violations as well as social and political problems in particular. I had the opportunity to meet other Tunisian and foreign bloggers longing for freedom and justice. I joined their different online actions mainly to denounce human rights violations or to uncover the misdeeds of the regime. I took part in different collective online campaigns to: claim freedom of speech, support people imprisoned for voicing their opinions, or denounce injustice. Nevertheless, the social movement of Gafsa Mining Basin has been a critical point in my blogging activity. At the time I was blogging on my own blog and different other collective blogs created to support the inhabitants of the area. The regime intensified the frequency of censorship actions targeting blogs. This drove bloggers, including me, to launch online campaigns against censorship. Censorship could have silenced bloggers but personally it drove me to speak louder and clear.

While blogs tend to be rather individual, bloggers connect to one another thanks to aggregators and hypertext links. This is why the information could not spread widely, as was the case with Mohamed Bouazizi's self-immolation. The dissemination of the information was limited only to bloggers and to those interested in following them.

Nevertheless, the turning point was the demonstration against censorship. Organized on May 22, 2010 as part of a worldwide event, Tunisian activists geared up to peacefully demonstrate against "Ammar 404". Ammar 404 is an imaginary (http://www.facebook.com/ammar404) person Tunisians have created to symbolize their country's *filtering* of the Internet, and a pun on the "error 404" messages users received when they tried to access censored content online. I call this "a turning point" because this demonstration allowed online activism to meet the real world. It paved the way for real-life participation and reopened the streets for protesters. Online activists left their screens and keyboards and challenged the authorities on the ground. They succeeded in mobilizing people to take to the streets through the use of irony, humor, videos, songs and various peaceful means of action. I was one of the organizers of that demonstration and this put me as a target of the wrath of the regime. Signing the notice to the ministry of interior had been considered as crime and there had been a price to pay. Few days, before the demonstration policemen broke into my parents' house to steal my laptop, cameras, and all my documents. But on the date of the demonstration I had on the street, facing the anger and violence of hundreds of policemen mobilized for the occasion.

Thus, not only did the Internet and online activism allow for the dissemination of information in a country characterized by information blackouts and the absence of freedom of speech; it also served as a catalyst and an agent of mobilization for concrete actions. The online and offline fields of battle merged as the virtual world met the real one.

Online activism presented a threat to the regime, which was why it resorted not only to censorship, but also to the arrest and the imprisonment of cyberactivists who had to pay the price for their activism efforts. Zouhair Yahyaoui, who was the first cyber dissident to be arrested and imprisoned in Tunisia, is considered as a martyr of the Internet as he died of a heart attack on March 13th, 2015 from the weakening of his body by hunger strikes, torture and ill-treatment. Similarly, Fatma Arabicca is another blogger who had been detained for seven days in 2009.

Therefore, online activism in Tunisia started long before the revolution. From the late 1990s, online activists used the Internet as a tool of contest and protest. In the beginning, online activists used forums and blogs to share their ideas and opinions and to denounce the wrongs of the regime, human rights violations, cases of censorship, and so on. They were tracked by the cyberpolice and faced censorship, assaults, and arrests. Nevertheless, the impact of the online activism movement remained relatively limited as it was mainly linked to blogs with a limited audience and was easily censored.

One of the important stages of the online activism movement had been the transition from online activism to real world activism through a demonstration against censorship organized on May 22, 2010. Subsequently, online activists (mainly bloggers), started to use social networks to disseminate their ideas and organize online campaigns to support a plethora of causes.

Role of Online Activism During the Uprising

When Mohamed Bouazizi set his body on fire on December 17, 2010, online activists used the Internet and their knowledge of ICT to spread the truth about what was going on and to mobilize their compatriots to act. They succeeded in showing that young Tunisians could challenge the regime and its oppressive forces. The youth offered their bare chests to the bullets and truncheons of the repressive forces. They inhaled tear gas and slept on public squares. Moreover, many of them mastered computer skills and new technologies of information, and managed to go through the threads of the wall of silence and the leaden shroud that muzzled our country for decades.

While the majority of local TV channels, radio stations, and newspapers continue to spread the propaganda of the regime and were working to falsify facts and fool the world, online activists were struggling to circumvent censorship, disseminate information, and mobilize the people. They also organized protest actions widely shared on social media and widely relayed by international media at a time when even foreign journalists were refused entry into the country. Some online activists traveled the country to cover live protest movements and show to the world that the situation in Tunisia was critical. Again online activists had to pay the price of their activism. Several of them were arrested in the beginning of January 2011. In his last speech, delivered on January 13, 2011, Ben Ali announced the lifting of censorship on the Internet as well as the release of arrested online activists in an attempt to placate the youth. However, this failed, as on the very same night online activists were mobilizing people to take to the streets on January 14, 2011 to demand the departure of Ben Ali.

As a blogger I didn't even think about what I had had to do when I had heard the news of the self-immolation of Mohamed Bouazizi. When Mohamed Bouazizi burned himself alive I was totally shocked, but not really surprised. A few months earlier other young Tunisians had done the same in Monastir out of their deep sense of despair. But let me say that at first the indifference of the majority of people around me stifled me. I was following the news of the demonstrations in Sidi Bouzid and I was at the same time bewildered by the indifference around me in the capital. We had to wait few days before seeing any reaction in the big cities of Tunisia. I started following what was happening and trying to write about it after checking the reliability of the news thanks to a network of friends: mainly activists and lawyers who had been eyewitnesses of the events in different areas and regions of the country. I had been sharing the news and the different developments on my blog, and Facebook and Twitter accounts. I could barely sleep at this time; I had to be connected 24/7. On December 25, 2010, I took part in the first demonstration to support the inhabitants of Sidi Bouzid and the different social movements. I had been there as an angry citizen, but also as a reporter, blogger. I had been taking photos, recording videos, but also sharing lives from the demonstrations. Until January 8, 2011, I did that work on a daily basis as the rhythm of demonstrations had been growing day after day. I had acquired a habit. Once at home, I shared all that I had gathered: information, photos, and videos on my blog with texts in Arabic, French, and English to reach a large audience around the world. International media started to contact me as a source of information and I also started to appear on news TV channels (using Skype) to give the latest information.

Starting from January 8, I had decided to go to Sidi Bouzid and Kasserine, the sites of the biggest and the most violent clashes between the security forces and protestors. There, I witnessed the atrocities that had been taking place. I took photos of the corpses of young people killed by bullets. I recorded the testimonies of their mothers. I had found myself in the middle of violent demonstrations, inhaling the tear gas and risking the truncheons of the police. As usual, I had been sharing all my work on social media, and answering the hundreds of e-mails I had been receiving from foreign journalists around the world, appearing on different programs and reporting what was happening.

On January 12, I returned to the capital. It was the first day of a curfew announced by the regime. Nevertheless, I kept on moving from one place to another to show what was happening. Violent clashes had been taking place in the poor quarters neighboring the capital.

On January 14, 2011, I had been protesting outside the Ministry of Interior, as was the case for hundreds of thousands of Tunisians who had taken to the streets to oust the dictator. That day also, I was a citizen, a blogger, and reporter. I had been using the Internet to share what was happening with the entire world.

I will underline the fact that the ouster of Ben Ali happened thanks to those women, men, the young and the old alike, and those who defied their fear and faced the indiscriminate violence and repression from the security forces. The presence on the ground, demonstrations, marches and sit-ins of hundreds of thousands of Tunisians made the regime wobble. There were more than 300 martyrs; women and men sacrificed their lives for freedom. It is important to note that this happened in real life, not online. It is true that online activists contributed in unveiling the truth and helped to mobilize people, but we must not forget that the hundreds of thousands of people and the different social organizations who supported them were the ones who made a difference and made the dream a reality. The revolt movement originated in the remote marginalized parts of the country, where people were demanding their right to employment, social justice, and dignity. It is true that the Internet played a role, but that role has been exaggerated. We must not forget that access to the Internet remains limited in Tunisia. According to Internet World Stats, the number of Internet users was estimated at 3.6 million for a total population of 11 million.

The Internet and social media attracted such attention that people turned to them as legitimate sources of information, including foreign media outlets that started sharing material produced by online activists. In fact, the Internet and social media replaced the mass media on the national level and were able to attract the interest of some foreign media that started to share materials produced by online activists before being able to send reporters to Tunisia. Online activists were successful in generating revolutionary content that they distributed to their online networks as well as to their families, friends, and acquaintances. The usually evoked conflict between traditional mass media and online media gave way to collaboration and complementarity. This complementarity facilitated the spread of information and the mobilization of people.

To conclude: While the role of social media was important during the revolution, it was the mobilization of people on the ground that proved to be the decisive factor.

Role of Online Activism in Tunisia after the Ouster of the Dictator

The departure of Ben Ali heralded a new phase of Tunisia's history. After a few months of revolutionary euphoria, however, Tunisians realized and understood that toppling a dictator was only the first step; it does not necessarily establish freedom and prosperity. This is why different demonstrations and sit-ins were held after the ouster of Ben Ali and the majority of people used social media to mobilize their compatriots and invite them to support their causes. In addition, many experts, researchers, journalists, and politicians around the world focused on the role of online activism in the Tunisian Revolution and in the outbreak of different revolutionary movements in the Middle East and in other parts of the world, such as the Occupy Movement in different parts of the world and the Indignant Movement in Spain. Online activism and social media were presented as unique tools that allowed these revolt movements to happen. Online activists and bloggers were glorified and gained acclaim. This focus on the role of ICT and online activism, and the illusion of infinite power that was linked to them, was tempting for most political parties and segments of civil society. They worked on exploiting the Internet and its networks to consolidate their position in a country that was going through a democratic transition. They wanted to acquire more space on the net, so they recruited young people and paid them not only to disseminate their propaganda but also to discredit and defame their opponents through rumors, lies and dishonest online campaigns. Some political parties were, in fact, so focused on gaining traction on the net that they forgot about the fieldwork, resulting in total failure. The miraculous tool became a double-edged sword. According to Internet World Stats, the number of Facebook users in Tunisia expanded exponentially, from 16,000 users in the beginning of 2008 to 1.8 million in 2011. Even professional journalists started relying on Facebook as a legitimate source of information, which led to unreliable information being reported and disseminated.

Importantly, the online activism landscape changed after the collapse of the previous Ben Ali regime. It is true that some people, groups, and civil society kept using this tool positively. However, some online activists, who were committed and devoted to the cause of their country, as well as a significant number of young people, became the lackeys of political parties, using their knowledge in the service of their interests. Unfortunately, clashes between different political parties and ideologies invaded the net.

In general, Tunisians overestimated the role of social networks and forgot that they had to combine real and online actions to achieve their goals. Today some people think that a simple click on a like button of an event or demonstration is sufficient to initiate change. This is why a gap exists between the number of online protesters and those who are really present on the ground. Generally, online support does not convert into real support.

Another alarming fact today is the invasion of the Internet by terrorists, who are using social media for different evil goals; to facilitate the recruitment of new members of terrorist groups and to allow for the rapid and widespread dissemination of propaganda that are produced by groups such as ISIS. Some people started to want to have recourse to censorship but online activists do not see it as the right solution. The debate is still ongoing.

Conclusion

For years, activist users of the Internet have helped to break the authoritarian control of the public space. During the Tunisian Revolution, the Internet, and Facebook in particular, had been used widely by Tunisians to circumvent censorship and regime propaganda that dominated traditional media. Despite the fact that the use of the Internet for protest purposes in Tunisia was not new and has steadily developed since the late 1990s, the significance of its role during the Tunisian Revolution—and in other Arab countries—turned it into a legitimate medium of information. However, while the Internet and online activism played a crucial role, we must not forget that it is just a tool. It is not an autonomous actor. Other factors are also important in achieving change.

After the liberation of the public space, online activism plays a different role; that of building a functional public space leading to the building of democracy. Some people are using it in the right way. Others are not.

Moreover, we have to keep in mind that the use of social media tools do not have a single preordained outcome. The failure of the Iranian Green Movement or of the Syrian Revolution are good examples of the arbitrariness of the efficiency of information and communication technologies (ICTs) and online activism.

Lina Ben Mhenni

INTRODUCTION

POLITICS AND MEDIA IN THE MIDDLE EAST:
CROSSING DISCIPLINES AND GEOGRAPHIES

Internet access is becoming more affordable and accessible the world over, and has had a particular impact on Middle Eastern countries. Satellite TV is also playing an increasingly larger role, both regionally and internationally, in spreading news and propaganda, while the local film and TV industries are also rapidly expanding in the Middle East. Internet connections and mobile applications have emerged as indispensable tools of information acquisition and dissemination, and, as a result, as activism. The result of this media explosion is that its role in political movements has become a prominent and often controversial topic of debate in the news and in academic circles. *Media in the Middle East: Activism, Politics, and Culture* brings together the insights and analyses of academic specialists best placed to investigate, evaluate, and understand the mounting issues and questions of emerging media trends in the region.

Recent political developments related to the media in the Arab World, Turkey and Iran are the subject of this volume and will be discussed with a focus on perceptions of the media's influence on regional and global change. The role of media will be evaluated through a variety of approaches: media studies, general Middle East studies, anthropology, film studies, linguistics and political science. In addition, first-hand accounts of media activists, as well as studies resulting from long-term field research by prominent scholars, contribute to a broad and interdisciplinary approach. Contributors to this volume offer perspectives from East Asia to West Asia, and from Europe to the USA.

This collection of research papers focuses on the broader aspects of media institutions, digital news and online activism, all of which continue to contribute to a rapidly growing media scene in the region. The wide range of chapters discuss political blogging and citizen journalism, social media and participation culture, as well as visual and textual cultural production.

One voice that many have deemed worth hearing is that of Lina Ben Mehnni, who runs the blog *atunisiangirl.blogspot.com*. Her Prologue, *Online Activism and the Arab Uprisings: Focus on the Tunisian Experience*, deals with online media's role during the Tunisian uprising, where she gives first- hand insights into a media activist's understanding of the events. As the only non-academic chapter in the volume, it provides a unique, insider perspective of Tunisian events as they unfold on the ground. After the ouster of Ben Ali from Tunisia and the spread of the uprisings in other parts of the Arab World, the role of online activism in the so-called "Arab Spring" have led some to call it the "Internet Revolution", the "Facebook Revolution", and the "2.0 Revolution". Ben Mehnni evaluates how much truth lies in these claims and identifies the role of online activists in the Arab uprisings in general, and in the Tunisian Revolution in particular.

Media in the Middle East: Activism, Politics, and Culture is divided into three parts that are connected through their analysis of media usage related to political activities; these can be state-run, activist-organized or political media usage connected to cultural production. Part I of the volume focuses on activism and social developments, while Part II investigates media usage by political bodies and terrorist organizations. Part III goes deeper into visual media and language-based media usage in the Middle East.

Part I, *On Media Activism and Political Involvement*, offers an introduction to ongoing activism and societal participation in political developments related to media usage. Media expert Sahar Khamis sets the context of this volume by providing a general evaluation of cyberactivisim in Egypt with her opening chapter *Revisiting Cyberactivism Five Years after the Arab Spring: Potentials, Limitations and Future Prospects*. Social media played a crucial role in the instigation and orchestration of the sweeping wave of political change that has taken place in the Middle East in recent years. She addresses the potential, limitations and future prospects of cyberactivism and the Arab Uprisings. In particular, Khamis revisits the role played by social media in aiding political transformation six years after the eruption of the "Arab Spring".

Gi Yeon Koo builds on this firsthand experience by delving into social media as an alternative public sphere for women in Iran. Like old media that produced the symbols and recognitions that contributed to the successful Islamic Revolution, new media is leading the discourses that threaten the current Islamic authority. In spite of the limitations on freedom of expression and Internet accessibility, satellite TV, and mobile phones, Iranians participate in creating transnational discourses concerning human rights or democratization in private spheres through social media. This chapter examines some of these narratives, which are built around the formation of alternative public and private social media spheres.

In her chapter *Women Working Around the State: Digital Activism & Everyday Life Resistance in the Middle East*, Deborah L. Wheeler shares her insights based on almost twenty years of women's interaction in Kuwait and Saudi Arabia. From the right to drive (Saudi Arabia), the freedom to vote and express themselves more openly (Kuwait), the right to fight back against sexual harassment (Egypt), and the smile as a resistance campaign (Turkey), women are using digital media to confront the state, enhance their agency, and change their life circumstances. Through this analysis of the use of new media amongst women in the Middle East, Deborah L. Wheeler examines some emerging implications for formal power relations and the role of women within them.

All of the chapters in Part I discuss social change and activist participation represented mostly in online media. In all three contributions, human interaction and development plays a central role in achieving change. The claiming of spaces on- and offline is an aspect that is emphasized in each of these chapters.

The second part of *Media in the Middle East: Activism, Politics, and Culture* deals with both the use of media by authorities and independent and governmental political organizations. Governmental media infrastructure, authoritarian media outlets, and terrorist organizations all use media for the purpose of conveying their political agendas in ways that are more closely connected than is commonly perceived. Messages to a larger audience can be conveyed when media usage is organized in an accessible form. Infrastructure facilitates this accessibility, especially in the case of traditional media.

Yushi Chiba's chapter, *Location & Media Production in the Middle East: A Case Study of Media Cities*, investigates the role of media cities in the region. In extensive field research and interviews, he compares the emergence of media cities in Jordan, Egypt and Dubai, and developments and changes in recent years, beginning with the inauguration of Egyptian Media Production City on the outskirts of Cairo in 1997. This is followed by an analysis of Jordan Media City and Dubai Media City, which were both established in 2001, with other countries following similar trends of establishing media cities. This chapter charts the development of these phenomena, and examines their contribution to creating multiplicity and diversity in the Arab broadcasting industry.

Matthieu Rey goes into detail and examines the state's perspective of social media interaction through an analysis of media strategies in Syria in his chapter *How to Prevent a Mobilization: Assad and the Electronic War*. In March 2011, a massive uprising broke out in Syria, which was helped and fuelled by social media activists, who worked together to connect the different protests across the country, and collected news to spread information outside Syria. Until today, the Assad regime has attempted to counter this by using different tools that allow the regime to survive by discrediting competing accounts and undermining public debate. The regime's own electronic services can be analyzed as an element of a broader partnership (with foreign experts and companies), but also as a team that is guided by self-preserving values and interests.

Suzi Mirgani uncovers a third perspective by showing how terrorists use Twitter and other social media tools to create media spectacles that generate attention for their cause, which she discusses in her chapter *Spectacles of Terror: Media and the Cultural Production of Terrorism*. The pervasiveness of mobile technology, social media connectivity, and corporate media network competition means that many of the recent tragic terrorists attacks against urban, commercial spaces are inevitably turned into global media spectacles. These attacks happen for home audiences in real time to the twin delight of both extremists, whose message reverberates internationally, and the media outlets, which received greater audience share and consequently, higher advertising revenues. In this chapter, Mirgani elaborates on how the conflation of corporate capitalism and terrorism can be most acutely read on a symbolic level in many of the images and recorded footage that has emerged during global terrorist attacks.

The chapters in Part II all draw on institutionalized and professionalized media support and practice. Each chapter represents a different aspect of this professionalization which has shaped contemporary means of media participation.

The third part of this volume shows political media usage from an arts and cultural angle. TV, film, poetry and language are represented in media production all over Arab, Turkish- and Persian-speaking countries. Arts and culture play an essential role when communicating social and political ideas. Language and poetry on the one hand and film and TV on the other, are fundamentally influential forms of expression that impact and are impacted by society.

In *Winning Hearts and Minds Through Soft Power: the Case of Turkish Soap Operas in the Middle East*, Jana Jabbour offers perspectives on the use of soft power in Turkish—Arab relations through the manipulation of television media. Her research shows how soap operas from Turkey are broadcast all over the Middle East, and aim to contribute to depicting a positive image of Turkey. The popularity of these TV shows in the greater region has the potential knock-on effect of impacting wider economic cooperation between Turkey and other countries in the Middle East.

Dale Hudson, in his chapter *Locating Emirati Filmmaking Within Globalizing Media Ecologies*, sets local film production in the UAE in a global perspective. Emirati filmmakers have produced more than twenty features since 1989, and this chapter situates the question of locating Emirati filmmaking within the context of competing expectations about audience. Drawing upon conventional models used throughout the MENASA regions alongside indigenous media, Nollywood, Hallyuwood, and the Morelia Film Festival, he argues that the UAE deepens our understanding of the broader region in relation to media industries and cultures.

In *Literature and Poetry Online in the Gulf: Global and Regional Interactions*, Nele Lenze examines how online publishing platforms enable writers to spread literary works to a broader public that are generally limited in freedom of speech through official and social censorship. Focusing on one influential example of protest poetry from Bahrain that spread through YouTube, Lenze argues that one of the most important aspects of online literature is interactivity, where the focus lies on the processes of participatory culture of this rapidly emerging form of literature. This kind of participatory interaction also influences other changes, such as those related to language.

Ivan Panovic's chapter, entitled *Arabic 2.0: Notes on a Sociolinguistic Revolution in Egypt*, explores the significant changes that have been taking place in Egypt in the domain of cultural and artistic production for quite some time, including the sociolinguistically significant changes in the Egyptian "linguascape". A number of examples of different, revolution-related, literacy practices serve as examples to discuss the ongoing reconfiguration of linguistic and semiotic repertoires used by (predominantly younger generations of) Egyptians when engaging in vernacular literacy events. With this contribution he picks up on Egypt, the country discussed in the first chapter of this book.

The chapters in Part III serve as counter viewpoints as well as to complement the stronger political focus in Parts I and II of this edited volume. They demonstrate another perspective of the multifaceted nature of media studies, while also referring to the first two parts by discussing topics such as gender roles, political participation and influences by independent and governmental organizations.

The chapters in Part III are connected through each author's perspective which values culture as having the potential to politically impact both society and the visual media industry. Each chapter offers its own unique version of political and cultural influence through and by media, selecting actors that cooperate interregionally and internationally.

The relevance and importance of media in the Middle East, and its increasing importance as a subject of both academic and popular discussion and debate is mirrored in the diversity of the chapters of this volume, through an attempt to form a general picture of the present variety of consumption and production of new and traditional media in the region. Although the volume does not cover every aspect of media in the region, the authors' lenses cover a wide range of topics for discussion, which helps to create a varied view from Tunisia and Turkey to Iran and Kuwait, from Syria and Egypt to Iran and the UAE. It is hoped that the results of these diverse and thought-provoking contributions provide insights to how the conversation may be further directed in gaining a better understanding of the politics, gender perspectives and arts in the region and their relationship within the broader study of media use in the Middle East.

Nele Lenze
Charlotte Schriwer
Zubaidah Abdul Jalil

PART I

On Media Activism and Political Involvement

Revisiting Cyberactivism Six Years after the Arab Spring: Potentials, Limitations and Future Prospects

Sahar Khamis

INTRODUCTION

Six years after the eruption of the so-called 'Arab Spring' or Arab Awakening movements, it became obvious that a myriad of factors have contributed to the varying outcomes in the so-called 'post-Arab Spring countries', most of which had far from smooth paths to democratization and reform. This necessitates revisiting the role of the process of 'cyberactivism'[1] in aiding political change and paving the road for socio-economic transformation and democratization. This introductory chapter sheds light on the most important lessons we can learn from analyzing this phenomenon and its manifestations, as it revealed itself before, during and after these waves of revolt and protest. In doing so, it pays special attention to highlighting the most important potentials, limitations and future prospects of this process of 'cyberactivism' and its implications.

S. Khamis (✉)
Department of Communication, University of Maryland,
College Park, MD, USA

© The Author(s) 2017
N. Lenze et al. (eds.), *Media in the Middle East*,
DOI 10.1007/978-3-319-65771-4_1

The Potentials of Cyberactivism

Many of the iconic, symbolic and historical images which spread all over the world highlighting the 'Arab Spring' movements were conveyed through social media.[2] These images were either directly posted or uploaded online, or were picked up by satellite television channels which broadcasted them to a much wider audience, as in the case of Al Jazeera television channel, for example, which relied in its coverage of the 'Arab Spring' on a lot of footage which was generated by citizen journalists.

This process of citizen journalism relies on average citizens to supply coverage and documentation of key events and significant developments.[3]

Moreover, other mediated images which were widely circulated at that time hailed and applauded the prevalence and significance of social media's role in sparking and aiding these popular, grassroots movements. In every case, these images framed and emphasized the centrality of social media's role in supporting these movements and giving momentum to these new waves of revolt.

In brief, there was a moment of social media euphoria at the inception of these new waves of sweeping revolt in the Arab World, which was reflected in the widespread description of these movements as 'Egypt's Facebook Revolution', 'Tunisia's Twitter Uprising,' and 'Syria's YouTube Uprising'.[4]

This process of using social media and new media in the realm of sociopolitical transformation has been referred to as 'cyberactivism', a term which refers to the use of new media to advance a cause which is difficult to advance offline.[5]

There were various strengths and potentials for using these new media in the midst of these growing waves of revolt and protest. First, they acted as catalysts for paving the way for the process of democratic transition and speeding it up. Second, they acted as amplifiers for the calls for reform. Third, they acted as platforms for self-expression, and as channels for communication, networking and organization. Fourth, they acted as bridge-builders between the young activists and their followers, whether inside the same country or in the diaspora, as well as between the 'virtual world' and the 'real world'. Finally, they also acted as avenues for civic engagement, popular participation and grassroots mobilization; and as arenas for a new form of citizen journalism.[6]

Citizen journalists[7] played a vital role in the 'Arab Spring', paving the way for the revolutions. For example, the political bloggers in Egypt and Tunisia revealed a lot of the human rights violations and regimes' corruption, which created the needed environment for public resistance and protest.

They also played an important role in the three areas of mobilization, documentation and education, and they influenced the agenda of mainstream media, through touching upon taboo issues in the political domain, such as governmental corruption, as well as taboo issues in the social domain, such as sexual harassment. By doing so, they spilled over to the realm of mainstream media and encouraged them to cover these issues for the first time.[8]

Social media also acted as two-way windows, allowing certain groups, especially those who were traditionally marginalized, such as women and underprivileged minorities, to see the rest of the world, while being seen by the rest of the world simultaneously for the first time. This was a unique opportunity which they were not offered in the past.[9]

Here, it is worth mentioning that various social media tools appeared best suited for performing certain functions. For example, Facebook appeared to be the best tool for networking and mobilization, since it helped to rally people around a certain cause and to gain public support for it. This was clearly evidenced in the case of the prominent Facebook page 'We are All Khaled Said,' which was significant and instrumental in raising awareness about violations of human rights and police brutality. Therefore, it was one of the major catalysts behind igniting the Egyptian revolution of 2011.[10]

Twitter appeared to be the best tool for on-the-ground organization and minute-by-minute coordination. The online book 'Tweets from Tahrir' documented all the tweets which were sent out and exchanged between the activists in Tahrir Square during the 18 historical days of the Egyptian revolution of 2011. This highlighted the importance of Twitter in the midst of this revolution as an organizational tool.

Blogs appeared to be the best tool for brainstorming and exchanging views, through offering platforms for self-expression, which helped break political and social taboos and pave the way for the eruption of revolutions, through raising awareness about pressing issues of public significance, such as governmental corruption, violations of human rights, and even sexual harassment.[11]

YouTube appeared to be the best tool for recording visual images and the documentation of all ongoing tragedies and transgressions, which may otherwise have never been revealed to the public. A good example was the crucial role citizen journalists played in covering the atrocities of the civil war in Syria, smuggling these video recordings outside of the country and uploading them on YouTube to inform the regional and international audience about Syria's tragedy. By doing so, they were able to overcome the imposed governmental ban on foreign correspondents and all international media personnel.[12]

Most importantly, in performing all of the above roles, these new media tools helped to transform the function of alternative venues for expressing oppositional voices from acting as safety valves[13] which provide a safe space for citizens to vent their anger, frustration and resentment, while avoiding a full-blown explosion of public protest against the regimes in power, to acting as mobilization tools, which are effectively deployed to aid the process of revolt and protest on a massive scale.

This is especially important since traditionally authoritarian regimes in the Arab World have deliberately tolerated a limited, and safe, margin of benign opposition to absorb the public's anger, through providing them with platforms to vent their frustrations and grievances, while simultaneously exploiting this safety valve mechanism to preserve the status quo in their respective countries.[14]

THE LIMITATIONS OF CYBERACTIVISM

It is essential to reassess the process of cyberactivism and its limitations and constraints six years after the eruption of the 'Arab Spring' uprisings, especially since it became obvious that the path to democratization in many of the so-called 'post-Arab Spring countries' is far from smooth or straightforward.

Syria is suffering from a brutal, ongoing civil war and an enormous, unprecedented humanitarian crisis. Egypt relapsed back to military rule, after overthrowing the first democratically elected president in 2013, in what has been described by some as a military coup, by others as a popular uprising, and by a third group as a popularly backed coup. Libya is in a state of total chaos and anarchy to the extent that it is becoming a stateless state.

Yemen has internal rifts and tensions, which escalated violently due to military intervention from other countries, especially its powerful neighbor Saudi Arabia. Bahrain became the forgotten and invisible revolution, to which no one pays sufficient attention, after crushing the popular uprising to maintain the status quo, which safeguards the strategic interests of the predominantly Sunni neighboring Gulf countries, as well as the strategic interests of Western superpowers, especially the United States.

The only exception to this twisted and bumpy road to democracy and reform is Tunisia,[15] which was recognized internationally by awarding the Nobel Peace Prize to some of its parties, hailing their peaceful and bloodless rotation of power, through effective coalition building.

These new realities in the Arab region necessitated moving away from the initial euphoria of hailing the role of cyberactivism in the 'Arab Spring' and perceiving social media as the key determinants of a revolution's success, as reflected in talking about 'Egypt's Facebook Revolution', 'Tunisia's Twitter Uprising' and 'Syria's YouTube Uprising', as previously mentioned.

Becoming more aware of the limitations of the role of social media is important, because while social media were proven to be important tools in assisting political change, it was also proven that they are not magical tools that can bring about political change all by themselves. It is always the people on the ground who can bring about the needed transition and enact the desired change.

Therefore, it is especially important to avoid the temptation of technological determinism, which overemphasizes the role of new media, especially social media, in aiding the process of political activism and democratic transformation.

This necessitates becoming more aware of the limitations of social media tools, and fully realizing what they can and cannot do. One of these limitations is the digital divide, which points to the discrepancy between the haves and the have nots in the realm of technological advancement. This is due to myriad factors, including low literacy rates, especially in rural areas and among certain groups, such as the less economically fortunate and women, as well as infrastructural barriers, and technical, technological and economic constraints which are widespread in many parts of the developing world, including the Arab region.

Another limitation is the danger of so-called 'clicktivism' and 'slacktivism', or replacing posting, sharing and tweeting for doing, a phenomenon through which individuals could cultivate a false sense of gratification and satisfaction by simply clicking the mouse and sharing a link or sending a tweet, without taking the necessary steps to change the realities on the ground and improve the actual situation in the real world.

Here, it is worth mentioning that we need to differentiate between a situation where someone has the capacity to take action, but chooses not to do so, and another situation where the only form of activism available is, in fact, online posting, sharing, and tweeting.

A good example is the case of Syrian opposition activists in the diaspora.[16] The same could be said about opposition activists from Egypt, Libya and Bahrain, who were also forced to flee their home countries and to exercise their activism in exile from the diaspora, because of fear of regime intimidation and retaliation.

Moreover, it is important to bear in mind the differing roles of social media, depending on the surrounding political environment and the degree of unity and solidarity, or division and fragmentation, which is demonstrated in it.

If there is a moment of unity and uniformity motivated by common goals, for example during the Egyptian revolution of 2011 when all Egyptians across the board chanted the same slogans: 'The people want to overthrow the regime' and 'Mubarak must go', social media can be very successful in increasing this unity and amplifying the voices of protest. They can help by acting as catalysts, mobilizers, and networking tools, which can aid the process of transformation and pave the way for change.

However, once this moment of solidarity is gone, it can be replaced by deep divisions, severe polarization, and dangerous fragmentation, as witnessed in many 'post-Arab Spring countries' today, including Egypt after June 2013.

In this case, social media can widen the gap between the different groups and increase the tensions and the divisions among them even more, since every group will use its social media venues as effective weapons to attack their opponents and defend themselves, while refusing to listen to their opponents' views.

This is directly related to the finding that many people either use social media as echo chambers, which allow them to stay within their own comfort zones, by adhering to similar people who share their worldviews, or they, to the contrary, use them as places to vent their anger, bash their opponents, and attack those who are different from them.

This leads to creating the two undesirable bipolar extremes of either collective, uninformed, emotional consensus, on one hand, or unjustified, aggressive divergence, on the other hand, while the favorable, desirable middle ground of rational, critical deliberation and sensible dialogue remains oftentimes absent or largely missing.[17]

It was also proven that social media cannot boost civic engagement on their own, and they are not sufficient to fill the power vacuum in a given society. Many of the countries which witnessed the 'Arab Spring' suffered from not having an active, well-entrenched civil society, organized opposition movements, or structured grassroots institutions and resistance mechanisms.

The absence of this civil society, coupled with semi-structured, loose leadership, rather than centralized, organized and experienced leadership, led to the creation of a power vacuum, which contributed to the democratic setbacks and current grievances witnessed in many parts of the Arab World.

Therefore, it could be said that while social media may have paved the way for political transition in the region by helping to provide an overall environment which is more welcoming and conducive to change and transformation, it did not, however, succeed to overcome the deficiencies which barred the full transformation to democracy in a smooth, successful, and peaceful manner.

Here, it is worth mentioning that the true meaning of democratization and the real practice of democracy should extend far beyond casting a ballot in an election.[18] It should ideally encompass all aspects of society, leading up to a comprehensive, holistic change which infiltrates every sphere, politically, economically, and socially. It is, indeed, this kind of overall transformation which remained largely missing in many of the so-called 'post-Arab Spring countries'.

Additionally, although citizen journalism played a crucial role in raising awareness about key issues and documenting important events, both before and during the 'Arab Spring' uprisings, it also has its shortcomings. Since most citizen journalists are not professionally trained to conduct media coverage, their reporting should not be taken at face value, as it may require a lot of fact checking and verification to detect any inaccurate, incomplete, or false content.

The fact that citizen journalists may lack the necessary qualifications needed to produce high-quality media content means that whatever content they may produce online needs to be taken with a grain of salt, as it may include inaccuracies or inconsistencies, or even fabricated or falsified content, in some extreme cases.[19]

Although the fabrication of news and the falsification of information may take place in any form of media, including mainstream media, the possibility is higher in the case of citizen journalism, in particular, due to the lack of institutional structures, control mechanisms, professional standards, and journalistic training.

FUTURE PROSPECTS FOR CYBERACTIVISM

In light of the major developments which have been unfolding in the Arab region before, during and after the 'Arab Spring' upheavals, and the multiple roles which social media played in them, as well as the previously discussed potentials and limitations of social media in the realm of sociopolitical transformation, it is essential to highlight some of the most important future prospects for the growing phenomenon of cyberactivism and its implications and manifestations.

One of the most important angles which deserve special attention and further analysis in the future is the phenomenon of 'cyberwars'.[20] This refers to the tensions and conflicts taking place between opposing parties in cyberspace, as manifested in the tug of war between regimes and their opponents in the Arab region, using new media technologies.

For example, the Syrian regime was more prepared and was not taken by surprise when the protests erupted, because it learned from the cases of Tunisia and Egypt, and it became more technologically savvy. A good example to illustrate this point was forming the 'Syrian Electronic Army', which was created by the Syrian regime to hack the activists' websites and to sabotage their initiatives and activities online. This means that regimes, not just activists, also build their own learning curves and sharpen their tools over time.[21]

It is wise to predict that this phenomenon of cyberwars will continue to grow and expand in the future. However, the exact shape, form, intensity, and direction of these future cyberwars deserve further investigation.

Therefore, some of the most pressing questions which need to be asked in this regard are: How are these cyberwars different now, compared to six years ago? What forms are they taking now, and what forms are they expected to take in the future? What tools are they using now, and what tools are they expected to use in the future? And how and why are they different across different Arab countries?

Another aspect which is worth further investigation in future research is the online and offline activism taking place outside of urban areas and away from elitist upper-middle-class circles. Most previous research on the role of social media in the 'Arab Spring' focused on urban areas, especially capitals and big cities. It also focused on the elitist, upper middle class, educated activists, who are technologically savvy.

More research has to be conducted on rural areas and small towns, as well as on average citizens and marginalized groups. This is especially important due to the digital divide factor, as previously discussed, which means that not all segments of society in the Arab world have equal access to online modes of communication or technology.

Yet it is interesting to note that even the less technologically advantaged areas and populations are not void of all forms of activism and political mobilization.

One good example is the activism which took place in rural areas in Egypt, calling for the release of ousted President Mohamed Morsi, the first democratically elected president in Egypt's history, and demanding his return to power.

In some of these protests, which erupted in a number of Egyptian villages and small towns, hundreds of peasants took to the streets riding their donkeys and holding banners with the word 'coup' written in English, in a smart and deliberate attempt to attract international media coverage and attention. Unfortunately, however, they did not receive sufficient media coverage, locally, regionally or internationally. They were also largely overlooked in academic research.

Therefore, this highly understudied phenomenon, which could be referred to as the ruralization of protest, with all its manifestations and implications, needs to be better studied and more deeply analyzed moving forward.

Moreover, the role of citizen journalists[22] and their activism has to be revisited six years later. This is especially true in the case of the activists in the diaspora, who played an important role in instigating the 'Arab Spring' movements in their own countries, by paving the road for them, through raising awareness about key issues, in their roles as citizen journalists, as well as boosting mobilization, expanding networking, and securing material and moral support.

A good example is the active role played by the Syrian opposition movement in the diaspora,[23] as well as exchanging useful knowledge and advice between Tunisian and Egyptian activists and protestors when the Arab uprisings erupted back in 2011.[24] It would be important and useful to analyze the changes and transformations in these activists' roles over time, and to unpack the factors behind their increased, decreased, or altered forms of activism, both online and offline, and across different countries.

Finally, Arab women, alongside youth, played an important, central and visible role in the instigation, continuation and amplification of the 'Arab Spring' movements. Many of these women engaged in a dual sociopolitical struggle to launch parallel social and political revolutions in their respective countries.[25]

Large numbers of these women became iconic figures and role models, not just for other women, but also even for fellow male citizens. For example, Tawakkul Karman, the Yemeni activist and journalist, who was the first Arab woman to win the Nobel prize, Asma Mahfouz, who was called 'the most brave girl in Egypt,' due to her very bold vlog on YouTube calling people to go out and revolt on January 25, 2011, and Ayat El Gomizi, the 20-year-old Bahraini young woman, who was arrested for publically reciting a poem against the king and the ruling family of Bahrain.[26]

Many Arab women, who became iconic figures of resistance, activism, and protest, relied on social media to enact their activism and to get their messages across.[27]

The roles of these Arab women activists six years later, and beyond, have to be closely reinvestigated and reassessed to better understand the political, social, cultural and communication factors which may be aiding, or hindering, their activism, both online and offline. This is especially important in attempting to forecast the future of Arab women's activism moving forward, as well as assessing the impact of the 'Arab Spring' uprisings on this phenomenon.[28]

Concluding Remarks

In (re)assessing social media's future roles in the Arab World, it would be wise to adopt the middle ground of cautionary optimism or 'cyber-realism', which avoids the two undesirable bipolar extremes of either 'cyber-pessimism' or 'cyber-optimism', which tend to either underestimate or overestimate the roles played by new media in the process of sociopolitical transformation.

This approach of cyber-realism[29] wisely acknowledges the new potentials and capacities which could be offered by the internet in terms of empowering certain marginalized groups. It avoids the two undesirable extremes of either cyber-optimism, which may magnify the internet's contribution to reducing inequality, ignorance and apathy, on the one hand, or cyber-pessimism, which tends to either underplay the internet's contributions, or to emphasize some of the negative implications of the new digital age, on the other hand.[30]

These include widening the digital divide, increasing the power differentials, or creating new possibilities for social control and manipulation, which could benefit the more economically advantaged and the more politically powerful groups in any society.[31]

As previously mentioned, social media are simply good tools for paving the way for change and transformation, through acting as *catalysts*, *mobilizers* and *amplifiers*, but they are not *magical tools* that can create this change all by themselves. It is always the people, as the *actors* on the ground, who can make that change happen, if, and when, they decide to do so.

Here, it is important to bear in mind, however, that in certain cases, such as the case of the Syrian opposition in the diaspora, for example, people cannot engage in activism on the ground in the real world, and, therefore, the virtual, online forms of activism become their only legitimate tools of resistance, mobilization and networking.[32]

In looking ahead, it would also be wise to adopt a balanced and realistic approach in predicting the Arab region's political future, in the midst of the current sociopolitical transformations, which acknowledges the valuable gains and victories which have been achieved, while taking into account the serious current challenges and the threats lying ahead.

Likewise, it is equally important to adopt a similarly balanced and realistic approach in reassessing the transformative Arab media landscape, with all its current changes and challenges. The key questions now are: How can we return back to constructive dialogue and democratization to build a better future for this region? And how can the media, especially social media, help in achieving this goal?

There are no easy, clear or straightforward answers to these pressing questions, since the future of the media landscape in the Arab region remains as uncharted, ambivalent, and in flux as the political landscape in this rapidly changing and dynamic region.

However, it is safe to predict that the tide of cyberactivism, with all its strengths and weaknesses, positives and negatives, and potentials and limitations, will, indeed, continue to grow and expand moving forward, especially in a region where more than 70% of the population are under the age of 30. This vibrant, energetic, change oriented and technologically savvy population will most likely continue to rely on the newest modes of communication to continue their struggle for self-expression, self-determination, and self-liberation.

The fruits of these efforts will certainly come to fruition one day, aided by the newest tools of communication in the hands of determined, young activists. When and how this will actually happen, however, remains to be as uncertain and unpredicted as the future of the Arab region itself.

NOTES

1. Philip N. Howard, *The Digital Origins of Dictatorship and Democracy: Information Technology and Political Islam* (Oxford: Oxford University Press, 2011).
2. Nahed Eltantawy and Julie Wiest, "Social Media in the Egyptian Revolution: Reconsidering Resource Mobilization Theory," *International Journal of Communication* 5 (2011): 1207–1224.
3. Lance W. Bennett, 'Changing Citizenship in the Digital Age' in *Civic Life Online: Learning How Digital Media Can Engage Youth*, ed. Lance W. Bennett (Cambridge: The MIT Press, 2008), 1–24.
4. Sahar Khamis and Katherine Vaughn, "Cyberactivism in the Egyptian Revolution: How Civic Engagement and Citizen Journalism Tilted the Balance," *Arab Media & Society*, Issue 13, (Summer 2011a), accessed 27 June 2016, http://www.arabmediasociety.com/?article=769; Sahar Khamis and Katherine Vaughn, "We are All Khaled Said: The Potentials and Limitations of Cyberactivism in Triggering Public Mobilization and Promoting Political Change," *Journal of Arab & Muslim Media Research*, 4, No. 2 & 3 (2011b), 139–157; Nahed Eltantawy and Julie Wiest, "Social Media in the Egyptian Revolution: Reconsidering Resource Mobilization Theory," *International Journal of Communication* 5 (2011): 1207–1224.

5. Philip N. Howard, *The Digital Origins of Dictatorship and Democracy: InformationTechnology and Political Islam* (Oxford: Oxford University Press, 2011).
6. Mohammed El-Nawawy and Sahar Khamis, *Egyptian Revolution 2.0: Political Blogging, Civic Engagement, and Citizen Journalism* (New York: Palgrave Macmillan, 2013).
7. Lance W. Bennett, "Changing Citizenship in the Digital Age," in *Civic Life Online: Learning How Digital Media Can Engage Youth*, ed. W. Lance Bennett (Cambridge: The MIT Press, 2008), 1–24.
8. Mohammed El-Nawawy and Sahar Khamis, *Egyptian Revolution 2.0: Political Blogging, Civic Engagement, and Citizen Journalism* (New York: Palgrave Macmillan, 2013); Courtney Radsch and Sahar Khamis, "In their own Voice: Technologically Mediated Empowerment and Transformation among Young Arab Women," *Feminist Media Studies*, 13, No. 5 (2013), 881–890.
9. Courtney Radsch and Sahar Khamis, "In Their Own Voice: Technologically Mediated Empowerment and Transformation among Young Arab Women," *Feminist Media Studies*, 13, No. 5 (2013), 881–890.
10. Sahar Khamis and Katherine Vaughn, "We Are All Khaled Said: The Potentials and Limitations of Cyberactivism in Triggering Public Mobilization and Promoting Political Change," *Journal of Arab & Muslim Media Research*, 4, No. 2 & 3 (2011b), 139–157.
11. Mohammed El-Nawawy and Sahar Khamis, *Egyptian Revolution 2.0: Political Blogging, Civic Engagement, and Citizen Journalism* (New York: Palgrave Macmillan, 2013).
12. Sahar Khamis, Paul B. Gold and Katherine Vaughn, "Propaganda in Egypt and Syria's Cyberwars: Contexts, Actors, Tools, and Tactics" in *The Oxford Handbook to Propaganda Studies*, eds. Jonathan Auerbach and Russ Castronovo (New York: Oxford University Press), 2013, 418–438.
13. Philip Seib, "New Media and Prospects for Democratization," in *New Media and the New Middle East*, ed. Philip Seib (New York: Palgrave Macmillan, 2007), 1–18.
14. Ibid.
15. Amel Mili, "Political-Social Movements: Community Based: Tunisia," in *Encyclopedia of Women & Islamic Cultures*, ed. Suad Joseph, 2015, accessed 9 March, 2017 http://dx.doi.org/10.1163/1872-5309_ewic_COM_002018
16. Sahar Khamis, Paul B. Gold and Katherine Vaughn, "Propaganda in Egypt and Syria's Cyberwars: Contexts, Actors, Tools, and Tactics" in *The Oxford Handbook to Propaganda Studies*, eds. Jonathan Auerbach and Russ Castronovo (New York: Oxford University Press), 2013, 418–438.

17. Mohammed El-Nawawy and Sahar Khamis, *Islam Dot Com: Contemporary Islamic Discourses in Cyberspace* (New York: Palgrave Macmillan, 2009).
18. Lisa Blaydes, *Elections and Distributive Politics in Mubarak's Egypt* (New York: Cambridge University Press, 2011); Steven A. Cook, *The Struggle for Egypt: From Nasser to Tahrir Square* (New York: Oxford University Press, 2012).
19. Lance W. Bennett, "Changing Citizenship in the Digital Age," in *Civic Life Online:Learning How Digital Media Can Engage Youth*, W. Lance Bennett, ed., (Cambridge: The MIT Press, 2008), 1–24.
20. Sahar Khamis, Paul B. Gold and Katherine Vaughn, "Propaganda in Egypt and Syria's Cyberwars: Contexts, Actors, Tools, and Tactics" in *The Oxford Handbook to Propaganda Studies*, eds. Jonathan Auerbach and Russ Castronovo (New York: Oxford University Press, 2013), 418–438.
21. Ibid.
22. Lance W. Bennett, 'Changing Citizenship in the Digital Age' in *Civic Life Online: Learning How Digital Media Can Engage Youth*, ed. Lance W. Bennett (Cambridge: The MIT Press, 2008), 1–24.
23. Sahar Khamis, Paul B. Gold and Katherine Vaughn, "Propaganda in Egypt and Syria's Cyberwars: Contexts, Actors, Tools, and Tactics" in Jonathan Auerbach and Russ Castronovo, eds., *The Oxford Handbook to Propaganda Studies* (New York: Oxford University Press), 2013, 418–438.
24. Sahar Khamis and Katherine Vaughn, "Cyberactivism in the Egyptian Revolution: How Civic Engagement and Citizen Journalism Tilted the Balance," *Arab Media & Society*, Issue 13 (Summer 2011a), accessed 27 June 2016, http://www.arabmediasociety.com/?article=769.
25. Kendra Heideman and Mona Youssef, eds., "Reflections on Women in the Arab Spring: Women's Voices from Around the World," Woodrow Wilson International Center for Scholars (2012), Washington, DC; Al-Malki, et al., *Arab Women in Arab News: Old Stereotypes and New Media* (Doha: Bloomsbury Qatar Foundation Publishing, 2012); Sahar Khamis, "The Arab 'Feminist' Spring?" *Feminist Studies*, 37, No. 3 (Fall 2011), 692–695; Courtney Radsch, "Re-Imagining Cleopatra: Gendering Cyberactivism in Egypt" (Paper presented at the Middle East Studies Association (MESA) annual conference, Washington, DC, December 1–4, 2011); Courtney Radsch, "Unveiling the Revolutionaries: Cyberactivism and the Role of Women in the Arab Uprisings," James A. Baker III Institute for Public Policy of Rice University, 2012, accessed 27 June, 2016, http://bakerinstitute.org/research/-and-the-role-of-women-in-the-arab-uprisings/

unveiling-the-revolutionaries-cyberactivism; Courtney Radsch and Sahar Khamis, "In Their Own Voice: Technologically Mediated Empowerment and Transformation Among Young Arab Women," *Feminist Media Studies*, 13, No. 5 (2013), 881–890.

26. Courtney Radsch and Sahar Khamis, "In Their Own Voice: Technologically Mediated Empowerment and Transformation Among Young Arab Women," *Feminist Media Studies*, 13, No. 5 (2013), 881–890.

27. Kendra Heideman and Mona Youssef, eds., "Reflections on Women in the Arab Spring. Women's Voices from Around the World," Woodrow Wilson International Center for Scholars (2012), Washington, DC; Al-Malki et al., *Arab Women in Arab News: Old Stereotypes and New Media* (Doha: Bloomsbury Qatar Foundation Publishing, 2012); Sahar Khamis, "The Arab 'Feminist' Spring?" *Feminist Studies*, 37, No. 3 (Fall 2011), 692–695; Courtney Radsch, "Re-Imagining Cleopatra: Gendering Cyberactivism in Egypt" (Paper presented at the Middle East Studies Association (MESA) annual conference, Washington, DC, December 1–4, 2011); Courtney Radsch, "Unveiling the Revolutionaries: Cyberactivism and the Role of Women in the Arab Uprisings," James A. Baker III Institute for Public Policy of Rice University, 2012, accessed 27 June, 2016, http://bakerinstitute.org/research/-and-the-role-of-women-in-the-arab-uprisings/unveiling-the-revolutionaries-cyberactivism; Courtney Radsch and Sahar Khamis, "In Their Own Voice: Technologically Mediated Empowerment and Transformation Among Young Arab Women," *Feminist Media Studies*, 13, No. 5 (2013), 881–890.

28. Haleh Esfandiari, "Is the Arab Awakening Marginalizing Women?" *Wilson Center Middle East Program Occasional Paper Series*, 2012. http://www.wilsoncenter.org/event/the-arab-awakening-marginalizing-women; Andrea Khalil, "Gender Paradoxes of the Arab Spring," *The Journal of North African Studies*, 19, No. 2 (2014), 131–136.

29. P. Muhlberger, "Access, Skill, and Motivation in Online Political Discussion: Testing Cyberrealism," in *Democracy Online: The Prospects for Political Renewal Through the Internet*, ed. P. Shane (New York: Routledge, 2004): 225–237.

30. Ibid.

31. Pippa Norris, *Digital Divide: Civic Engagement, Information Poverty, and the Internet Worldwide* (Cambridge: Cambridge University Press, 2001).

32. Sahar Khamis, Paul B. Gold and Katherine Vaughn, "Propaganda in Egypt and Syria's Cyberwars: Contexts, Actors, Tools, and Tactics," in *The Oxford Handbook to Propaganda Studies*, eds. Jonathan Auerbach and Russ Castronovo (New York: Oxford University Press), 2013, 418–438.

BIBLIOGRAPHY

Al-Malki, Amal, Kaufer, David, Ishizaki, Suguru, and Dreher, Kira. *Arab Women in Arab News: Old Stereotypes and New Media*. Doha: Bloomsbury Qatar Foundation Publishing, 2012.

Bennett, W. Lance. "Changing Citizenship in the Digital Age." In *Civic Life Online: Learning How Digital Media Can Engage Youth*, W. Lance Bennett, ed., 1–24. Cambridge: The MIT Press, 2008.

Blaydes, Lisa. *Elections and Distributive Politics in Mubarak's Egypt*. New York: Cambridge University Press, 2011.

Cook, Steven A. *The Struggle for Egypt: From Nasser to Tahrir Square*. New York: Oxford University Press, 2012.

El-Nawawy, Mohammed and Khamis, Sahar. *Egyptian Revolution 2.0: Political Blogging, Civic Engagement, and Citizen Journalism*. New York: Palgrave Macmillan, 2013.

El-Nawawy, Mohammed and Khamis, Sahar. *Islam Dot Com: Contemporary Islamic Discourses in Cyberspace*. New York: Palgrave Macmillan, 2009.

Eltantawy, Nahed & Julie Wiest. "Social media in the Egyptian revolution: Reconsidering resource mobilization theory," *International Journal of Communication* 5 (2011): 1207–1224.

Esfandiari, Haleh. Is the Arab Awakening Marginalizing Women? *Wilson Center Middle East Program Occasional Paper Series*, 2012. http://www.wilson-center.org/event/the-arab-awakening-marginalizing-women.

Heideman, Kendra & Youssef, Mona (eds.). "Reflections on Women in the Arab Spring. Women's Voices from Around the World." Woodrow Wilson International Center for Scholars, Washington, DC, 2012.

Howard, Philip N. *The Digital Origins of Dictatorship and Democracy: Information Technology and Political Islam*. Oxford: Oxford University Press, 2011.

Khalil, Andrea. "Gender paradoxes of the Arab Spring," *The Journal of North African Studies*, 19, No. 2, (2014): 131–136.

Khamis, Sahar. "The Arab "Feminist" Spring?" *Feminist Studies*, 37, No. 3 (Fall 2011): 692–695.

Khamis, Sahar and Vaughn, Katherine. "Cyberactivism in the Egyptian Revolution: How Civic Engagement and Citizen Journalism Tilted the Balance." *Arab Media & Society*, Issue 13, (Summer 2011a). Accessed 27 June 2016. http://www.arabmediasociety.com/?article=769.

Khamis, Sahar and Vaughn, Katherine. "We are All Khaled Said: The Potentials and Limitations of Cyberactivism in Triggering Public Mobilization and Promoting Political Change." *Journal of Arab & Muslim Media Research*, Volume 4, No. 2 & 3 (2011b): 139–157.

Khamis, Sahar, Gold, Paul B. and Vaughn, Katherine. "Propaganda in Egypt and Syria's Cyberwars: Contexts, Actors, Tools, and Tactics." In *The Oxford Handbook to Propaganda Studies*. Jonathan Auerbach and Russ Castronovo (eds.), 418–438. New York: Oxford University Press, 2013.

Mili, Amel (2015). "Political-Social Movements: Community Based: Tunisia." In *Encyclopedia of Women & Islamic Cultures*. Edited by Suad Joseph, 2010. Accessed 9 March, 2017. http://dx.doi.org/10.1163/1872-5309_ewic_COM_002018.

Muhlberger, P. "Access, skill, and motivation in online political discussion: Testing cyberrealism." In *Democracy online: The prospects for political renewal through the Internet*, P. Shane, (ed.), 225–237. New York: Routledge, 2004.

Norris, Pippa. *Digital Divide: Civic Engagement, Information Poverty, and the Internet Worldwide*. Cambridge: Cambridge University Press, 2001.

Radsch, Courtney. "Re-Imagining Cleopatra: Gendering Cyberactivism in Egypt." Paper presented at the Middle East Studies Association (MESA) annual conference, Washington D.C., Dec. 1–4, 2011.

Radsch, Courtney. "Unveiling the Revolutionaries: Cyberactivism and the Role of Women in the Arab Uprisings." James A. Baker III Institute for Public Policy of Rice University, 2012. Accessed 27 June 2016. http://bakerinstitute.org/research/unveiling-the-revolutionaries-cyberactivism-and-the-role-of-women-in-the-arab-uprisings/.

Radsch, Courtney and Khamis, Sahar. "In their own Voice: Technologically Mediated Empowerment and Transformation among Young Arab Women." *Feminist Media Studies*, 13, No. 5 (2013), 881–890.

Seib, Philip. (2007). "New Media and Prospects for Democratization." In *New Media and the New Middle East*. Philip Seib, ed., 1–18. New York: Palgrave Macmillan, 2007.

CHAPTER 2

Constructing an Alternative Public Sphere: The Cultural Significance of Social Media in Iran

Gi Yeon Koo

Happiness brings people together.
Happiness is our right.
Nobody can stop our laughter.
I am a happy Iranian.
#freehappyiranians.

This work was supported by Laboratory Program for Korean Studies through the Ministry of Education of Republic of Korea and Korean Studies Promotion Service of the Academy of Korean Studies (AKS-2015-LAB-1250001). This chapter expands upon Koo Gi Yeon, "Constructing an Alternative Public Sphere: Social Media and Their Cultural Meaning in Iran" (paper presented at the National University of Singapore, MEI (Middle East Institute) Media Conference, Singapore, September 3–4, 2015 and Koo Gi Yeon, "Making an Alternative Public Sphere: New Media and Their Cultural Meanings in Iran" (paper presented at the Middle East Studies Association, Denver, Colorado, November 21–24, 2015.

G.Y. Koo (✉)
Institute of Cross-Cultural Studies, Seoul National University,
Gwanak, South Korea

21

In March 2014, a YouTube video called "Happy We are From Tehran" made in Iran became known throughout the world. This clip was a music video that showed Iranian youths dancing to Pharrell Williams' song "Happy". In it, young men and women are dancing in the streets and rooftops of Tehran, and the women are not wearing veils. The video had almost 300,000 views within five days, and 2.32 million views were recorded by November 2015. However, the seven men and women who uploaded the video were arrested for undermining 'public chastity'. They were sentenced last September to three years of imprisonment and lashing.

Efforts to free these youths mobilized under the hashtag *#freehappy-iranian* on Twitter and through the "Free Happy Iranians" Facebook page. Similarly, the current Iranian president Rouhani also took a critical stance towards the arrest, by retweeting one of his own past tweets, "Happiness is our people's right. We should not be too hard on behavior caused by joy." In Iran, where such expression of happiness and joy on social network services (SNS) can become a crime (Koo 2016a), critical voices continue to emerge against this reality. Iranians, both within the country and abroad, are uniting in solidarity and collective opposition towards governmental policies through their posts on Twitter or Facebook.

Reform-oriented urban upper-middle-class youths have a strong dissatisfaction towards the Islamic government and dream of social change; in reality, however, they face too many obstacles in which reform is a slow and laborious process (Yaghmaian 2002). In contemporary Iran, we see a muddle of features that include aspects of the pre-modern ruling system and the modern state system, mixed in with recent attributes of globalization. Within this social context of colliding values, it is only natural that the Iranian urban upper middle-class youths feel confused. As a result of globalization, the influences of new media and the introduction of a new culture of consumption have rapidly transformed the cultural configuration of the Iranian city dwellers. New media, satellite media and social media have seen an explosive growth despite governmental censorship and restrictions. In the present, the "mediated experience" conveyed through mass media has deeply influenced the basic tissues of self-identity and social relations, and, as a result, it has developed the self-identity of the Iranians in a more reflective manner. In contemporary Iranian society, electronic devices and social media have changed the "situational geography" of social life (Giddens 1991), which has allowed continuous and direct communication with the globalized world.

Iranian media, which has its roots in the small media from the times of the Iranian Islamic Revolution and the foundation of the Islamic Republic (Sreberny-Mohammadi and Mohammadi 1994), has always maintained an important position in public and private discourses. Sreberny-Mohammadi and Mohammadi emphasize the importance role played by small media in the success of the 1979 Revolution. In this context the term small media refers to the alternative media vehicle that counters the state authority or companies' big media (national broadcasts or public television). During the Islamic Revolution, various forms of small media, including flyers, audio cassettes, Polaroid photographs, etc., led those of opposing opinions into social mobilization. Small media functioned as a successful media vehicle that targeted the audience in spite of the pressures and controls of the then-authoritarian administration (Sreberny-Mohammadi and Mohammadi 1994). Just as small media led the Islamic Revolution to success in the past, personal and new media in contemporary Iranian society are becoming consolidated into a political public space of their own.

The Ahmadinejad administration has had a great influence upon Iranian modern history and its current media environment. By attempting to enforce a new policy of Islamization on all aspects of Iranian society, it has strongly confronted the infiltration and penetration of individualistic, secular values of Western culture through media. It has issued fines on the installation and use of illegal satellite media, while trying to strengthen the capacity of the national television stations. The Iranian administration has increased the budget for the production of state broadcasts to effectively convey the voice and vision of the Islamic Republic, and has tried to produce and distribute an increased number of programs (Piri and Halim 2011). Nonetheless, although the government tries to prohibit access to information through worldwide channels and satellite television, in reality, it is difficult to maintain such control or censorship. For example, global human rights discourses regarding democratization and the rights of women—among others—has already filtered deeply into Iranian society (Koo 2013).

This chapter is a qualitative study based on research around the adoption of new and social media by the urban upper middle class of Tehran, based on fieldwork carried out over a year in 2009, during the Mahmud

Ahmadinejad administration, followed by two shorter terms of fieldwork carried out in January 2015, 2016, 2017. It will explore the Iranian media environment that have been changing with the distribution and expansion of new and social media, and analyze—from an anthropological perspective—how Internet and social networks have been introduced into Iranian society and function as sociocultural devices in the lives of the urban population. The visible and invisible wars between the state and citizen that began in urban areas have now moved onto the arena of new and social media. Social media is currently one of the most responsive and interactive mediums of communication. There are numerous case studies of how social media such as Facebook and Twitter have been used as instruments of political activity around the world (Loader and Mercea 2011; Van Laer and Van Aelst 2010), and it is within this perspective that we will explore the political significance of social media in Iran.

Furthermore, I seek to emphasize the role of online media and social networks as an "imagined community" (Anderson 2006) and a space of solidarity and resistance. Shirky (2011) argues that social media creates a "shared awareness", "the ability of each member of a group to not only understand the situation at hand but also understand that everyone else does, too" (Shirky 2011). In other words, social media, as an instrument of communication between friends and colleagues, allows for the "second step" in the formation of political opinion. As Shirky (2011) points out, the "more promising way to think about social media is as long-term tools that can strengthen civil society and the public sphere", we can expect social media to be the cornerstone for the development of, not just an alternative public sphere, but of civil society in Iran. In other words, I will consider how the domain of media has transformed into a platform for heated political debate between the state and its citizens. By actively revealing the voices of the interviewees through their experiences, I plan to follow the processes by which private discourses about social media construct the vast public discourse.

CURRENT USE OF SOCIAL MEDIA IN IRAN[1]

"Internet? Internet is my life itself!" said a 16-year-old girl from the upper-middle class of Tehran, her eyes locked on her mobile all day long. She was constantly communicating to her friends and family through mobile applications, and they all shared their daily lives as well as "anti-Islamic" content that was being transmitted through illegal satellite channels. This phenomenon is not limited to teenagers, however. Family entertainment had been, until a few years ago, shows and soap operas shown through cable television, but now every family member in the upper urban classes has smartphones and tablets through which they have access to media from all around the world, particularly media that are censored by the Iranian government.

For Iranian youths nowadays, the actors of the American TV series "Bones", The Oprah Winfrey Show and The Doctor Oz Show, pop stars such as Beyoncé or Rihanna, football players such as Lionel Messi or Wayne Rooney, and even the Korean pop singer Psy are familiar figures. New technology such as satellite broadcasts, smartphones, bluetooth, personal computers, digital cameras and the Internet, have functioned as important devices that set new standards and norms for cultural life in Iranian society. The media industry is one of the fastest-growing sectors of the Iranian economy, and it is this unprecedented growth rate that demands our attention. Furthermore, new communication technologies have had a greater influence upon the youth's culture and mass culture in a relatively short period of time, and they are changing the cultural landscape of the urban upper-middle classes, particularly for the younger Iranian generations.

The following are some data charts from the World Bank database that give us an idea of the extraordinary growth of new media in Iran over the past few years. Figs. 2.1, 2.2 and 2.3 show the number of Internet users, of mobile cellular subscriptions, and of broadband subscriptions, per 100 people. In order to provide a comparison, world and Arab world figures have also been included.

Let us first consider the use of broadband Internet in Iran. Iranian Internet users amount to 56% of the total number of Internet users in the wider Middle East (Amir-Ebrahimi 2009). As can be seen in Fig. 2.1, the number of Internet users has increased in the past 10 years by almost 25 times, from 610,421 in 2000 to 15,707,706 in 2014. Furthermore, the number of mobile phone users has grown from only 5 in every 100 people in 2003 to 87.8 of every 100 people in 2014. This is one of the clearest examples of the astonishing growth in the distribution of new technologies in Iran over the past decade. Similarly, the number of smart phone users has also been increasing exponentially since 2011. Recent fieldwork in Iran (carried out in January 2015, January 2016, and January 2017), showed that the demand for smartphones is increasing

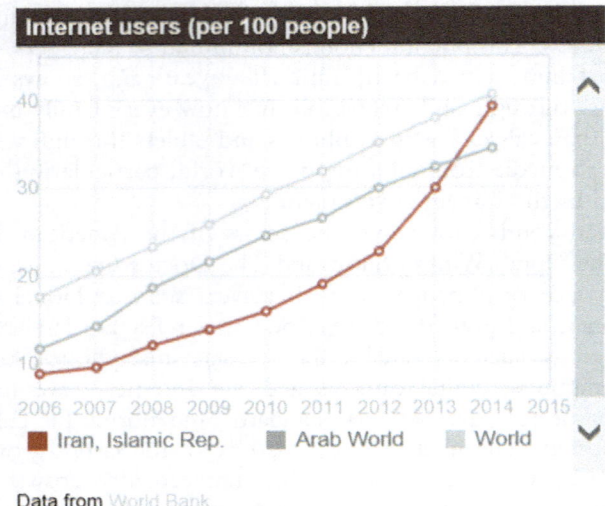

Fig. 2.1   Internet Users (Per 100 People)

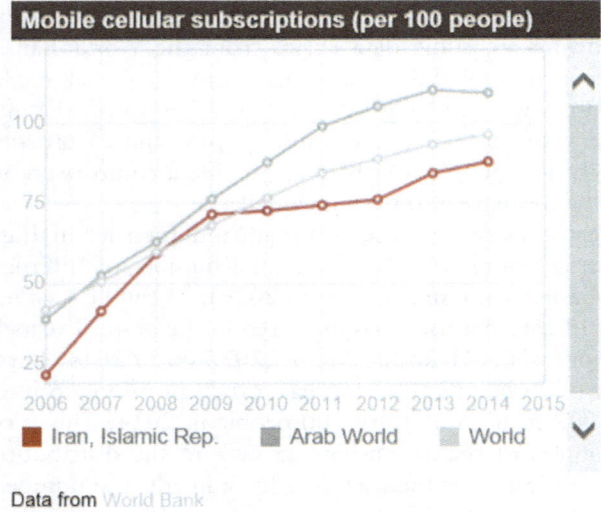

Fig. 2.2   Mobile cellular subscriptions (per 100 people)

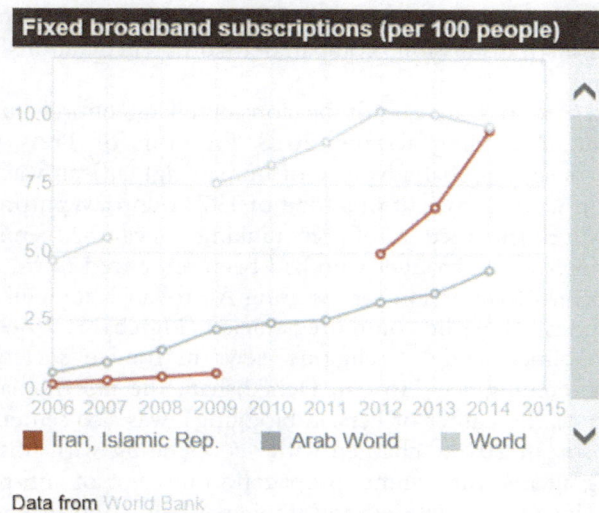

Fig. 2.3 Fixed Broadband Subscriptions (per 100 people)

rapidly, in particular among the upper-middle-class youths, despite the high prices.[2] According to a study published in 2015 by Iran's Academic Center of Education, Culture and Research, "over 20 million of Iran's 78 million people are smartphone users."[3]

Similarly, the use of social networks such as Facebook[4] to send messages, share music and photos has become a popular trend amongst the younger generations. In major cities, almost all of the young people in their 20s and 30s, even high school students, possess mobile phones, which they use to send text messages and share videos and photos through Bluetooth. Broadband networks have expanded from schools and public offices to home and personal computers, which has resulted in the increase of Internet bloggers and greater access to information that had been previously restricted by official Iranian media.

In 2011–2012, Wojcieszak et al. (2012) carried out research regarding Iranian media consumption and found that only 4% of those over 59 years of age accessed the Internet, whereas almost 61% of the youths between 18 and 28 years of age used the Internet at home. According to this study, for Iranian youths (those aged 18–28 years), the Internet and SMS (text messaging) were the most important means of information transmission, compared to other generations' access to information.[5]

The Internet in Iran cannot be considered an entirely uncensored environment. According to the 2013 Freedom of Press report by Freedom House, a global advocate of human rights, Iran was ranked at 192nd along with Cuba, out of a total of 197 countries, putting it in the bottom seven of the freedom of press ranking. As can be seen in the case of Omid Mir Sayafi, a blogger who had been sentenced to thirty months in the notorious Evin prison for insulting Ayatollah Khomeini and other religious clerics, where he committed suicide (March 18, 2009),[6] openly expressing political and/or religious views in Iranian society can still be a life-threatening act. Hossein Derakhshan, the first Iranian blogger (also known as the Father of Persian blogging), was also sentenced to 19 years in prison in 2010,[7] charged with "cooperating with hostile states, propagating against the regime, propagation in favor of anti-revolutionary groups, insulting sanctities, and implementation and management of obscene websites".[8]

Despite these difficulties and obstacles imposed by the regime, there are approximately 65,000 active bloggers in Iran and the total number of Internet users in 2015 amounted to over 46,800,000.[9] The penetration of digital devices such as personal computers and laptops has opened a new stage for the fomentation of public opinion and transfer of information, and young people are the main pillar of this rapidly expanding digital society. However, with the increase of information and the development of an eye for the outside world, those urban youths who have greater access to new media and social media have come to be considered dangerous by the Islamic government. The expansion of the Internet and various digital devices has become reflected as one of the most threatening forces of resistance against the government pushing for a strong Islamic state. As can be seen in the following interview, the number of new media users in Iran is multiplying rapidly and, in the process, they are gaining access to information from which they had hitherto been cut off. The incapacity to discuss issues freely in the public sphere has caused a movement to the online space, and now, despite governmental restrictions, they are constantly attempting to stay online and connected.

MALE, 26 YEARS, GRADUATE STUDENT, TEHRAN, NOVEMBER 20, 2009

Unlike other generations, the younger generations in Iran are encountering a reality ridden with social problems, and in this context, we are experiencing foreign cultures 'with our own eyes' through new media such as the Internet and satellite television. With the increase in the number of Internet users in the population over the past 10 years, the government has implemented censorship institutions, but these do not pose severe obstacles for the young people. Everybody downloads programs that deactivate firewalls and access the Internet, unrestricted.

Although people maintain a public image of themselves vis-à-vis the government and in public spaces, they show their true selves to their closest friends and family in private, and also on their blogs (Koo 2008). The rapid changes of the communications industry, greater economic wealth, the increased demand for communication channels, the upsurge of use of personal technologies has led to an extraordinary growth of blogging and SNS activity in Iran. Whilst the early uses of the Internet were limited to chatting on certain websites, in recent years, the trend has moved from chatting rooms to blogs, to social media sites and smart phones.

One historic incident that best shows political importance of new media is the 2009 Green Movement. Green cloth wristbands and small media mixed with social media to create a "Green Wave". Just as the Arab Spring was coined a Twitter Revolution, so also was the impact of the Internet War around the 2009 presidential elections, where political slogans were shared through Twitter and Facebook, while posters and flyers that had filled the streets in the past came to fill the screens of mobile devices through the use of social networks. In fact, Candidate Mousavi targeted the youth and reform-oriented population by opening a Twitter[10] and Facebook[11] account, and carrying out an online electoral campaign. In response, those young people in their 20s and 30s who supported Mousavi began sharing posts and home-made videos showing their support on their SNS accounts such as those of Twitter, Facebook and their personal blogs. Furthermore, these young supporters shared with each other emails with photos or other materials satirizing the shortcomings of the Ahmadinejad administration. To further support this, Iranian diaspora from all around the world participated actively alongside the Iranian electorate, thanks to the capacities of new media, for which the forces of the reform-oriented Iranians, including expatriates and those in exile, began to gather in this virtual space (Koo 2012).

People refer to the Iranian Green Movement of 2009 as the SNS Revolution, but we need to take into account that, until 2009, there was a very low level of smartphone penetration in Iran. In fact, a closer look at the period shows that it was mainly through the SNS activity of the Iranian diasporas that the world was informed about the Iranian Green Movement. Nevertheless, this does not undermine the fact that the internet had become one of the most important channels of Iranian social and democratization movements, and that the 2009 Green Movement would be a starting point in the history of new media and social media as transmission tools for political propaganda and public protests. (Fig. 2.4).

Smartphone penetration in Iran increased abruptly in 2012. Unofficial statistics suggest that at the time of writing there are at least 5 million Iranians using mobile SNS applications such as WhatsApp, Telegram and Viber.[12] During the short-term fieldwork carried out in January 2016, I was able to gather that mobile phone users were switching from Viber to Telegram for instant messaging while Instagram was more popular, relative to Facebook, among the younger generations. Whilst this seems to be in line with global demographics of social network users, which indicate that Instagram is, indeed, more popular amongst teens than Facebook or Twitter, in the case of Iran, the major reason behind the popularity of Instagram is simply the fact that it has not yet been censored by the government, meaning that currently anybody can access it.

It should be noted that several of world's most popular networks, such as Twitter and Facebook, are banned in Iran while users are still able to access them via proxies.[13] (Figs. 2.5 and 2.6).

Among these are Facebook and Twitter—for which nowadays, there is an increasing tendency for people to hide in the more private spaces of mobile messaging applications such as Telegram.

While it is possible to "access" Facebook and Twitter through aforementioned proxies or programs, expressing one's opinions or political stance through Facebook or a blog is considered a cultural crime in Iran and can lead to either imprisonment or execution. In other words, despite the fact that so many people utilize SNS through their smartphones, the users are prevented from voicing their opinions freely.

(a)

(b)

Fig. 2.4 Some pictures used as Facebook profiles during the Green Movement

They are forced to be very cautious about their online activities and are required to wear a political mask in their personal online spaces, such as their Facebook profiles. However, in mobile messaging applications such as Telegram, Iranian users can share their latest news and voice anti-governmental opinions freely with their personal contacts.

THE POTENTIAL OF SOCIAL MEDIA TO TRANSITION TO SOCIAL MOVEMENTS

In this section, I will explore—through various examples—the potential of social media to transition into social movements in Iranian society. The Facebook page "My Stealthy Freedom" was created in 2014 by an UK-based journalist from the Iranian diaspora, and has subsequently

Access to this site is Denied

برابر قوانین جمهوری اسلامی ایران و دستور مقامات قضایی دسترسی به این سایت مجاز نمی باشد.

در صورتیکه این سایت به اشتباه فیلتر شده است , جهت بررسی مجدد دکمه Submit را بزنید.
If you think this site is incorrectly blocked please press the Submit button.

Fig. 2.5 Screenshot of forbidden website, taken by researcher in 2009

received over 945,000 "likes". By addressing the lack of freedom of choice regarding the Iranian government's hijab policy, it has gained the attention of many Iranian studies researchers (including, among others, Hamzehei 2014; Karimi 2014; Koo 2016b; Lewis 2015; Novak and Khazraee 2014; Sreberny 2015). (Fig. 2.7).

On the cover picture of this Facebook page, we find the following greeting in Persian, "I want to say to all of you: Come and shake my hand, I am not your enemy, I just do not want to breathe any more of my freedom stealthily, simple freedom that does no harm to others... We do not want to be sentenced forever to this stealthy freedom. That's it! We want to walk, shoulder to shoulder with those who believe or do not believe in Hijab, with dignity and freedom. That's it."

What is surprising is the high level of participation this social media campaign involved, despite the possible dangers entailed. Numerous Iranian women are uploading their stories and photos without their hijabs. One woman posted, "I do happily request you to publish my

Fig. 2.6 Screenshot of forbidden websites, taken by researcher in 2014

Fig. 2.7 "My Stealthy Freedom" Facebook page ("My Stealthy Freedom," Facebook, accessed February 20, 2016, https://www.facebook.com/StealthyFreedom.)

photo in your page so that you can deliver to the entire world not only our desire for freedom and our quest to be respected, but also our pursuit of dignity to those dictatorial authorities of Iran who have been turning a deaf ear to our aspirations. I hope they will be able to see vividly our request of freedom for our most basic rights."

As can be seen in the following post, the most common themes recurrently discussed on "My Stealthy Freedom" are freedom of choice and women's rights:

> *Equality is my right. Freedom is my right.*
> *And I want to enjoy this right while I'm alive.*
> *Until we unite our voices, we won't be able to decide for our simplest of rights.*
> *That is the right to choose how to dress, let alone our great right.*

Furthermore, in the next post, reform-oriented women maintain that it is not their true "self" that submits to the government's compulsory hijab policy:

> The international sanctions against Iran are lifted, let's stand shoulder to shoulder and raise our voices so that the domestic sanctions would be lifted as well. Each one of us lives once and only once. But we don't live, even this one time the way we like, the way we are entitled to and the way we deserve. It seems we are kept in captivity. The freedom to choose what to wear is only one simple example. We cannot even take the risk of being happy. Look at those men behind me, I am as much a human being as they are and I don't wish to die before I have lived my true self.

Nonetheless, in reality, even such secretive instances of freedom of expression on social media can be dangerous. Although most women agree with these opinions, they are afraid of the negative consequences that may arise from revealing themselves and posting photos without the hijab.[14]

> We don't have freedom even in social media. We are being judged just because of what we wear. Some people think that if we don't dress as they wish, then they can insult us. That all means we have a long way to go. So we need to be strong and stand together.

This Facebook page also addresses women's rights issues beyond the enforced wearing of the hijab, expanding to issues such as women singing in public spaces, watching public sports matches, and travelling. For example, women singing in public or on stage were considered a sin, and the conservative religious leaders considered these women a target of hatred and blame. As a result, and, in resistance, Iranian women uploaded videos of themselves singing. This page serves as a platform to criticize not only the mandatory use of the hijab, but recently, it has also uploaded posts with the hashtag "*#Myforbiddensong*", referring to the official verdict to forbid a female singer's song.

"My Stealthy Freedom" further expanded its political significance as it began to incorporate endorsements of men for women's rights, as seen in the hashtag "*#ItsMensTurn*". Men's social movement on SNS is closely related to a recent incident that caused much controversy in Iranian society. The captain of the Iranian women's futsal team, Niloufar Ardalan, was unable to participate in the 2015 AFC Futsal Championship held in Malaysia because her husband did not allow her to renew her passport.[15] However, once the Iranian team won the championship, they brought this issue to the center of attention of both national and international media. Ardalan made a call for change in Iranian laws on her Instagram, so that married women may travel abroad without their husbands' consent. After this incident, the Facebook page that had featured mostly women without their hijabs, began to be covered with posts by men, wherein they showed themselves holding up a statement saying, "Iranian law states women need their male guardians' permission to travel abroad. I support my wife's rights to travel freely without anyone's consent".

In addition, freedom of expression and the subject of individual human rights are important issues that are yet to be resolved in Iran. Individuals are still under surveillance and censored for the way they present themselves and how they act in public as well as in private. As Rahimi (2015) analyzed, censorship is continuously and systematically taking place in Iran, both officially and unofficially. New media, with its immense power of influence, has become the greatest battlefield between the government and the civilians. Nonetheless, as pointed out by Rahimi (2015), the Iranian government's cultural policies on media censorship has an omnidirectional impact on "division of labor, with regards to visual art, crafts, cinema, print publication, music, research, press relations, and tourism". Recently, two poets, Mehdi Mousavi and Fateme Ekhtesari, were sentenced to long prison terms for crimes including "insulting the holy sanctities", one of the charges being shaking hands and kissing on the cheeks with strangers. The judge sentenced both of them to 99 lashes. In response, on "My Stealthy Freedom", couples posted themselves holding up statements like "Shaking hands is not crime! A poet's place is not the prison! Break the cruel sentence!"

Furthermore, this page shows the potential of social media to move from an online social movement to an offline civil movement. As Sreberny (2015) said, "The My Stealthy Freedom page is an online activity that is putting new issues into public contention", giving the issue a sense of political significance. In other words, this page brings Iran's internal problems to the outside world, and allows the different debates of the private sphere to be discussed in the virtual space of social network. Thus, the online community is becoming an alternative public sphere, a platform for political debate. The issues that are raised on social networks have been contended in the Iranian private sphere for a long time. After the Islamic Revolution, the secretive discourses of the private sphere have moved to the platform of social media such as Facebook and, in this process, are becoming part of a new public discourse. It is true that the resistance towards the hijab policy that is active online has yet to become an offline social movement. For this, the authority of Islamic law in Iranian society is too strong. Nonetheless, just as women have now been allowed to enter sports stadiums,[16] we can expect this movement against the compulsory use of hijab to soon flare up in the Iranian social scene.

As we can see, the Facebook page "My Stealthy Freedom" is gaining more and more symbolic and political power within Iranian society. Although it is a social movement that began abroad to criticize the enforcement of the hijab, we can expect much more from this movement, in that it is dealing with the rights of Iranian women in general and is gaining support from both men and women. Overall, we can say that social media has become the new platform where public opinion is created, fomented and transmitted (Koo 2016). As the public interested in women's issues such as the hijab policy meet the opinions of discontent of the private sphere on this Facebook platform, this page has become a form of alternative public sphere. Whilst it is still difficult for this online movement to evolve directly into an active offline civil moment, it is a development we can hope to see in the close future.

CONCLUSION

Iran is no exception to the worldwide trends of neoliberalism and globalization. Iranian people are watching Psy's "Gangnam Style" through YouTube, and different parodies of the same by Iranian diasporas around the world. Furthermore, through new media and diverse forms of personal media, they are encountering the flow of information that had hitherto been controlled and restricted. The new media audience is continuously met by modernity, and in this process, the urban Iranians are establishing a world of their own, an alternative public space online. New media in Iran is engaging with political situations to produce various discourses and the competition between the state-centered media and social media that arises in this process can be ultimately explained as an extension of the conflicting ideologies and classes in Iranian society.

The use of SNS, such as Facebook and Twitter, has seen explosive growth since 2011, and we can expect Iranian media around social media and smartphones to expand even more rapidly and more multidimensionally in the future. After a large-scale anti-governmental uprising in 2009, the government has realized the threat of SNS and the Internet, declaring a "Soft War" and devoting itself to blocking the influx of Western culture via social media networks. In particular, the government is taking a strong stance against the Internet and illegal copies of Western cultural products. However, Iranian Facebook users have found their way around the restrictions through programs that disable Internet firewalls, or other proxy servers.

Abadpour and Anderson (2013) stated that the media space in Iran is functioning as an important medium for expression and is one of the few spaces left where debates can still take place. Furthermore, Wojcieszak (2013) said that the act of connecting onto the Internet, which is under censorship, is a political act in itself, and a form of day-to-day treason. Although the act itself is not a direct act of resistance against the administration, it is essentially a political act that mocks the restrictions on access to information. Thus, the viewing and embracement of new media means more than simple media intake. For this reason, research on Iranian new media should extend beyond the field of communications, and consider the fact that it is possible to extract political and cultural significance from this phenomenon.

Just as the role of new media in Iran is currently one of the most heated issues in contemporary Iranian political society, the observation of social media becomes thus an important resource for predicting the future state of Iranian politics and society. During the Green Movement that process took place around the 2009 presidential elections. New media had a greater significance above all other types of media (Koo 2012). Furthermore, the rapid growth in supply of smartphones since 2011 is expected to instigate yet another Media Revolution. The election of the moderate president Hassan Rouhani in 2013 has led to careful speculations for progressive reforms in Iran, and his statement on "the expansion of liberty through new media", right after his inauguration, leads us to pay greater attention to the outlook of new media in Iran. In this context, we can say that media is the most important factor determining the Iranian political scene, meaning that new media and social media are research topics that need to be expanded and studied in greater depth.

So far, we have seen the development of new media in Iran, centered around SNS and its impact on society. SNS is consolidating an alternative public sphere for Iranian people where they are expressing and sharing their thoughts and voices, safe from persecution. This is achieved by the collective enjoyment of illegal popular culture and communication with the outside world using new media and technology in the private space. Social media functions as an imagined community and a space of solidarity and resistance. In other words, recent trends of globalization and transnationalism are communicating and conflicting with the specific sociopolitical context of Iran as an Islamic state. What remains in question is whether the social movements that develop over online social networks can extend into the physical world.

NOTES

1. This chapter expands upon a part of Koo, Gi Yeon. "The Study on the Acceptance of New media in Iran: Focusing on Ahmadinejad Regime" *Collection of In-Depth Studies about the Strategic Region* (2013).
2. There are certain limitations to presenting accurate statistics on smartphone penetration in Iran. However, according to a report by an Iranian 3G carrier, Tamin Telecom, smartphones are predicted to take up around

40% of the Iranian mobile market. Referencing a study carried out by Freedom House (2012) about Iranian mobile communication, Fars News Agency estimates that 9% of the total Iranian population use mobile Internet, while almost 100,000 text messages are sent daily. However, this study is from 2012, but, considering the smartphone dissemination has rapidly increased since the end of 2011 and 2012, we can expect the current mobile Internet access rate through smartphones to be much higher than predicted in this report.

3. Umid Niayesh, "Over 20 Million Iranians Use Smartphones", *Trend News Agency*, June 10, 2015, accessed January 5, 2016, http://en.trend.az/iran/society/2404528.html

4. It is not easy to verify the number of Facebook users in Iran. Access to Facebook has been restricted as it is considered a forbidden site. For this reason, Facebook users resort to programs that deactivate government firewalls, or access Facebook indirectly through proxy servers or virtual private networks (VPN), which makes the collection of data extremely difficult. Nonetheless, "Iran Web 2.0" published in 2012 indicated that 58% of Iranians use Facebook regularly, while Iranian Minister of Culture and Islamic Guidance estimated there to be 4–4.5 million Facebook users in Iran by 2015. However, according to an article from Yonhap News on "The sudden rise in Facebook and Twitter from September", the number of Facebook users in Iran reached 17 million at that time. (*Yonhap News*, August 17, 2013, accessed September 28, 2013, http://www.yonhapnews.co.kr/bulletin/2013/09/17/0200000000AKR20130917112451009.HTML?from=search).

5. It means that the other generations' main source of information is not the Internet, but rather, the newspapers or even religious leaders. For example, people of 40–50 years generally access information through newspapers, radios and close relatives and family. According to Magdalena, Wojcieszak, Briar Smith and Mahmood Enayat, *Finding a Way: How Iranians reach for News and Information* (Pennsylvania: University of Pennsylvania Press, 2012), 30% of youths between 18 and 28 years of age acquired information through the Internet, as opposed to reform the 59 and above age group. A greater proportion of the older generations received their information from the mosque or other religious leaders.

6. "Iran Blogger Dies in Evin Prison," *BBC News*, March 19, 2009, accessed January 6 2016, http://news.bbc.co.uk/go/pr/fr/-/2/hi/middle_east/7953738.stm

7. Although precise circumstances remain unknown, he was pardoned in 2014 by Supreme Leader Ayatollah Khameini.

8. "Iranian Blogger Hossein Derakhshan Sentenced to Over 19 Years in Prison," International Campaign for Human Rights in Iran,

September 28, 2010, accessed January 6 2016, https://www.iranhumanrights.org/2010/09/iranian-blogger-hossein-derakhshan-receives-19-5-years-in-prison/

9. Different sources present different figures for the number of internet users in Iran. However, according to "Iran," Internet World Stats, accessed February 7, 2016, http://www.internetworldstats.com/me/ir.htm, there were approximately 46,800,000 internet users, that is, 57.2% of the entire population, in 2015. A recent report by the Ministry of Youth and Sports stated that 67.4% of the youth use the Internet but we can expect actual figures to be much higher than officially announced.

10. "Mir Hossein Mousavi," Twitter, accessed February 20, 2016, http://twitter.com/#!/mousavi1388.

11. "Mir Hossein Mousavi," Facebook, accessed February 20, 2016, https://www.facebook.com/mousavi.

12. Iran's Minister for Culture Ali Jannati said that 9.5 million Iranians use the social app Viber and 4–4.5 million use Facebook: Michael Pizzi, "Iranian leaders sign on to social media, call for end to Twitter ban," *Al Jazeera America*, November 5, 2013, accessed February 20, 2016, http://america.aljazeera.com/articles/2013/11/5/iranian-govt-signingontosocialmedia.html.

13. A proxy allows users to bypass firewalls that block certain censored sites.

14. It is particularly dangerous when the woman is question is a public figure. For example, recently, two famous Iranian actresses were suspended from acting for posting photos of themselves without hijab on their social network pages, and raising their voices against its compulsory use. Governmental officials announced that they would be allowed to return to acting if they were to apologize for such political treason.

15. Saeed Kamali Dehghan, "Husband Bars Iranian Footballer from Asian Championships," *The Guardian*, September 16, 2015, accessed February 20, 2016, http://www.theguardian.com/world/2015/sep/16/husband-bars-iranian-footballer-from-asian-championships.

16. These activists had started a campaign called "Rusari Sefid-ha", which means "those wearing white scarves." The campaign aimed at "defending women's right to attend stadiums freely." Its motto was, "My share, half of Azadi." ("Azadi" also means freedom.) Read more: Mani Fardad, "Iranian Women Still Banned from Stadiums," *Al-Monitor*, July 3, 2014, accessed February 20, 2016. http://www.al-monitor.com/pulse/originals/2014/06/iran-womens-volleyball-barred-entry.html#ixzz3zOmuUTV3.

BIBLIOGRAPHY

Abadpour, Arash, and Collin Anderson. "Fights, adapts, accepts: Archetypes of Iranian internet use." *Iran Media Program and Annenberg School for Communication, University of Pennsylvania*, 2013.

Amir-Ebrahimi, Masserat. "Weblogistan: The emergence of a new public sphere in Iran." In *Publics, Politics and Participation: Locating the Public Sphere in the Middle East and North Africa*, edited by Seteney Shami, New York: Social Science Research Council, 2009.

Anderson, Benedict. *Imagined communities: Reflections on the origin and spread of nationalism*. New York: Verso Books, 2006.

Giddens, Anthony. *Modernity and self-identity: Self and society in the late modern age*. California:Stanford University Press, 1991.

Hamzehei, Pegah. "Iranian Women's Experience of Mandatory Hijab: A Case Study of a Campaign on Facebook." Independent thesis Advanced level, Stockholm University, 2014.

Karimi, Sedigheh. "Iranian Women's Identity and Cyberspace: Case study of Stealthy Freedom." *Journal of Social Science Studies* 2 (2014): 221.

Koo, Gi Yeon. "Media as a Political Ideology and Its Cultural Meaning in the Transnational Era: Focusing on the Iranian Society." *Korean Journal of the Middle East Studies* 28 (2008).

Koo, Gi Yeon. "The Study on the Acceptance of New media in Iran: Focusing on Ahmadinejad Regime." *Collection of In-Depth Studies about the Strategic Region* VI (2013).

Koo, Gi Yeon. "Constructing an Alternative Public Sphere: Social Media and Their Cultural Meaning in Iran." Paper presented at the National University of Singapore, Middle East Institute (MEI) Media Conference, Singapore, September 3–4, 2015.

Koo, Gi Yeon. "Making an Alternative Public Sphere: New Media and Their Cultural Meanings in Iran." Paper presented at the Middle East Studies Association, Denver, Colorado, November 21–24, 2015.

Koo, Gi Yeon. "Politics of Sorrow: Dynamics and Control of Emotion in Iran" *Cross-Cultural Studies* 22(2016a): 137–168.

Koo, Gi Yeon. "To be Myself and Have My Stealthy Freedom: The Iranian Women's Engagement with Social Media." *Revista de Estudios Internacionales Mediterráneos* 21 (2016b): 29–51.

Loader, Brian D., and Dan Mercea. "Networking democracy? Social media innovations and participatory politics." *Information, Communication & Society* 14 (2011): 757–769.

Novak, Alison N., and Emad Khazraee. "The Stealthy Protester: Risk and the Female Body in Online Social Movements." *Feminist Media Studies* 14 (2014): 1094–1095.

Piri, Daryuosh and Adlina Ab Halim. "Diplomacy of Iran towards Globalization: The Tension between Globalization and Islamization in Iran (Diplomatie de l'Iran vers la mondialisation: La tension entre la mondialisation et l'islamisation en Iran)." *Cross-Cultural Communication* 7 (2011): 82.

Rahimi, Babak. "Censorship and the Islamic Republic: Two Modes of Regulatory Measures for Media in Iran." *The Middle East Journal* 69 (2015): 358–378.

Shirky, Clay. "The political power of social media." *Foreign Affairs* 90 (2011): 28–41.

Sreberny, Annabelle, and Ali Mohammadi. *Small media, big revolution: Communication, culture, and the Iranian revolution.* Minnesota: University of Minnesota, 1994.

Sreberny, Annabelle. "Wome's Digital Activism in a Changing Middle East." *International Journal of Middle East Studies* 47 (2015): 357–361.

Van Laer, Jeroen and Peter Van Aelst. "Internet and social movement action repertoires: Opportunities and limitations." *Information, Communication & Society* 13 (2010): 1146–1171.

Wojcieszak, Magdalena, Briar Smith and Mahmood Enayat. *Finding a way: How Iranians reach for News and Information.* Pennsylvania: University of Pennsylvania, 2012.

Yaghmaian, Behzad. *Social Change in Iran: An Eyewitness Account of Dissent, Defiance, and New Movements for Rights,* New York: SUNY Press, 2002.

Online sources

BBC News. "Iran blogger dies in Evin prison." March 19, 2009. Accessed January 6 2016, http://news.bbc.co.uk/go/pr/fr/-/2/hi/middle_east/7953738.stm.

Chen, Hui and Maihemuti Sali, "A Qualitative Study of Iranian Facebook Users' Perceptions of Using Facebook in Iran's Participation Activities." Master Thesis , Örebro University, 2010. Accessed August 25, 2016. http://www.diva-portal.org/smash/get/diva2:372479/FULLTEXT01.pdf.

Dehghan, Saeed Kamali. "Iranian women post pictures of themselves without hijabs on Facebook." *The Gurdian*, May 12, 2014. Accessed February 20, 2016. http://www.theguardian.com/world/2014/may/12/iran-women-hijab-facebook-pictures-alinejad.

Dehghan, Saeed Kamali. "Husband bars Iranian footballer from Asian championships." *The Guardian*, September 16, 2015. Accessed February 20, 2016. http://www.theguardian.com/world/2015/sep/16/husband-bars-iranian-footballer-from-asian-championships.

Fardad, Mani. "Iranian women still banned from stadiums," *Al-Monitor*, July 3, 2014. Accessed February 20, 2016. http://www.al-monitor.

com/pulse/originals/2014/06/iran-womens-volleyball-barred-entry. html#ixzz3zOmuUTV3.

International Campaign for Human Rights in Iran. "Iranian blogger Hossein Derakhshan sentenced to over 19 years in prison." September 28, 2010. Accessed January 6 2016. https://www.iranhumanrights.org/2010/09/iranian-blogger-hossein-derakhshan-receives-19-5-years-in-prison/.

Internet World Stats. "Iran." Accessed February 7, 2016, http://www.internetworldstats.com/me/ir.htm.

Niayesh, Umid. "Over 20 million Iranians use smartphones." *Trend News Agency*, June 10, 2015. Accessed January 5 2016. http://en.trend.az/iran/society/2404528.html.

Pizzi, Michael. "Iranian leaders sign on to social media, call for end to Twitter ban." *Al Jazeera America*, November 5, 2013. Accessed February 20. 2016.http://america.aljazeera.com/articles/2013/11/5/iranian-govt-signingontosocialmedia.html.

World Bank. "Internet users (per 100 people)." Accessed February 20, 2016. http://data.worldbank.org/indicator/IT.NET.USER.P2.

World Bank. "Fixed broadband Internet subscribers (per 100 people)." Accessed February 20, 2016. http://data.worldbank.org/indicator/IT.NET.BBND. P2.

World Bank. "Mobile cellular subscriptions (per 100 people)." Accessed February 20, 2016. http://data.worldbank.org/indicator/IT.CEL.SETS.P2.

Yonhap News. "The sudden rise in Facebook and Twitter from September." August 17, 2013. Accessed September 28, 2013, http://www.yonhapnews. co.kr/bulletin/2013/09/17/0200000000AKR20130917112451009. HTML?from=search.

CHAPTER 3

You've Come A Long Way Baby: Women's New Media Practices, Empowerment, and Everyday Life in Kuwait and the Middle East

Deborah L. Wheeler

In 1968 the Philip Morris Company defined a new American woman by the brand of cigarette she smokes. The ad campaign presented a brief history of women's lives, through the lens of "The right to smoke" and declared "You've come a long way baby" (Fig. 3.1).

With hindsight, to measure women's empowerment via the Virginia Slims marketing strategy seems too small a victory to warrant such celebration. Equality achieved through thinner, more womanly cigarettes, which encourage women to develop a life-threatening habit, raises interesting questions about the meaning of empowerment.

How should we best understand women's empowerment in the digital age? Patterns of Arab women's empowerment in the twenty-first century are more "ceiling breaking" and progressive than the forms of

D.L. Wheeler (✉)
Department of Political Science, United States Naval Academy, Annapolis, MD, USA

© The Author(s) 2017
N. Lenze et al. (eds.), *Media in the Middle East*,
DOI 10.1007/978-3-319-65771-4_3

Fig. 3.1   You've come a long way baby?

transformation Philip Morris and American society imagined for women in the 1960s and 70s. Some Arab women have come a long way, "leap-frogging" to new heights of social and political engagement, both liter-ally and figuratively. In the digital age, we see Arab women flying fighter jets in active combat (2015), summiting Mount Everest (2014), winning the Nobel Peace Prize (2011), running universities and businesses, pat-enting new medical devices, and making revolution. This chapter focuses on the changing representation, voice, and engagement of Arab women in cyberspace, with a particular emphasis on women in Kuwait, and asks what role, if any, new media tools play in such processes of empower-ment. While there are clearly numerous variables at play in the process of Arab women's enhanced agency, the participants in this struggle often highlight the utility of new media tools in projecting power and voice, for reasons explored more thoroughly in what follows.

For the purposes of this analysis, new media are understood as com-munication devices that are: personalized, portable, many-to-many, virtual, social, and made publicly available sometime in the last three decades. New media include mobile phones, the Internet, Facebook, Twitter and tablets. In this chapter what is most important is not what device women use to engage publicly and privately with information and virtual civic space, but, rather, what they do with such experiences to enable processes of empowerment in their lives. Thus, social media and the Internet can be understood as shared pathways to new forms of rep-resentation and voice. Collectively, new media form an ecological space within which people interact and represent both themselves and their communities. Together women form new relationships and experiences in these virtual environments, with clear implications for their "real" lives.

The Middle East is an increasingly contentious place, especially when it comes to women's lives. Women's representation, social role, and political activism are being renegotiated throughout the region (Dubai Social Media Report 2014). As Coleman (2011) states, during the Arab Uprisings, for example, "Women are on the front lines of change: protesting alongside men, blogging passionately and prolifically, cov-ering the demonstrations as journalists and newscasters, leading pub-lic demonstrations and launching social media campaigns" (Coleman 2011, p. 215).[1] With regimes collapsing and public demands for good governance more widely vocalized in the region, will women find greater opportunities for empowerment? What future for the Middle East, and what role for women within it? What role, if any, will new media tools play in enabling women to change their lives, economies, societies, and politics? These issues form the core questions of this chapter, focussing on data collected in Morocco, Tunisia, Egypt, Jordan, Israel/Palestine, Syria, Turkey, Saudi Arabia, Oman, the United Arab Emirates, Qatar, and Kuwait, between 1990 and 2014. Based upon these investigations and data, I argue that new media empower women in everyday life, giving them new access to information, helping them to find a life partner, enabling them to obtain advice on socially sensitive topics (divorce, sexuality, relationships, and sex), making lives easier and more fun, and enabling them to develop and project opinions on politics, religion, and social issues. Women are actively involved in redefining their roles in Middle Eastern society and new media use enhances their abilities to achieve new forms of civic engagement. But the impact of women's voices and agency is best assessed in processes of empowerment localized in their everyday lives, because it is in the politics of small power negotiations that women's empowerment is most generally felt (Hofheinz 2011; Bayat 2010; Goldfarb 2006). In order to ground this analysis in the particulars of Arab women's lived experience, this chapter focuses particularly on the use of the Internet by women in Kuwait.

Kuwait is an important case study, because it is one of the most digitally connected countries in the Gulf/MENA region (the 4th most connected; see Table 3.1 below). Moreover, recent analysis indicates that women in the small emirate have achieved forms of empowerment and equality that are unprecedented in the region. For example, the *World Economic Forum Global Gender Gap Report 2014* states that Kuwait is the region's top-performing country in terms of closing the Middle East gender gap, having increased its position to number one in the region (global ranking 113th), mostly because of its earned income rankings for women.[2]

Between 1996 and 2014, I have seen women come a long way in terms of their Internet use, activism, and empowerment. Women in Kuwait dress more freely than in the rest of the Arabian Gulf. They expect more from their professional lives and more equality within marriage than other places in the Middle East. Women in Kuwait achieve more education wise than in many places regionally. And Kuwaiti women are more vocal in their demands for change.

While it was an isolated incident, for me the most meaningful representation of this change is a young Kuwaiti woman who filled out her Internet use survey and under gender put "female; gay." The sense that her sexual identity was primary in understanding who she is; and that she felt agentive enough to say "I am GAY and proud of it!" epitomizes the processes explored more completely below.

Given increased the activism and resistance of Middle Eastern women in the region, including, for example, the Saudi women's driving campaign,[3] the Turkish Smile campaign,[4] women's activism in the Arab Uprisings,[5] and women's participation in the Green Movement in Iran (2009),[6] this analysis attempts to identify regional patterns of new media activism and resistance as a backdrop to the particulars of the Kuwaiti case. The data yielded by these two approaches, one focused on the particulars of Kuwait, and a second, more attuned to transregional patterns of representation and new media resistance by women, seeks to confirm the initial hypothesis that clear links exist between new communication patterns and women's empowerment in the Middle East.

STARTING POINTS AND EVOLUTIONS

My first experience of Arab women's lives came in 1990, in an East Jerusalem Dojo. I was studying popular culture and resistance in the first Intifada for my doctoral thesis, and my ethnographic pathway into the Palestinian community was through women's classes, at the Palestinian Judo and Karate Association. At the time, the Internet did not exist in Palestine, satellite TV was in its infancy, and "new media" meant cassette tapes, fax machines, leaflets, word of mouth, and graffiti. The martial arts were a more expedient pathway to empowerment than mere words and images, or so the women of the dojo argued.

My instructor was a black belt, and an activist for an independent Palestine. She was physically strong and mentally cunning. At the same time she was a mother, nurturing of her students, combining physical powers and feminine influence into a complex, yet highly capable life. She was also a Palestinian living under occupation, which meant she lacked a passport, freedom of movement, and real opportunities for personal and national growth. In daily life, she experienced dangers and discrimination, and had to repress her political opinions for fear of arrest.

My judo instructor's story reminds us that although women can make their own forms of empowerment, even in contexts of adversity, they do not act with complete liberty. As Marx had noted more than a century earlier, "Men make their own history, but they do not make it as they please. They do not make it under self-selected circumstances" (Marx 1852). The same is true for Arab women. As argued below, however, the advent of cyberspace provides some women a shared space within which to be partially liberated from their context. Online environments allow Arab women to transcend national boundaries, and social class, aesthetic values such as beauty, sectarian differences, cultural norms, social categories (hetero-sexual/homo-sexual; male/female), and barriers to voice, participation and information. In the words of one Kuwaiti female interviewed for this project, when asked if the Internet has made a difference in her life, she responds, "Yes and hell yes. I'm more aware of what's going on around me" (Interview #255, Kuwait City, July 2010).

How to Recognize Arab Women's Empowerment

Every woman in the world is the product of her environment, her geography and national status, her sexual orientation, her physical appearance and family name, her level of education and social class, her employment status, her relationship to patriarchies and matriarchies that shape her identity and expectations, and, last but not least, her access to information technology (IT). All of these factors influence her ability to have the life she wants, as well as what society wants for her life. So how can we measure empowerment objectively, and across cultures, without marginalizing the role those women's desires and circumstances play in the quest for a meaningful life? How can we understand the impact of context on women's lives, without failing to recognize women's ingenuity and creativity in carving out spaces for autonomy and influence?

The film *Wadjda*[7] illustrates this need for contextualized knowledge of women's empowerment, and reminds us that women can use the structures that bind, to resist. We see this when Wadjda uses a Quran recitation contest to obtain a bike. With financial independence from the prize money, won craftily through a traditional, Islamic practice, she works to redefine the boundaries of acceptable public behavior for women. By challenging society's rules that women shouldn't ride bikes because they might risk their virginity by breaking their hymen, Wadjda embodies new forms of empowerment. Wadjda represents a new reading of women's resistance: from the woman who works in a hospital, with men, to Wadjda's boundary-breaking victory, to her male friend's acceptance of her public bike riding, to the shopkeeper's agreement to hold the bike for Wadjda until she earns the money, each of these individuals play a role in women's transformational social roles. The school's headmistress, Wadjda's mother, the Indian driver, and Wadjda's father, who divorces her mother and marries another because she is unable to bear a male heir and brother for Wadjda, represent patriarchy in its most limiting form. The more constraining the patriarchy, the wider the range for resistance. The Saudi filmmaker's act of narration, filming on location by a woman for the first time in history, in a country where public screening of film is illegal, also represents processes of boundary shattering. The film is a meta-narrative of women's resistance in Saudi Arabia. It is also a reminder of distinct forms of empowerment. In Kuwait or Cairo, riding a bike or making a film might not be a revolutionary act for a woman, while in Saudi Arabia the accomplishment of these small acts of defiance is comparable to reaching the summit of Mount Everest.

The story of Wadjda, and narratives like hers, raises the question of how to measure women's empowerment in the Arab World. Are more universal constructions of empowerment, like counting seats in Parliament, measuring women's participation in the labor force, and educational attainment sufficient? How can we better understand empowerment and the gender gap in the Arab World? What if a woman finds her joy and purpose in maintaining a household, raising children and loving a spouse, yet resists by allowing her daughters, for example, to ride a bike, to marry for love, or to work or study abroad? Wouldn't such acts ultimately contribute to women's empowerment; both the mother's, through her resistance of the norms of patriarchy; and the daughter's, by allowing her opportunities to shape her destiny?

What if a woman lives under occupation, or in an authoritarian political system, in a strictly Islamic state, in a context of civil war or an abusive family? Do structural differences, those circumstances, which exist outside of a woman's choices, provide a need for nuance in empowerment measures, something beyond an abstract set of global standards? In general, regardless of context and personal circumstance, scholars of women's empowerment argue that "when girls receive more education, their children are healthier. When women have more ownership of property, domestic violence often drops. When more women work outside the home, a country's economic output rises. And when women hold elective office, government corruption is lower" (Skoler 2015). With these examples of the ways in which women's empowerment equate with a society's overall health and wellbeing, we have incentives for considering women's empowerment in general terms. But when wanting to understand processes of resistance and targets for change, then more contextualized framing of empowerment illuminates women's lived experiences and the deeper meanings of empowerment particulars.

Objective measurements of women's empowerment in the Arab World highlight the challenges women face in the region. It is these circumstances which lead Arab feminist Fatima Mernissi to ask, "Why on earth is the Arab World so hostile to women? Why can it not see women as a key force for development building? Why so much desire to humiliate and retard us?" (Mernissi 1996, p. vii).

Women's Empowerment Measurements: All data are sourced from the World Bank Indicators: http://data.worldbank.org/indicator and the Global Gender Gap Rankings 2014 http://reports.weforum.org/global-gender-gap-report-2014/report-highlights/).

The data in Table 3.1 represent a general picture of women's empowerment in the Middle East. From this chart, we can see that Bahrain has the highest Internet penetration rate (91%). Kuwait has the highest percentage of female participation in the labor force (44%). Lebanon has the highest life expectancy for women (82 years). Tunisia has the highest percentage of female MPs (31%; ranked 30th globally—beating the UK, 36th globally (24%); and the USA, 71st globally (20%)). Kuwait is also the country in the region with the smallest gender gap; or with the highest level of overall equality (measured in terms of economic, health, political and education indicators). But what do these rankings really tell us about women's lived experience and empowerment in the Middle East? And what role is played in new media in such empowerment?

WOMEN'S VOICES: HOW NEW MEDIA
USE EMPOWERS KUWAITI WOMEN

Since December 1996, Kuwaiti women have provided me with windows into their lives and the gender challenges they face. Within the two decades of observing everyday life in Kuwait, I have learned to admire, respect, and resist aspects of patriarchy at work in this conservative, mostly Muslim society. Kuwait is a survivalist landscape, from resilience required to recover from Iraqi occupation (1990–1991), to staying clean

Table 3.1 Women's empowerment measurements

Country	Labor force % female (2000/2013)	Life expectancy female (2013)	% Seats in parliament held by women (2014)	Internet access per 100 people (male and female, 2014)	Global gender Gap 2014 Rank/ 1 = equality 0 = inequality
Bahrain	35/39	77	8	91	124/ (0.6261)
Egypt	19/24	73	2	31.7	129/ (0.6064)
Iraq	13/15	73	25	11.3	No data
Jordan	13/16	76	12	44.0	134/ (0.5968)
Kuwait	44/44	76	2	78.7	113/ (0.6457)
Lebanon	19/23	82	3	74.7	135/ (0.5923)
Libya	27/30	77	16	17.8	No data
Morocco	29/27	73	17	56.8	133/ (0.5988)
Oman	28/29	79	1	70.2	128/ (0.6091)
Qatar	38/51	79	0	91.5	116/ (0.6403)
Saudi Arabia	16/20	78	20[a]	63.7	130/ (0.6059)
Syria	20/14	78	12	28.1	139/ (0.5775)
Tunisia	24/25	76	31	46.2	123/ (0.6272)
UAE	34/47	78	18	90.4	115/ (0.6436)
Yemen	22/25	64	0	22.6	145/ (0.5145)

[a]When this change was implemented, it was not just a publicity stunt. They even had to remodel the Shura building to allow women to participate. And in terms of Saudi politics, the Shura council is the highest form of political engagement in the country. If you look at the biographies of the women who were appointed, this also illustrates how serious the Saudi state is about empowering women, of course, in ways that are compatible with their own version of 'acceptable' roles for women. The definition of 'acceptable' roles for women—from women entering the commerce realm (including store clerks, which illustrates that this is not just about empowering a handful of elite women) sports, climbing Mt. Everest, or entering into the highest levels of advising the government, or publicly resisting driving rules is changing very rapidly in Saudi

and healthy in sand storms, to maintaining hydration, physical activity, and leisure during the summer months, especially when Ramadan coincides with extremely hot temperatures and long days. Kuwait City is one of the hottest cities on the planet.[8]

Kuwait is a very small country, and a very rich country. The economy is dominated by petroleum resources, controlled almost exclusively by the ruling Sabah family. Most Kuwaitis work for the government, receiving large stipends for housing, health care, food, water, electricity, education, and retirement.

Kuwait is a patriarchal society in which citizenship is awarded by birth, through the father's kinship line. Accordingly, a Kuwaiti woman who marries a non-Kuwaiti man cannot pass her Kuwaiti citizenship on to her offspring. A Kuwaiti man, however, who marries a non-Kuwaiti (a very common practice) can pass Kuwaiti citizenship on to his children. The non-Kuwaiti spouse also gains citizenship through marriage to a Kuwaiti.

Nearly half of all Kuwaiti women are employed. Most receive a post-secondary education, though not always in the field of their interest. During several years of teaching at the American University of Kuwait, I have had numerous female students tell me that they wanted to study business or politics, but were told by their parents to study graphic design or interior design because these fields were considered more suitable for a woman.

Most Kuwaiti women have domestic help: maids for cleaning, cooks, gardeners, drivers, and nannies. Kuwaiti women are liberated from a wide array of domestic responsibilities, which are generally faced by women in other countries. At the same time, the pressures on Kuwaiti women to care for the needs of immediate and extended family members, to host family gatherings, to attend weddings and engagements, to be actively involved in charity and the community, to provide for the physical and emotional needs of husbands, children, and relatives (many of whom live in the same household) is more than a full-time job. In addition, responsibilities to manage the household staff, and to maintain a career or extended educational development, in addition, caring for one's physical appearance and health, all add stress to Kuwaiti women's lives.

So what role does Internet use play in Kuwaiti women's lives? The following paragraphs will closely examine a representative handful of "empowerment" narratives regarding women's Internet use in Kuwait. Students at the American University of Kuwait, in a class on Arab Human Development, collected the narratives for an assignment on

Internet use and development. One of our main concerns as a class was to study the gender gap and women's empowerment, and whether or not Internet use would change women's lives.

Many women interviewed for the study viewed the Internet as a tool for empowerment because it was "a source for all knowledge" (Interview #125 July 2010, Kuwait City). Interestingly, the woman who gave this interview is 42, employed in the IT field, and taught her husband to use the Internet. She uses the Internet for email, health concerns and to get advice. She has a Facebook page and her favorite website is www.alseraj. net, an Islamic advice and Quran site.

Another woman interviewed for this study states that she met her husband on the web and that Kuwaiti society "is less conservative because of the Internet" (Interview #126, Kuwait City July 2010). Several women interviewed for this study stated that they had met their spouse through the Internet. Interestingly, her favorite website is Koora.com—a soccer website! This seemed an unusual choice for a young woman.

Several women highlighted the ease with which the Internet allowed them to maintain or expand their social networks, or to save money on international calls. One woman said that Internet use was fun, but it made her fatter, because of long hours of sitting.

Many of the women interviewed for this project highlighted more typical "empowerment" narratives, with a distinctive political twist. For example, a 38-year-old Muslim Kuwaiti who is not employed, but did teach her sisters to use the Internet, and has an interest in sports, specifically tennis (frenchopen.com and wimbledon.com are her favorite websites) observes that Internet use "allowed people to know more about other countries policies so we become more involved in government decisions. We find out other countries styles, culture, politics and business and this has an impact on Arab society" (Interview #155 July 2010, Kuwait City).

Similarly, a 24-year-old Kuwaiti explains that the Internet is "a place to share ideas and opinions and this has an impact on politics in the Arab world" (Interview # 158, Kuwait City, July 2010). Another young woman explains that exploring the Internet "has allowed me to understand the outside world with a simple click of my fingers. It helped me to learn a lot" (Interview #161, Kuwait City, July 2010).

If we were looking for Arab Uprisings—like activism and resistance in Kuwaiti women's Internet narratives, we might be disappointed in the testimonies above. No one claims that they are organizing for change, resisting patriarchy, and demanding more equality in citizens' right. Instead, in these narratives we see that Kuwaiti women are empowered by saving time, money, meeting new people, learning new things, and becoming more aware of politics and foreign culture.

While these micro-changes might seem mild (mildly boring in fact) they do illustrate something important about Kuwaiti society, and the relatively good lives women lead there. Among younger women, however, there are signs of overt resistance. Girls dressing "butch" embracing their gayness; women wearing mini-skirts and skinny jeans, low-cut blouses; young women dating and flirting in more daring ways; women wanting careers and spouses that they choose for themselves, using the Internet to discover pathways to their own individual desires and purposes. Many young women I interviewed for this project stated that they did not want to get married, in order to have more time and opportunity to make a difference in the world, and they were overtly resisting family pressures to maintain their autonomy. All of these processes of dismantling patriarchy through subtle forms of resistance are, however, aided by new media practices.

Beyond Palestine: Understanding the Challenge of Arab Women's Dis-Empowerment

Two direct experiences of violence in Arab women's lives motivate this study of empowerment. One occurred in Amman, Jordan in 2004; and the second emerged in Kuwait City, in 2011. Both of these encounters illustrate the degree to which some women are not empowered, even in the digital age.

Muhajiba

The cold February day in Amman started out relatively normally, with a trip to the market located in the City Center mall in West Amman. We had just parked the car and were walking into the mall, when our gaze was drawn to a muhajiba woman (a Muslim conservative woman, wearing a hijab, niqab, abaya, and gloves). The only part of this woman's body that was visible, were her eyes, magnified by heavy eye make-up and stylish glasses. She walked briskly, as if being tracked or in danger, which drew our attention. Behind her trailed two bearded men wearing

Arabian Gulf dress, a long dishdasha gown, an igal and ghitra head covering. They rapidly approached the young woman, grabbing her arm aggressively and spinning her around to face them. The younger of the two backhanded the woman across the face, launching her glasses through the air. Her glasses hit the floor with a smack, and slid into the wall near us. We froze in fear for this woman's life. What were we supposed to do to protect her; to stop the violence? Although my husband was with me to witness this fight, we were foreign and not wanting to make the situation worse.

Suddenly a crowd of 10 or so local men encircled the three Gulfis. They stopped the men from beating up the woman, temporarily. Who are the men issuing the beating? What relation to the woman? What was the justification for the public display of violence? The questions flew in heated Arabic. After a few minutes, the men dispersed, and the beating continued. The two men dragged the woman out of the mall, and one of the bystanders handed the eldest man her glasses. They dragged her out of the mall, and shoved her into the back seat of a car that was presumably being driven by another family member.

One of the men who intervened explained when we asked that the men were the father and brother of the young woman. The young woman had disgraced the family's honor, and the father and brother had an obligation to put an end to it. Once the crowd of men learned that family members were acting to protect their honor, they left the scene. The man who stopped to explain to us what happened said she deserved what she had coming for disgracing the family.

A father and brother were judge, jury and executioner—their sister/daughter was guilty, but of what crime? Whose honor and what violation would warrant such embarrassment and spectacle, such pain and suffering? Most importantly, where is this woman today? Did she find a way to resist and to live her own life?

Had it been 2015, instead of 2004, I could have used my smartphone to film the event, to show you what I saw, to inhibit the beating and, perhaps, to protect the woman; to enable the police to arrest the violators. Social media access might have allowed me to get involved without experiencing harm myself. I could have been like an anonymous observer in Riyadh, where two Saudi men were filmed beating a female family member; or this most recent case, which involves an expat who beat a Saudi woman in the souk; the film footage of which went viral, resulting in the man's arrest.[9] Citizens throughout the world are leveraging new communication tools to resist bad governance and social injustice through processes of digital disclosure, which intensify civic engagement and encourage processes of better governance.

If It's in a Marriage, It's not Rape

A second incident happened during a class I was teaching at the American University in Kuwait in the summer of 2011. We were having a discussion on women's rights and human development in the Middle East in an Arab Human Development seminar. Classes at AUK are segregated by gender. In the women's section about half-way through the summer course, we were talking about women's rights and domestic abuse. One of the studies we were discussing talked about a lack of protection for Arab women from marital rape. One of the young women in the class, a member of the Sabah family, who was married, raised her hand. She explained that the study is wrong, because in the Muslim world, there can be no rape within a marriage. A woman is not allowed to say no to sex with her husband, she explained. Thus, if she refuses, and he takes it anyway, it is not considered rape. I was shocked. How was I supposed to respond? Is this a problem with Islam; a cultural problem; a problem of false consciousness, not my business, or all of the above? The students were 30 women, some liberal, some religiously conservative, and no one objected to the young royal's observations about marital obligations. I was uncertain about how to proceed, as I was a guest, brought into educate, not to colonize or to force my culture on theirs. But wasn't marital rape a violation of women's empowerment no matter what the cultural or religious justification?

This was a cultural impasse—my upbringing and culture would not let me accept this ultimate disempowerment by relinquishing control over one's body, one's desire. And they, raised with the notion that their job is to keep their husbands satisfied, lest the husband take another wife or look outside the marriage for sexual satisfaction.

I turned to the digital universe on a quest for empowerment. Certainly, I would find a way to learn more about what Islam teaches about a women's rights within marriage. If Islam, as a part of the marital contract, prescribed relinquishing control over a woman's body, I wanted evidence. Multiple sources were available online. I chose to rely on *Dar al Ifta al Masriyya*, as the organization is reputable; as the "pioneering foundation for fatwa in the Islamic world"... and the "flagship

for Islamic legal research" worldwide, as described on the organization's home page.[10] *Dar al Ifta al Masriyya* is physically located in
Cairo, Egypt, but also has a significant online presence, including a rich
archive of questions and answers about the conduct of everyday life for
Muslims.

According to *Dar al Ifta*, it is illegal for a husband to forcibly engage
in sex with his wife. For example, one the "most viewed" fatwa pages on
the site is an entry entitled "marital rape."[11]

The topic of sex, marriage, and relations between men and women are
popular subjects on Islamic guidance websites. The only more popular
category is food rules. For example, in the *Dar al Ifta* website, among
the "most popular" fatwas are questions about whether or not it is
against Shariah for women to post photos of themselves on Facebook?
The answer according to the Dar al Ifta imams is yes, it is allowed.[12]
Another question is: is it permissible for a woman to chat with men on
social media? The answer is yes, so long as the purpose is for study, work,
or something else "chaste."[13]

Muslim women have used online fatwa services to specifically ask
questions about sex within marriage. For example, on the *Islamicity*
website, a woman asks, "with my husband, sex is always painful as he
never engages in any foreplay or kindness. I feel like an animal and I
want to reject painful sex. Is this permitted in Islam?" The fatwa from
Dar Al-Ifta would say yes, you can reject painful sex, and your husband
should not behave like an animal. The Islamicity fatwa says, "Islam's
main focus is on building a stable marital life." In the service of a good
marriage, "it is the duty of the husband and wife to see that they are a
source of comfort and tranquility for each other." Moreover, "intimacy
is a mutual right for both husband and wife." Therefore, "the husband
should not deny himself to his wife, and the wife should also not deny
herself to her husband."[14] To use such online fatwa services would be a
microform of empowerment and a demonstration of how the Internet
can promote women's rights within a marriage.

Part of the process of enabling men to see us differently is representational. How we look, how we are portrayed, sets expectations for wom-
en's lives. Embedded in representations are layers of power, which shape
and constrain what is expected, and what is possible for women's lives. It
is in this sense that Philip Morris did women a favor by showing how far
they had come, by giving them a cigarette all of their own, that looked
different, and met women's specific needs. While this might have been a

small and dangerous victory in hindsight, the ad campaign still illustrates the power of representation. How are Arab women represented, and how are these images changing over time? Are Arab women becoming more empowered in how they are portrayed? What role does new media usage play in Arab women's representation?

REPRESENTING ARAB WOMEN: YOU'VE COME A LONG WAY BABY?

On a recent visit (June 2015) to the Metropolitan Museum of Art in Manhattan, the following image captured my attention (Fig. 3.2).

Even from a distance, without reading the caption, my eyes were drawn to this generic orientalist representation of an Arab woman, which contained all of the layers of stereotype characteristic of Western understandings of the subject. The painting was created in the early 1900s, although its message and meaning are still relevant as a marker of women's representational leaps forward.

Fast-forward about a century, and see how significantly some women's representation and lived experience have changed. Ms. Eltahawy is an outspoken critic of Arab culture. In her book *Headscarves and Hymens: Why the Arab World Needs a Sexual Revolution*, she issues a call to action: "To the girls of the Middle East and North Africa: Be immodest, rebel, disobey and know you deserve to be free" (Eltahawy 2016). In her own life, Eltahawy has practiced what she preaches. She has defaced NY City subway advertising and gone to jail for her publiSc statement of opposition to anti-Muslim advertising.[15] She has marched and reported from Tahrir Square during the Arab Uprisings, where she was sexually assaulted, an experience which launched her book project. Eltahawy's call to action is revolutionary, because, as Fatima Mernissi argues, "the ideal model of femininity upheld by orthodox Sunni Islam is that of an obedient woman, one who is physically modest. Such a woman does not challenge laws and orders. She veils her body and keeps it available for her husband only (Mernissi 1996, p. 113). Eltahawy's model of femininity turns this traditional model on its head, so to speak.

While responding to their own unique calls to action, Arab women are setting new standards for their social roles and representation. For example, Emirati fighter pilot Maj. Mariam al Mansour, who assisted her country with the air campaign against ISIS, has broken barriers for women in combat.

Fig. 3.2 Arab Woman, 1905–1906; John Singer Sargent. Metropolitan Museum of Art, New York

Similarly, Saudi citizen Raha Moharrak records a milestone of women's achievement by being the youngest woman and the first Arab woman to reach Everest's summit with her successful 2013 climb.

Immodesty and political activism have become a form of extreme sport for a few Arab women. For example, Tunisian Femen Amina Tyler extended the bare-chested protest for women's rights to North Africa, an act that landed her in jail.

Her resistance, and the freedom poaching response of the Tunisian government, sparked a global "topless jihad day" to contest her arrest. Topless activists launched protests in front of Arab embassies worldwide. Images posted on the web of the global solidarity movement with Amina illustrate the geographic reach the topless jihad achieved.[16] While many of the protesters were perceived as attacking Islamic culture in ethnocentric ways, counter-responses by Muslim women globally, defended Islam, and made the mobilization more inclusive and impactful. A dialogue emerged. The fact that a Tunisian woman's norm-violating Facebook post started the mobilization process is a sign of both Arab women's enhanced risk taking and engagement, as well as the role of new media in supporting and spreading women's calls to action globally. Sisterhood is more powerful in the digital age, because the message can reach more people (women and men) and agency is concentrated and shared. The same process can be seen, for example, in videos posted globally by women in support for the Arab women's driving campaign in Saudi Arabia.

The Uprising of Women in the Arab World Facebook campaign (https://www.facebook.com/intifadat.almar2a) provides another example of global mobilization for women's empowerment via social media. It also illustrates that a partnership between the genders expands the reach of the mobilization. A point the Femen appear to reject, the Uprising of Women in the Arab World suggests that empowering women is at least 50 percent about mobilizing men to see women differently. Moreover, calls to action, which avoid offensive representations, have the potential to appeal to a wider audience. Their mainstream images and moderate voices embraced by both men and women reveal the subtlety and promise of new media agency. Images from the campaign are multifaceted in their message and their messenger: I don't need a guardian; I don't need to obey a man, and he is no better than me. The man on the right says he supports the movement, "because I can't think of a single good reason not to."[17] The man on the left explains that he supports the movement, to paraphrase, because states run by men have ruined the world, and he thinks empowering women would result in political change for the betterment of all.

A visit to the website of the movement presents the visitor with a wide range of new frames of women—their changing social roles, voices, and capabilities. The calls to action presented by the site include bridge-building messages spanning the globe and gender gaps. But what do these new narratives and representations mean? Are they as token in significance as the one Arab woman who reached the summit of Everest; or the one Arab woman who bombed ISIS from a fighter jet? Do images and calls to action have wider consequences for other women's empowerment? Do they set leading examples of what Arab women can achieve? By pressing the boundaries of what is normal and acceptable for Arab women's lives, we see negotiations of power and purpose in everyday life. Cyberspace and the voices and representations within this realm give us hints of the forms of liberation and resistance taking place on the ground, potentially more widespread, in Arab women's lives. They indicate forms of change which deserve narrative analysis as a means for verifying the everyday struggles which women in the Arab world confront, in part aided by new media tools.

Conclusion

This chapter argues that new media, defined as communication tools that are personalized, portable, many-to-many, virtual, social, and made publicly available sometime in the last three decades, play a role in Arab women's empowerment. In the service of this argument, this chapter examines ethnographic evidence on women's lived experiences in the Middle East, collected during many years of travel and research in the region. This chapter also uses digital examples of tools available for Arab women's empowerment, as well as Arab women's representations in cyberspace as evidence of everyday forms of resistance. The analysis compares images and experiences of Arab women with aggregate empowerment indicators and argues that although statistics provide important benchmarking for women's achievements in the Middle East, they tell us little about the everyday life struggles and opportunities for women in the region. Instead, this study examines women's digital practices in

Kuwait and detects subtle forms of empowerment through information access, social networking, human capital development, and civic engagement. In these small pathways to empowerment Kuwaiti women illustrate the importance of new media in Arab women's lives.

The turbulence of the Middle East's political and social environment offers freedom to shape new power relationships between rulers and the ruled, men and women, but the riskiness of destabilizing political structures and social norms simultaneously can make some women hesitant to act up, like my AUK students who refused to consider rape in a marriage illegal. Others, like Mona Eltahawy, find the chaos a liberating environment for smashing patriarchy in the service of equality and shared rule, over women's bodies, over their social roles, over their cyberpractices and -desires. In the wake of such unrest, we can only wait and see what Arab women will do next. The sky is the limit, both literally and figuratively.

In closing, we might ask, what do Arab women want? In the spirit of this chapter, I would say, we need to ask Arab women this question within their individual contexts; to locate women's voices and images in everyday life and cyberspace as they articulate their desires, according to their interests, and capabilities. On various pathways to empowerment, however, I have found that Arab women share globally in what we don't want. That is, "what women don't want is to be told how we should act or how we should feel… The goals we set for ourselves are based upon personal emotional and financial needs and therefore are the right choices because they stem from our hearts, and not societal expectations." (Krasnow 2014). Much like other places in the world, new media help Arab women discover what they want, who they are, and to resist societal expectations in ways great and small, with the results still emerging.

NOTES

1. Women's involvement in the Arab Uprisings is defined here in relation to new media practices—so I don't see the need to bring in other past revolutionary settings. For example, during the first Intifada, women baked bread, pickled vegetables, passed through word of mouth information about strikes, but these practices are different from the more overt and discursive forms of resistance in the Arab Uprisings of 2011.

2. "The Global Gender Gap Index 2014," World Economic Forum, accessed February 20, 2016, http://reports.weforum.org/global-gender-gap-report-2014/report-highlights/

3. "Video Shows Saudi Woman Being Slapped While Crowd Watches!" Saudi Women to Drive, April 22, 2015, accessed February 20, 2016, http://saudiwomentodrive.com/.

4. "#direnkahkaha," Twitter, accessed February 20, 2016, https://twitter.com/search?q=%23direnkahkaha.

5. David Harris, "Dr Grami: Feminism, Activism and the Arab Spring," *The Clarion Project*, February 2, 2014, accessed February 20, 2016, http://www.clarionproject.org/analysis/dr-grami-feminism-activism-and-arab-spring.

6. GlobalPost, "Iran's Women A Driving Force Behind Green Movement," *The World Post*, May 25, 2011, accessed February 20, 2016, http://www.huffingtonpost.com/2009/07/24/irans-women-a-driving-for_n_244218.html.

7. Wadjda, directed by Haifaa Al-Mansour (2012; Iceland: Razor Film Produktion GmbH).

8. Liz Osborn, "Hottest Cities in the World," *Current Results*, accessed February 2016, http://www.currentresults.com/Weather-Extremes/hottest-cities-in-the-world.php

9. Za, Sa, "Man Slaps a Saudi Lady in Public in KSA". YouTube video, 0:55. Posted April 22, 2015. Accessed February 20, 2016, https://www.youtube.com/watch?v=7msKrdBGw7A.

10. Dar al Ifta al Masriyya, accessed February 20, 2016, http://eng.dar-alifta.org/foreign/default.aspx.

11. "Does Marital Rape Exist in Islam," Dar al Ifta al Masriyya, accessed February 20, 2016, http://eng.dar-alifta.org/foreign/ViewFatwa.aspx?ID=6033.

12. "I Am a New Female Convert to Islam. Is It Wrong to Post My Photos on Facebook?" Dar al Ifta al Masriyya, accessed February 20, 2016, http://eng.dar-alifta.org/foreign/ViewFatwa.aspx?ID=10437.

13. "I am a Teenage Girl and I Wonder if Chatting with Boys on Social Media is Considered a Sin?" Dar al Ifta al Masriyya, accessed February 20, 2016, http://eng.dar-alifta.org/foreign/ViewFatwa.aspx?ID=9386&LangID=2.

14. "Question #44816," Islamicity, accessed February 20, 2016, http://www.islamicity.com/qa/action.lasso.asp?-db=services&-lay=Ask&-op=eq&number=44816&-format=detailpop.shtml&-find.

15. Amanda Holpuch, "Activist Mona Eltahawy Released After Arrest in New York Subway Protest," *The Guardian*, September 26, 2012, accessed February 20, 2016, http://www.theguardian.com/world/2012/sep/26/mona-Eltahawy-released-new-york-subway.

16. Eline Gordts, "International Topless Jihad Day: FEMEN Activists Stage Protests across Europe," *The World Post*, April 05, 2013, accessed February 20, 2016, http://www.huffingtonpost.com/2013/04/04/international-topless-jihad-day_n_3014943.html.
17. "The Uprising of Women in the Arab World," Facebook, accessed February 20, 2016, https://www.facebook.com/intifadat.almar2a.

BIBLIOGRAPHY

Bayat, Asef. (2010) *Life as Politics: How Ordinary People Change the Middle East.* Stanford: Stanford University Press, 2010.

Coleman, Isabell. "Women and the Arab Revolts." *Brown Journal of World Affairs* 18 (2011): 215–228. Accessed July 14, 2015. http://www.brown.edu/initiatives/journal-world-affairs/181/women-and-arab-revolts.

Dar al Ifta al Masriyya. Accessed February 20, 2016, http://eng.dar-alifta.org/foreign/default.aspx.

Dar al Ifta al Masriyya. "Does Marital Rape Exist in Islam?" Accessed February 20, 2016, http://eng.dar-alifta.org/foreign/ViewFatwa.aspx?ID=6033.

Dar al Ifta al Masriyya. "I Am a New Female Convert to Islam, Is It Wrong to Post My Photos on Facebook?" Accessed February 20, 2016. http://eng.dar-alifta.org/foreign/ViewFatwa.aspx?ID=10437.

Dar al Ifta al Masriyya. "I am a Teenage Girl and I Wonder if Chatting with Boys on Social Media is considered a Sin?" Accessed February 20, 2016. http://eng.dar-alifta.org/foreign/ViewFatwa.aspx?ID=9386&LangID=2.

Dubai Eye 1038. "Raha Moharrak First Saudi Woman to Climb Mount Everest." http://dubaieye1038.com/raha-moharrak-first-sausi-woman-climb-mount-everest/.

Dubai School of Government. (2011) "Role of Social Media in Arab Women's Empowerment," *Arab Social Media Report* 1 (2011). Accessed August 17, 2015. http://www.arabsocialmediareport.com/UserManagement/PDF/ASMR%20Report%203.pdf.

Eltahawy, Mona. *Headscarves and Hymens: Why the Arab World Needs a Sexual Revolution.* New York: Frarar, Straus and Giroux, 2016.

GlobalPost. "Iran's Women A Driving Force Behind Green Movement." *The World Post*, May 25, 2011. Accessed February 20, 2016, http://www.huffingtonpost.com/2009/07/24/irans-women-a-driving-for_n_244218.html.

Goldfarb, Jeffrey C. *The Politics of Small Things: The Powers of the Powerless in Dark Times.* Chicago: University of Chicago Press, 2006.

Gordts, Eline. "International Topless Jihad Day: FEMEN Activists Stage Protests across Europe," *The World Post*, April 05, 2013. Accessed February 20, 2016, http://www.huffingtonpost.com/2013/04/04/international-topless-jihad-day_n_3014943.html.

Harris, David. "Dr Grami: Feminism, Activism and the Arab Spring." *The Clarion Project*, February 2, 2014. Accessed February 20, 2016, http://www.clarionproject.org/analysis/dr-grami-feminism-activism-and-arab-spring.

Hofheinz, Albrecht. "Nextopia? Beyond Revolution 2.0." *International Journal of Communication* 5 (2011):1417–1434. Accessed July 14, 2015. http://ijoc.org/index.php/ijoc/article/view/1186.

Holpuch, Amanda. "Activist Mona Eltahawy released after arrest in New York subway protest." *The Guardian*, September 26, 2012. Accessed February 20, 2016. http://www.theguardian.com/world/2012/sep/26/mona-Eltahawy-released-new-york-subway.

Islamicity. "Question #44816." Accessed February 20, 2016, http://www.islamicity.com/qa/action.lasso.asp?-db=services&-lay=Ask&-op=eq&number=44816&-format=detailpop.shtml&-find.

Krasnow, Iris. (2014) "What Don't Women Want?" *Capital Gazette*, October 5, 2014. Accessed July 17, 2015. http://www.capitalgazette.com/entertainment/pc-ac-cl-talk-to-iris-10-05-14-20141005-story.html.

Marx, Karl. *The Eighteenth Brumaire of Louis Bonaparte*. New York, 1852. Accessed August 17, 2015. https://www.marxists.org/archive/marx/works/1852/18th-brumaire/ch01.html.

Mernissi, Fatima. *Women's Rebellion and Islamic Memory*. London: Zed Books, 1996.

Musaiger, Abdulrahman O. Hamed R. Takruri, Abdelmonem S. Hassan, and Hamza Abu-Tarboush. "Food-Based Dietary Guidelines for the Arab Gulf Countries," *Journal of Nutrition and Metabolism* (2012). Accessed July 31, 2015. http://www.hindawi.com/journals/jnme/2012/905303/cta/.

Skoler, Michael. "When A Country Has Problems, Women are Often the Answer." *PRI* February 3, 2015. Accessed July 10, 2015. http://www.pri.org/stories/2015-02-03/when-country-has-problems-women-are-often-answer.

The National. "Emirati woman who reached for the skies." June 11, 2014, http://www.thenational.ae/uae/government/emirati-woman-who-reached-for-the-skies.

Wheeler, Deborah. "Blessings and Curses: Women and the Information Revolution in the Arab World." In *Women and the Media in the Middle East: Power through Self-Expression*, edited by Naomi Sakr, 138–161. London: Tauris, 2004.

Wheeler, Deborah L. "Empowerment Zones? Women, Internet Cafes and Life Transformations in Egypt." *Information Technologies and International Development* 4(2007): 89–104.

Wheeler, Deborah and Lauren Mintz. "Girls Just Want to Have Fun? Internet Leisure and Women's Empowerment in Jordan." In *Handbook of the Economics of Leisure*, edited by Sam Cameron, 496–516. Northhampton: Edward Elgar, 2012.

World Economic Forum. "The Global Gender Gap Index 2014." Accessed February 20, 2016. http://reports.weforum.org/global-gender-gap-report-2014/report-highlights/.

PART II

On Governmental and Non-Governmental Media Organisations

Location, Regulation, and Media Production in the Arab World: A Case Study of Media Cities

Yushi Chiba

Location, regulation, and media production are closely related to one another. Looking back into modern Arab history, at least to the 1970s, Cairo and Beirut were two centers for Arabic publications and attracted many journalists and thinkers from all over the Arab World. The former, particularly in the 1950s and 1960s, flourished regardless of tight media regulations although the latter flourished amongst political polarization. Not only Arab cities, but also some European cities played important roles in the development of Arabic media. For instance, from the mid-1970s, cities such as London and Paris became safe havens for Arabic presses in exile and broadened the margin of freedom of expression. Furthermore, in the 1990s, some broadcasters, most of which were funded by Saudi capitalists, started Arabic satellite TV channels and headquartered their offices in London and Rome. Both cities became *sine qua non* for the development of private Arabic broadcasters.

Y. Chiba (✉)
Organization for Islamic Area Studies, Waseda University, Tokyo, Japan

N. Lenze et al. (eds.), *Media in the Middle East*,
DOI 10.1007/978-3-319-65771-4_4

However, these situations changed dramatically after the 2000s because of two primary factors. First, since the mid-1990s, Arab states have been establishing free zones, called media cities, for private media entities to propel their knowledge-based economies and catch up with global trends. Media cities, like other free zones, are characterized by attractive features, including tax exemptions, an up-to-date infrastructure, and limited government interference. Several leading private broadcasters, including the Middle East Broadcasting Center (MBC), the Arab Radio and Television Network (ART), and Orbit,[1] which began broadcasting in Europe in the 1990s, moved their headquarters to the Arab World after the establishment of these media cities. Second, a number of countries revised their laws and began to allow private media entities to operate their businesses within their boundaries while governments obligated broadcasters to obtain licenses before they began their operations and even after licenses were issued, these governments imposed several restrictions on their activities.

Regardless of the restrictions, these institutional and legal changes contributed to a dramatic increase in the number of Arabic satellite broadcasters. Now, more than one thousand channels, most of which are operated by private broadcasters, are on the air and competing for the hearts and minds of Arab audiences. Having breathed new life into the hitherto monotonous broadcasting scene, these private broadcasters have reshaped the Arab broadcasting industry. According to a recent statistic, Arab stakeholders occupy 38% of the world's satellite channels, a figure which indicates that the Arab world is the most competitive satellite market in the world.[2] Without doubt, this transformation is considered to be both a direct and an indirect response to globalization.

As Tyler Cowen uniquely demonstrates,[3] in contrast to the hypothesis proposed by cultural/media imperialism theorists that globalization devastates "indigenous" culture, globalization is not always a destructive force for local cultures. In fact, even though cultures become more like each other, globalization tends to diversify the choices within society and, under some conditions, can contribute to the continuance of local culture by broadening the market and increasing the number of supporters in every corner of the globe. This argument helps us understand globalization and its practical meaning for Arab media. If someone supposes that the recent increase of channels is just a reflection of westernization or the unification of broadcasting content, he/she is seeing only half the picture and has clearly not looked into the complexity and dynamics of contemporary Arab broadcasting. It is important to consider not only the destructive side of globalization but also its constructive aspects and to clarify how it has been reshaping the Arab broadcasting scene.

This chapter aims to clarify how the media city, which is considered to be a unique local response to globalization, first appeared in the Arab World and the way in which it has contributed to the diversification of contemporary Arab broadcasting content. Although there are already plenty of studies that discuss media cities,[4] most seem to lack a systematic analysis of the broadcasters that contract with these cities. In other words, although some pioneering studies have already revealed several aspects of media cities, they have not fully revealed the dynamic between media cities and broadcasters, thereby failing to shed light on the practical implications of media cities in the contemporary Arab broadcasting scene.[5] This chapter is an attempt to bridge the above-referenced research gap. To determine the significance of media cities in the Arab broadcasting industry, a comparative analysis will be conducted on media cities established in Egypt, Jordan, and the United Arab Emirates (UAE) and their contracting broadcasters.[6]

THE ECONOMIC AND POLITICAL MOTIVATION BEHIND THE MEDIA CITY

Attempts to provide special locations for media entities can be traced back to the 1970s and 1980s. Jordan was the first Arab country to develop the concept of a media city. The Jordan Production Company, the predecessor of the current media city in Jordan, was built in 1978 and it began its operation in 1982 as a semi-government entity.[7] This venture ended in 1991 as a result of the financial crisis. Another local attempt was undertaken in Oman by Halley Media Production, which was established in 1986, and continues to thrive today. However, these pioneering attempts differ from contemporary media cities in that they did not specifically target private media entities. In this sense, Egyptian Media Production City (EMPC), inaugurated in 1997, can be regarded as the first media city that clearly declared its ambition to attract private media entities. The year 2001 saw the opening of two new media cities in the region—Dubai Media City (DMC) and Jordan Media City (JMC).

The concept of a media city soon spread across the Arab World. Currently, ten media cities operate in Egypt, Jordan, and the UAE.

Although the period of political turmoil since the end of 2010 has disrupted the emergence of new media cities, the phenomenon of establishing media cities will likely continue in the long run. Indeed, in 2014, both Tunisia and Morocco announced plans to establish media cities.[8] Even Saudi Arabia, one of the most conservative countries in the Arab World, has recently contracted with Arabsat and Media Speed Company in order to establish a digital satellite TV platform in Riyadh to invite private broadcasters and develop a private media sector in the kingdom.[9]

However, this kind of convergence, or accumulation, of private media entities is not limited to the Arab World. Turning to other parts of the world, there are many media companies, both software and hardware companies, that have clustered in special zones such as Silicon Valley in the USA, Silicon Glen in the UK, Zhongguancun in China, and Bangalore in India. With regard to content-based entities, Hollywood in the USA and Bollywood in India are among the most famous examples of prime locations for entertainment industries. Furthermore, in 2002, the Korean government embarked on establishing Digital Media City as a media complex comprised of software companies, broadcasting companies, cultural centers, and other media-related entities. Compared with the other "cities" referenced above, Digital Media City is similar to DMC in Dubai in terms of both its size and its role in the industry.

Although it would not be an easy task to compare all of these different cities in the same way, some economic studies can help us understand the mechanism behind this type of convergence in order to highlight their similarities. Specifically, economic geography and spatial economics offer reasons for such convergence in terms of cost, synergy, innovation, path dependence, and other economic factors. In certain cases, companies cluster voluntarily in one location. Alternatively, governments allot special districts for private companies in commerce, media, and manufacturing industries, expecting to benefit from the expansion of the private sector and through attracting foreign companies. In all likelihood, the Arab states that constructed media cities had the same motivation and tried to benefit from a process of media liberalization. In other words, through establishing media cities and inviting private companies, the Arab states expect to develop their knowledge-based economy, generate synergies among domestic industries, and catch up with global trends.

Nonetheless, when we consider Arab cases, other specific factors come into play. That is, political motivation provides a strong driving force in the construction of media cities and, in some cases, the politics might actually come first. Since the early 1990s, the number of Arabic satellite channels has increased dramatically, leading to a rise in the number of Arab viewers who watch foreign and private satellite channels instead of their states' channels. In other words, satellite television posed a challenge to government policies that attempted to control citizens' access to non-state-sponsored programs that might include harsh criticizes of the government. In the face of this reality, several states started to establish free zones for private broadcasters, courting, in particular, influential broadcasters rather than offering special economic benefits.

Therefore, despite advertisements that the government would not interfere with broadcasters located in media cities, there have been several incidents involving the denial of operating licenses, the shutting down of offices, and acts of censorship.[10] For instance, during the period of political turmoil in Egypt in early 2011, the Al-Jazeera bureau was shut down and the staff were forbidden from operating in Egypt. Even media cities in Dubai, which are considered the least restrictive places for foreign broadcasters in the region, punished two private Pakistani channels, stating that the channels had stirred up political tensions in Pakistan. Such incidents show clearly that media cities are not only projects for privatization and democratization in the Arab World; they are also a means to regulate the media in the age of satellite television. In other words, the media cities in the Arab World are often the tools of the cunning authoritarian governments who use them to control the political threat posed by satellite television and media globalization, as well as to generate profits.

Media Cities as a Reflection of the Sociopolitical Climate

I would now like to take a closer look at the media cities in three specific countries: Egypt, Jordan, and the UAE. Although all media cities share a common ambition to be both regional and global media hubs through hosting foreign broadcasters, every media city tends to reflect its respective sociopolitical climate, thereby generating fundamental differences in the capabilities of hosting foreign broadcasters.

The Case of the Egyptian Media Production City

Envisioned as the "Hollywood of the Middle East," the Egyptian Media Production City (EMPC) was inaugurated in 1997 in the outskirts of Cairo. It now boasts of a huge area of approximately 35 million square meters. This contains six complexes housing around 70 studios equipped with broadcasting and shooting facilities, an expansive outdoor shooting area (particularly for cinema production), theaters, and other facilities such as an academy for media science and engineering.[11]

Like other media cities, EMPC aims to be a global media hub and this was strongly reflected in the remarks of Safwat Sharif, the then-Egyptian Minister of Information who took the initiative of establishing EMPC: "Egypt wants to continue leading in information, in media, and Arabic production."[12] However, from the beginning, government policies toward EMPC were contradictory. For instance, regardless of its manifesto about welcoming foreign broadcasters, Sharif had been reluctant to open the market to foreign broadcasters. Furthermore, the lack of clear criteria for issuing operating licenses for foreign broadcasters hindered their entrance into the Egyptian media market. Although the situation appeared to change after the fall of the Mubarak regime, its contradictory policies continue to this day. Indeed, Mubarak and his henchmen were purged; however, the situation surrounding EMPC is still far from ideal. What is worse, political instability since that time has posed additional difficulties for non-Egyptian broadcasters to utilize EMPC. For instance, in April 2015, a militant group from Egypt bombed the electricity towers outside of EMPC, leaving all TV and radio channels from the city off the air for almost 45 minutes.[13]

After the January 2011 revolution, media in Egypt became a primary battlefield for those with different beliefs and different interests. For instance, following the clash between the military and the Muslim Brotherhood in 2013, the Muslim Brotherhood, its supporters, and channels such as Al-Jazeera continuously denounced the brutality of the military's actions and repeatedly questioned the legitimacy of the new government. Facing this situation, the military-supported government tried its best to silence the critical voices and did not permit pro-Brotherhood channels to operate in Egypt. While EMPC continues to boast of its openness, it is far from open.

Furthermore, a recent situation illustrates the persistence of the industry's closed characteristics. Just two months after Abdel Fattah Al-Sisi assumed the presidency, Osama Heikal, former information minister and a known pro-Sisi figure, was nominated as the new EMPC chairperson.[14] In October 2015, some private Egyptian media accused Heikal of allowing his comrades from "For the Love of Egypt," a pro-Sisi party in which Heikal plays a leading role, to shoot TV spots in EMPC studios at reduced rates.[15] Considering these allegations, EMPC lacks transparency. Thus, EMPC seems to be failing to establish itself as a global information hub, despite its ambitions, because it cannot fully appeal to foreign broadcasters.

The Case of Jordan Media City

Compared with EMPC, Jordan Media City (JMC) was more consistent in its strategy and proved successful in attracting many foreign broadcasters. JMC was established as a private free zone by Dallah Media Production Company in Jeddah, Saudi Arabia, owned by media mogul Saleh Kamel, under the auspices of Jordan's Information and Communication Technology (ICT) program.[16] Compared with other media cities, JMC is relatively small. Therefore, many broadcasters locate their offices outside of JMC and then contract with JMC to uplink their programs to the satellite.

Although JMC is a private media city, the project, similar to that of other media cities, was a product of government policy. King Abdullah II has always fully supported JMC. Indeed, his support stemmed from the clear expectation that JMC would generate jobs and advance the nation's economy through promoting knowledge-based activities. Similarly, Saleh Kamel had a strong economic reason for building JMC, which is to reduce the operational costs of ART (which he founded and later moved from Italy to Jordan). Consequently, regardless of its status as a private entity, JMC maintains a strong relationship with the Jordanian government.[17]

JMC seems to be fully aware of its advantages.[18] Compared with EMPC, JMC is more open to foreign broadcasters and is more willing to court them. Unlike other media cities in the UAE, JMC charges reasonable fees and offers the services of skilled engineers and technicians. Thus, JMC's strategy is to offer a comparatively attractive location to relatively unknown broadcasters who aspire to reposition themselves in the regional media market, regardless of whether or not they are Jordanian.

Taking recent circumstances into consideration, the Arab upheavals that have occurred since the end of 2010 did not pose any serious threats to the Jordanian government. Instead, the Jordanian government strategically took on the role of buffer zone and has successfully sold itself to the global society as one of the few safe countries in the Arab World, thereby continuously accommodating humanitarian and international organizations. This political stability benefits JMC, and the Arab upheavals might generate a favorable wind for JMC because it can market itself as a stable, safe zone for broadcasters in exile. As with the Egyptian case, JMC tends to reflect the circumstances of its home country.

The Case of Two Media Cities in Dubai

Like JMC, media cities in the UAE have clear visions and consistent strategies. Media cities in the UAE are the projects of each of the individual emirates. Four of the seven emirates have their own media cities,[19] with Dubai boasting the largest. Similar to Egypt and Jordan, each emirate aims to become a regional and global information hub and aims to use its media city to create synergy between media and other economic activities. Compared with EMPC and JMC, the motivation to establish media cities in each emirate must be more economic than political. However, not all media cities in each emirate have fully opened to broadcasters. They are inevitably the project of each emirate and thus deeply embedded in the UAE's politics. Therefore, channels that may contradict each government's policy are carefully excluded at its registration phase. For this reason, the degree of freedom of expression enjoyed by each broadcaster within media cities in the UAE is allowed on condition that it does not seriously challenge the UAE's interests.

Of all of the emirates, Dubai leads the trend because it has established four media cities: DMC, Dubai Studio City (DSC), Dubai Internet City (DIC), and the International Media Production Zone (IMPZ). In terms of broadcasting status, in particular, DMC and DSC hold the most important positions because most broadcasters in Dubai have their offices in either one or the other.

DMC was inaugurated in 2001. In the set-up period, it boasted an area of two million square meters and several skyscrapers; at the time of writing, the size and number of the buildings continue to expand. DMC was established to help the UAE become a regional and global media hub. To this end, it undertook several media activities: marketing, broadcasting, new media, publishing, music production, film production, and event services. DMC stands out among other media cities and has attracted many investors with its up-to-date facilities, its attractive location, and its capacity to offer skilled technicians. In addition, DSC was established to complement DMC. Currently, many broadcasters and content production companies operate both in DMC and DSC.[20]

Instead of impressing clients with their size and low costs, both DMC and DSC focus on providing advanced infrastructure and creating synergy between media and other activities (such as economic and academic enrichment) as their primary strategy. With regard to infrastructure, DMC and DSC provide state-of-the-art facilities while their rivals in Egypt and Jordan do not provide any such facilities. Superior technology and facilities are important when thinking about the capability to attract international broadcasters.[21]

Synergy is another important factor. For instance, other free zones such as DIC and Dubai Knowledge Village accommodate global, knowledge-intensive companies and offer attractive incentives for international broadcasters. Furthermore, Dubai could successfully establish itself as a global transportation hub and accommodate multinational companies, thereby creating easier access to CEOs, politicians, and celebrities.[22] These aspects make DMC and DSC appealing not only to local and Arabic broadcasters but also to global media giants.[23]

MEDIA CITIES USERS

Each media city, especially in Jordan and the UAE, has unique characteristics and adopts different strategies to attract broadcasters. Differentiating themselves from others can benefit broadcasters because it allows them to choose a location accordingly.

EMPC Users

According to Mervat Abou Oaf, professor at the American University in Cairo, EMPC was home to 18 studios in 2003, 13 of which were occupied by non-Egyptian channels and the rest by private Egyptian channels.[24] This means that EMPC's studios housed more non-Egyptian channels in its early days. However, this trend has changed in recent years. According to my field research conducted in EMPC in early 2011, the number of studios in EMPC had more than doubled and housed at least 30 channels. Although the number of non-Egyptian channels did not increase, the number of Egyptian channels rose steadily. Seventeen studios were occupied by Egyptian channels, including Dream TV, Melody TV, Mazzika TV, and Mihwar, whereas 13 studios were occupied by non-Egyptian Arabic channels, including MBC, Al-Nas, and Al-Baghdadiya.[25]

Soon after the January 2011 revolution, new Egyptian broadcasters began to successfully emerge, launching new channels in EMPC because many Egyptians dreamed of an end to any form of media censorship. According to one estimate, 16 new channels began operating directly after the revolution.[26] Regarding this situation, Sayed Helmi, the then-chairperson of EMPC, remarked "[c]ompanies operating in Dubai or in Jordan could soon want to benefit from the removal of restrictions here and decide to transfer their business to Cairo."[27]

However, this euphoria did not last long and the situation that followed was deeply disappointing. Currently, as discussed above, the situation surrounding EMPC is far from attractive. Though many local channels may broadcast from EMPC,[28] it does not accommodate enough foreign broadcasters. Instead of EMPC, some foreign broadcasters such as Saudi Broadcasting Center (SBC) lease space outside of EMPC and operate there. A staff member working for a foreign broadcaster mentioned that the degree of governmental interference between operating in and outside of EMPC is superficial and EMPC facilities are not always attractive to broadcasters.[29] For this reason, as opposed to EMPC's ambition, the primary users are still Egyptian broadcasters.

JMC Users

As of 2004, the number of channels that contracted with JMC was less than one hundred.[30] By 2011, the number of channels whose transmissions and retransmissions were supervised by JMC had increased dramatically to 247.[31] Specifically, JMC was in charge of uplinking 68 channels to the satellite. As was the case with EMPC, the majority of channels that contracted with JMC were Arabic. However, JMC is much more open than EMPC to broadcasting channels from outside its borders and it has successfully attracted several foreign channels. In addition, with the exception of channels under the ART network's umbrella, most of the channels were relatively new.[32]

For satellite channels that do not have the financial strength to rent offices in Dubai but wish to enjoy the advantages of media cities, it is only natural that they would choose JMC over the alternative, EMPC, which is not as open as other non-Egyptian entities. Thus, in the words of Radi Al-Khas, CEO of JMC, JMC plays a vital role as a platform for channels that "would not have started if JMC was not there" and JMC "made it very easy for them [these low-budget channels] to get satellite."[33]

According to my research conducted in 2011, the number of Jordanian channels with uplinked programs via JMC was 11 out of a total of 68.[34] JMC was established by a Saudi entrepreneur and tended to be more open to non-Jordanian entities. In addition, as Jordan was more politically stable than other Arab states, many Arabic channels with different nationalities preferred to use JMC as their platform. For example, as of 2015, 10 Algerian TV channels were being transmitted from JMC.[35] Furthermore, the official Libyan channels recently chose JMC as their main platform for security reasons.[36] Through JMC, Jordanian as well as other Arab private broadcasters could launch their satellite channels much more easily.

DMC and DSC Users

The strategy of DMC and DSC was to invite famous broadcasters by offering them what other media cities could not. These benefits mainly stemmed from the technological and economic edge of Dubai. According to Saeed Al-Muntafiq, former CEO of DMC, its vision is "not to be a regional base for broadcasters, but to be one of four or five global bases for broadcasting."[37] Through the statements of media companies located in DMC, we discover that media companies share DMC's vision. For instance, the manifest vision of MBC reflects this tendency well: "[W]ith our heart in the Arab world, we are forging a global media group that enriches people's lives through information, interaction, and entertainment."[38]

Both DMC and DSC successfully attracted several famous broadcasters from inside and outside the Arab World. According to one estimate, as of 2009, DMC was home to over 60 broadcasters operating approximately 150 channels.[39] Presently, with the inauguration of DSC, channels previously located in DMC have moved to DSC. As of 2013, there were 1,400 corporations in DMC and 350 in DSC.[40] Under the category "radio and television stations," 26 and 23 satellite broadcasters were registered in DMC and DSC, respectively. Thus, as of 2013, at least 49 broadcasters operated their satellite channels in DMC and DSC. Those 49 broadcasters comprised 25 Arab and 24 non-Arab broadcasters, including a number of famous broadcasters operating several channels. Some examples include MBC and the Al-Majd Network of Saudi Arabia and Spacetoon of Syria. Similarly, the non-Arab broadcasters include several global broadcasters such as BBC, CNN, NBC, and NTV. In addition, DMC and DSC were home to several Asian media giants, including Geo TV of Pakistan, Zee TV of India, and CCTV of China. Compared with EMPC and JMC, media cities in Dubai successfully attract both Arab and non-Arab media giants.

CONCLUSION

As illustrated above, broadcasters tend to choose their locations according to the characteristics of each media city. Media cities, in turn, tend to reflect the social and political climate of their respective locations, targeting different clients, and enjoying various advantages. Therefore, they play different roles and are not always in competition with each other. Instead, this trend gives broadcasters multiple choices that match their individual goals and visions. EMPC, which aims to be a global media hub, has failed to attract non-Egyptian broadcasters because of its inconsistent strategies, its non-openness, and the continuing government regulation in the country. Therefore, EMPC has more private Egyptian channels than non-Egyptian channels. In contrast, JMC, which is open to foreign channels, has successfully attracted many non-Jordanian channels. However, with regard to its goal to become a global media hub, JMC has been eclipsed by its counterparts in Dubai. Presently, Dubai remains the preferred location for the headquarters and regional offices of many famous Arab and global broadcasters.

This study has revealed the significance of media cities in the contemporary Arab broadcasting industry. That is, media cities have facilitated the entrance of many broadcasters into the Arab satellite market. Although EMPC does not fully appeal to non-Egyptian broadcasters, it benefits many Egyptian channels and has helped them to connect with Arab audiences. JMC has enabled many unknown and newly established channels to easily enter the Arab satellite market, thereby playing an important role in removing some of the barriers to the satellite market.

Similarly, through DMC and DSC, many famous non-Arab broadcasters have also gained easy access to the Arab satellite market.

In summary, the establishment of media cities has enabled both Arab and non-Arab channels to enter the Arab satellite market regardless of their net worth. In addition, these zones have facilitated the migration of broadcasters and enabled many broadcasters that could not have otherwise entered the Arab satellite market to initiate broadcasting activities. In this regard, media cities have served as gateways to lower the entry barriers to the satellite market and created a foundation for the multiplicity and diversity of the present-day Arab broadcasting industry. Going beyond the governments' original intentions to gain profits and reduce political threats through regulation, media cities, as a whole, globally contribute to the increased number of satellite channels and to the diversification of broadcasting content.

NOTES

1. In 2009, Orbit merged with Showtime Arabia and became Orbit Showtime Network (OSN).
2. Ahmed Ghazali, "Médias et développements politiques dans le Maghreb et le monde arabe," *Toripodos*, 30 (2012), 33; Joan Barata, "Tunisian Media under the Authoritarian Structure of Ben Ali's Regime and After," In Tourya Guaaybess (ed.), *National Broadcasting and State Policy in Arab Countries* (Palgrave Macmillan, 2013), 126.
3. Tyler Cowen, *Creative Destruction: How Globalization Is Changing the World's Cultures* (Princeton University Press, 2004).
4. On EMPC, see the following articles: Hamdy Kandil, "The Media Free Zone: An Egyptian Media Production City Finance," *TBS Archive*, 5 (2000); Chris Forrester, "High Hopes for Egyptian Media Production City," *TBS Archive*, 7 (2001); Mervat Abou Oaf, *Egyptian Media Production City (EMPC): Prospects and Future Concerns (A Case Study)*, Master's Thesis submitted to the American University in Cairo (American University in Cairo, 2005); Naila Hamdy, "Latest Tenants at EMPC: Private Egyptian Channels, and One Million-Dollar Show," *TBS Archive*, 8 (2002). On JMC, see the following article: Sarah Sullivan, "Private-Sector Media City Launched in Amman," *TBS Archive*, 7 (2001). On media cities in Dubai, see the following articles: Abdallah S. Shleifer, "The Dubai Digital Broadcasting," *TBS Archive*, 5 (2000); Dana El-Baltaji, "Dubai: An Emerging Arab Media Hub," *Arab Media and Society*, 3 (2007); Marwan M. Kraidy and Joe F. Khalil, *Arab Television Industries* (Palgrave Macmillan on behalf of the British Film Institute, 2009).

5. The following reference is one of a few articles that steps into the analysis realm of the relation between media cities and broadcasters, although its primary focus is Dubai Media City. See Joe F. Khalil, "Towards a Supranational Analysis of Arab Media: The Role of Cities," In Tourya Guaaybess (ed.), *National Broadcasting and State Policy in Arab Countries* (Palgrave Macmillan, 2013), 88–108.

6. As for comparative studies, see the following articles: Stephan Quinn, Tim Walters, and John Whiteoak, "A Tale of Three (Media) Cities," *Australian Studies in Journalism*, 12 (2003); Pawel Krzysiek, "Testing Legal Boundaries within Arab Media Hubs: Reporting, Law and Politics in Three Media Cities," *Westminster Papers in Communication and Culture*, 6: 1 (2009), 69–91. At the same time, it is necessary to caution against a simple comparative study of media cities. For instance, Joe F. Khalil emphasizes the difficulty of comparing different types of media clusters because most media clusters emphasize different purposes, histories, structures, and sectors (see Joe F. Khalil, "Modalities of Media Governance in the Arab World," In Danatella Della Ratta, Naomi Sakr, and Skovgaard-Petersen (eds), *Arab Media Moguls* (I.B. Tauris, 2015), 13–30).

7. Sarah Sullivan, "Private-Sector Media City Launched in Amman," *TBS Archive*, 7 (2001).

8. Sami-Joe Abboud, "Tunisia Economic City Aims to Boost Economy," *Al-Monitor*, September 11, 2014, accessed September 17, 2016, http://www.al-monitor.com/pulse/business/2014/09/tunisia-economic-city-project-major.html; "Media city to be launched soon in Morocco," *Moroccan World News* (December 14, 2014), accessed September 17, 2016, http://www.moroccoworldnews.com/2014/12/145684/media-city-to-be-launched-soon-in-morocco/.

9. Rebecca Hawkes, "Saudi Arabia embarks on digital satellite TV platform," *Rapid TV News*, February 6, 2015, accessed June 5, 2015, http://www.rapidtvnews.com/2015020637089/saudi-arabia-embarks-on-digital-satellite-tv-platform.html#axzz3iICrHRFX.

10. Regarding this detail, see the following article: Yushi, Chiba, "The Geographical Transformation of Arab Media: The Decline of Offshore Media and the Rise of the Media City," *Asia and African Area Studies*, 12: 1 (2012), 79–103.

11. EMPC website, accessed May 5, 2015, http://empc.com.eg/wordpress-en/.

12. Forrester, "High Hopes for Egyptian Media Production City."

13. Ahmed Fouad, "Who is Bombing Egypt's Electricity Towers," *Al-Monitor*, May 5, 2015, accessed September 26, 2016, http://www.

al-monitor.com/pulse/originals/2015/05/egypt-power-plants-bomb-ings-brotherhood-electricity-ministry.html.

14. "Osama Heikal Chosen New Egyptian Media Production City Chairman," *Arab Today*, August 26, 2014, accessed September 2016, http://www.arabtoday.net/home-335/osama-heikal-chosen-new-egyptian-media-production-city-chairma.

15. "Top Media Execs Accused of Campaigning in their Own News Outlets," *Mada Misr*, October 15, 2015, accessed September 26, 2016, http://www.madamasr.com/news/top-media-execs-accused-campaigning-their-own-news-outlets.

16. Sullivan, "Private-Sector Media City Launched in Amman"; Krzysiek, "Testing Legal Boundaries within Arab Media Hubs: Reporting, Law and Politics in Three Media Cities."

17. The fact that Radi Al-Khas, former director general of the Jordan Radio and Television Corporation, has been JMC's CEO demonstrates the close relationship between JMC and the Jordanian government. Radi Al-Khas was director general of Jordan Radio and Television between 1989 and 1994. Then, he moved to ART as the vice president of technology and development. As a professional technician, he helped further the technological development of ART broadcasting. He initiated the media city project and, since 2002, has been the CEO of JMC.

18. "Mid-East's other TV hot-spot," *The IBC Daily*, September 13, 2008, accessed March 25, 2011, http://www.jordanmediacity.com/pdf/The_ibc_daily.pdf.

19. Dubai has four media cities and Ras al-Khaimah has Ras al-Khaimah Media City (RAK Media City). Fujairah has Fujairah Creative City (FCC) and Abu Dhabi has Twofour54.

20. TECOM Group website, accessed January 28, 2014, http://www.tecom-directory.com/.

21. As for a recent example, CNN opened a new hi-tech studio in DMC. See Eleanor Dickinson, "CNN opens new hi-tech studio in Dubai Media City," *Gulf Business*, January 25, 2016, accessed October 27, 2016, http://gulfbusiness.com/cnn-opens-hi-tech-studio-in-dubai-media-city/.

22. Zafar Siddiqi, "Featured Interview with the TBS staff," *TBS Archive*, 7 (2001).

23. Saeed Al-Muntafiq, "Featured Interview with the TBS staff," *TBS Archive*, 7 (2001).

24. Mervat Abou Oaf, *Egyptian Media Production City (EMPC)*.

25. Interview with EMPC staff member, January 23, 2011.

26. Emad Mekay, "TV stations multiply as Egyptian censorship falls," *The New York Times*, July 13, 2011, accessed June 5, 2015, http://www.

nytimes.com/2011/07/14/world/middleeast/14iht-M14B-EGYPT-MEDIA.html.

27. Ibid.

28. "Egyptian Media Production City aims to pay off debts by December: Chairman." *Ahram Online*, August 4, 2015, accessed September 27, 2016, http://english.ahram.org.eg/NewsContent/1/64/136914/Egypt/Politics-/Egyptian-Media-Production-City-aims-to-pay-off-deb.aspx.

29. Interview with SBC staff member, August 25, 2016.

30. Interview with JMC staff member, November 21, 2011.

31. These 267 channels comprise four types of channels: pass-through channels, play-out channels, fiber channels, and internet channels. See JMC website, accessed July 4, 2015, http://jordanmediacity.com/en/9/News.

32. Interview with JMC staff member, November 21, 2011.

33. Keach Hagey, "Golden Age of the Media City," *The National (Business)*, November 19, 2008, accessed April 5, 2015, http://www.thenational.ae/business/golden-age-of-the-media-city?pageCount=0.

34. Those Jordanian Channels include Roya TV, Arab Motors TV, Seven Stars TV, ShooFee TV, Jo Sat, Spin Jordan Raio, Nourmina, Ayyam FM Radio, Quran Kareem Radio, Mazaj FM, and Hayat FM.

35. JMC website, accessed July 4, 2015, http://jordanmediacity.com/en/9/News.

36. "Libya's official TV channel broadcasting from Jordan," *The Jordan Times*, March 3, 2015, accessed July 4, 2015, http://www.jordantimes.com/news/local/libya%E2%80%99s-official-tv-channel-broadcasting-jordan.

37. Saeed al-Muntafiq. "Featured Interview with the TBS Staff."

38. MBC website, accessed May 10, 2015, http://www.mbc.net/portal/site/mbc-en/.

39. Kraidy and Khalil, *Arab Television Industry*, 135.

40. TECOM Group website, accessed January 28, 2014, http://www.tecom-directory.com/.

BIBLIOGRAPHY

Abboud, Sami-Joe. "Tunisia Economic City Aims to Boost Economy," *Al-Monitor*, September 11, 2014. Accessed September 17, 2016, http://www.al-monitor.com/pulse/business/2014/09/tunisia-economic-city-project-major.html.

Abou Oaf, Mervat. *Egyptian Media Production City (EMPC): Prospects and Future Concerns (A Case Study)*. Master's Thesis submitted to the American University in Cairo (American University in Cairo, 2005).

Al-Muntafiq, Saeed. "Featured Interview with the TBS staff." *TBS Archive*, 7 (2001).

Arab Today. "Osama Heikal Chosen New Egyptian Media Production City Chairman." August 26, 2014. Accessed September 2016, http://www.arabtoday.net/home-335/osama-heikal-chosen-new-egyptian-media-production-city-chairma.

Barata, Joan. "Tunisian Media under the Authoritarian Structure of Ben Ali's Regime and After." In Tourya Guaaybess (ed.), *National Broadcasting and State Policy in Arab Countries* (Palgrave Macmillan, 2013).

Chiba, Yushi. "The Geographical Transformation of Arab Media: The Decline of Offshore Media and the Rise of the Media City." *Asia and African Area Studies*, 12: 1 (2012).

Cowen, Tyler. *Creative Destruction: How Globalization Is Changing the World's Cultures* (Princeton University Press, 2004).

Dickinson, Eleanor. "CNN opens new hi-tech studio in Dubai Media City." *Gulf Business*, January 25, 2016, Accessed October 27, 2016, http://gulfbusiness.com/cnn-opens-hi-tech-studio-in-dubai-media-city/.

El-Baltaji, Dana. "Dubai: An Emerging Arab Media Hub." *Arab Media and Society*, 3 (2007).

Forrester, Chris. "High Hopes for Egyptian Media Production City." *TBS Archive*, 7 (2001).

Fouad, Ahmed. "Who is Bombing Egypt's Electricity Towers." *Al-Monitor*, May 5, 2015, Accessed September 26, 2016, http://www.al-monitor.com/pulse/originals/2015/05/egypt-power-plants-bombings-brotherhood-electricity-ministry.html.

Ghazali, Ahmed. "Médias et développements politiques dans le Maghreb et le monde arabe." *Toripodos*, 30 (2012).

Hagey, Keach. "Golden Age of the Media City," *The National (Business)*, November 19, 2008. Accessed April 5, 2015, http://www.thenational.ae/business/golden-age-of-the-media-city?pageCount=0.

Hamdy, Naila. "Latest Tenants at EMPC: Private Egyptian Channels, and One Million-Dollar Show." *TBS Archive*, 8 (2002).

Hawkes, Rebecca. "Saudi Arabia embarks on digital satellite TV platform." *Rapid TV News*, February 6, 2015. Accessed June 5, 2015, http://www.rapidtvnews.com/2015020637089/saudi-arabia-embarks-on-digital-satellite-tv-platform.html#axzz3iICrHRFX.

Kandil, Hamdy. "The Media Free Zone: An Egyptian Media Production City Finance." *TBS Archive*, 5 (2000).

Khalil, Joe F. "Modalities of Media Governance in the Arab World," In Danatella Della Ratta, Naomi Sakr, and Skovgaard-Petersen (eds.), *Arab Media Moguls* (I.B. Tauris, 2015).

Khalil, Joe F. "Towards a Supranational Analysis of Arab Media: The Role of Cities." In Tourya Guaaybess (ed.), *National Broadcasting and State Policy in Arab Countries* (Palgrave Macmillan, 2013).

Kraidy, Marwan M. and Joe F. Khalil. *Arab Television Industries* (Palgrave Macmillan on behalf of the British Film Institute, 2009).

Krzysiek, Pawel. "Testing Legal Boundaries within Arab Media Hubs: Reporting, Law and Politics in Three Media Cities." *Westminster Papers in Communication and Culture*, 6: 1 (2009).

Mada Misr. "Top Media Execs Accused of Campaigning in their Own News Outlets." October 15, 2015. Accessed September 26, 2016, http://www.madamasr.com/news/top-media-execs-accused-campaigning-their-own-news-outlets.

Mekay, Emad. "TV stations multiply as Egyptian censorship falls," *The New York Times*, (July 13, 2011). Accessed June 5, 2015, http://www.nytimes.com/2011/07/14/world/middleeast/14iht-M14B-EGYPT-MEDIA.html.

Moroccan World News. "Media city to be launched soon in Morocco." December 14, 2014. Accessed September 17, 2016, http://www.moroccoworldnews.com/2014/12/145684/media-city-to-be-launched-soon-in-morocco/.

Quinn, Stephan, Tim Walters, and John Whiteoak. "A Tale of Three (Media) Cities." *Australian Studies in Journalism*, 12 (2003).

Shleifer, Abdallah S. "The Dubai Digital Broadcasting." *TBS Archive*, 5 (2000).

Siddiqi, Zafar. "Featured Interview with the TBS staff." *TBS Archive*, 7 (2001).

Sullivan, Sarah. "Private-Sector Media City Launched in Amman." *TBS Archive*, 7 (2001).

The IBC Daily. "Mid-East's other TV hot-spot." September 13, 2008. Accessed March 25, 2011, http://www.jordanmediacity.com/pdf/The_ibc_daily.pdf.

CHAPTER 5

Preventing a Mobilization from Spreading: Assad and the Electronic War

Matthieu Rey

"No… using Skype is not secure. Do you remember how they arrested Mr. X? They had access to his personal data and they picked him up thanks to that."[1] These few sentences encapsulate Syrian opinion towards the use of the Internet during the revolution. They highlight the immediate difference from other Arab contexts, such as the situations in Tunisia and Egypt. In December 2010 and January 2011, the wave of protests suddenly shed light on the importance of social media in the Arab World in the eyes of Western public opinion. Certainly, their social and political aspects have been scrutinized by researchers for a decade, but they remain marginalized in the scope of scholarly work.[2] The successive overthrow of Ben Ali and then Mubarak shook the Arab World and triggered extensive analysis of the recent trends which have shaped public opinion. Controversially, analysts and commentators apologized for not taking these developments into account; namely that social media, mainly Facebook and Twitter, and satellite channels trigger contributed to these movements. They looked to new heroes such as Egypt's

M. Rey (✉)
Iremam (CNRS), Aix en Provence, France

Walid Ghonim and often overstressed their roles.[3] From this perspective, a new dominant narrative emerged from the turmoil: of youth using social media to bring down old autocratic regimes.[4] This approach did not work in the case of Syria.

In contrast to previous uprisings, the regime did not shut down the Internet but allowed access to new sites; it did not crumble in a few weeks, but instead proved extremely resilient. This development needs some further explanation. Studying the electronic response to the protest by the Syrian regime may help us understand this particular evolution of events.

Is Syria an example of the official repression of the state against activists by deploying coercion? This chapter will detail the coercive processes; this perspective is useful as many aspects of the electronic repression are not well known. A first analysis of this topic has been advanced by Delshād`Uthmān.[5] I would like to outline the different aspects of the repression and, by connecting them, to shed light on the concrete procedure of how public policymaking is implemented in Syria.

Scholars have tackled the issue of policy building in Syria with the intention of shedding light on political practices.[6] However, they have not provided any insight into the policies and the apparatus of power on a day-to-day basis. The new context which emerged from the uprising of 2011 clarified the relationship between institutions and their actions. Legal institutions such as the intelligence services or the army can also implement informal activities that depart from their scope of competencies.

In order to analyze the use of social media and electronic repressions, a few theoretical stances help to qualify the main stakes. First, I will argue that an institutional process is ongoing to curb the revolutionary process that was sparked by the new behaviors that emerged from the protest.[7] Management of digital content is part of a broader scope of public policies implemented in reaction to the unrest.[8] I will argue that even if neither the Syrian uprising nor any of the other Arab revolutions were sparked by Internet activity, electronic counter-attacks shed light on how the movement was prevented from growing. Institutions conceive their aims with regards to the collective values of their members. Negotiations and institutional effects unify these different voices in a single policy.[9]

From this perspective, electronic repression highlights the importance of the informal aspects of the political fabric in Syria. Furthermore, this point of view underlines the importance of framing reality. Erwin

Goffman was the first to insist on how interactions alter the views of the actors.[10] Daniel Snow and Daniel Cefai underscore the relations between perceptions and facts. They show that framing reality creates important material and symbolic resources.[11] However, building the narrative—the dominant one against the others—cannot be understood without taking into consideration the actors who produced the discourses. Finally, as David Hakken notes, studying the Internet sphere leads to the focus being placed on three levels—micro, meso and macro—each revealing different elements.[12] I will mainly focus my attention on the meso level.

From this perspective, two different approaches are relevant in shedding light on the institutional processes which affect policymaking. First, Baathist regimes have been compared to a form of totalitarianism.[13] These approaches highlight the classical dilemma of characterizing the decision-making process in policy planning. Do they result from a personal initiative or is it several interplaying voices? In this matter, Syrian electronic activists reveal the connection between the first circle[14] and the specific team targeting the Internet.

Consequently, the present study clarifies internal procedures which shape the decisions. Arguing with Paul DiMaggio, Walter Powell and the neo-institutionalist approach,[15] electronic repression points to the outcome of an institutional dialogue. Therefore, curbing protest and promoting a new discourse on the regime and the opposition are converging in highlighting internal dynamics of formal and informal institutions. However, it seems necessary to firstly examine the role of the Internet and social media before the crisis to assess how important they were.

At the beginning of the twenty-first century, the new president, Bashar al-Assad, came to power. The "young president with blue eyes" had been head of the Syrian Computer Company[16] since the late 1990s, following the death of his elder brother, Bassel al-Assad.[17] In this structure, the leader recruited his men, who took over various positions from the old guard. This very first step in "electronic" history of the regime highlights the connection between the Internet and the rise of Bashar al-Assad.[18] If he initiated changes in matters of infrastructure and modernization of the country, the new president would not be able to maintain the long seclusion of the country.

As a result, Internet providers and users remained few until the very end of the twentieth century[19] (Table 5.1).

The increase in usership reflected the rocky path of the Internet's development in Syria. As Delshād 'Uthmān points out, the whole system

Table 5.1 Internet coverage in Syria since 2000

Date	2000	2005	2011	2012
Percentage of users	0.5	6.5	17	19.5

has been controlled by the regime from the very beginning. The geography of the network depended on its will to monitor the activity with distribution of the electronic links from the capital and the coast, where cables arrived, and subsequently reached second-tier cities.[20] Considering this aspect, two different dynamics informed the use of Internet in Syria.

As the figures show, 2005 was a turning point. Internet activity reached a certain level and reflected the contradictions of the new Syria. On the one hand, it was a sensitive issue, as reports mentions, the regime ordered different companies to track down all electronic activities.[21] Basic laws allowed the regime to control how the Internet was used. If Internet cafes proliferated, each user was supposed to present an identity card and a log of the different screens were kept at the end of each session.[22] The mukhabarat (Intelligence Services) colluded in the process, as a consequence, the Internet did not offer real free space.

On the other hand, online access was part of the new modern Syria. In 2006, the president defended his new economic plan and the focus on the Internet and telecommunications was correlated to economic growth of two percentage points.[23] New technology became the new pillars of the Syrian economy. (It also allowed the businessman Rami Makhluf, a relative of Bashar al-Assad, to build his fortune.) Homes in the main cities had Internet access, as Syrians emphasized:

> It was still expensive to buy a computer and to obtain access to the Internet. The connection was very slow. It nevertheless created a new life. We could have access to the world without being restricted by official media. Of course, many websites remained forbidden. Any pages containing "Israel" for example could not be accessed. However, it changed our view.[24]

These few sentences highlighted the relationship between the Internet and certain segments of the population. Mostly, in Damascus, then in Aleppo, it was an important part of the new way of life that the regime promoted. From this perspective, it facilitated a new kind of socialization—the process of individualization. In the insightful remarks of Asef Bayat, the Internet exemplified the urban effect on youth. In urban areas, they learnt the social skills and resources to obtain independence from the family.[25] The differences in Internet connectivity between the Syrian provinces eventually increased.[26]

Both capitals—Aleppo and Damascus—were well-equipped and directly connected to external points. Secondary cities, such as Homs and Hama, also received attention. However, networks went through the capital and, therefore, the level of traffic was lower than in other places. Gradually, the Internet reached other parts of Syria. However, this did not narrow the spatial inequality between the cities. On the contrary, it marginalized these territories still further. Internet distribution reflected how Syria was modernized during the early part of the century.[27] Transport and educational institutions improved and were able to bring people closer together. However, they led to centralizing activity in both capitals.

> "The University of Aleppo welcomed more than 55% of students who were not from the city. Most of them came here, as there was no opportunity to pursue studies in their homeland. In Aleppo, the students met and discussed. We first organized informal talks."[28]

> I entered the University of Aleppo. We were living in dorms and shared several activities, such. as watching TV, discussing classes, etc. When we saw the downfall of Saddam Hussein on TV in 2003, we immediately went into the street and demonstrated. It was not legal nor was it forbidden as the regime was against the USA.[29]

The new capitals were the new places where a specific socialization took place and Syrian youth interacted with one another. The Internet fuelled these processes during the decade leading up to the uprising. However, its use was restricted to a small minority. Assessing the number of users and the nature of their activity is relatively hard as a certain amount of data can only be surmised—age, number of computers, literacy, family relationships, number of Internet cafés—were all interplaying factors in the use of the Internet. These inequalities and the two different aspects of the Internet largely underpinned the role of the Internet in the uprising and the electronic repression.

> "Come see! There was a demonstration! Yes, in Damascus!"[30]

Early February 2011, YouTube, newly authorized, helped to spread the video of the first gathering in Damascus. Naturally, this website did not trigger the revolt, nor was it decisive in setting Syrians against the regime. On the contrary, the social and political dynamics of the revolt were not sparked by the use of social media and the Internet. It was attributed to peripheral marginalization and resentment against the abuse of dignity.[31] It first took place in Deraa and in coastal towns, before spreading to new areas. In these developments, the Internet played a secondary role, but demonstrated being a decisive part of the events in April and May 2011, by proving to the protesters that others were indeed participating. In the words of an activist from Homs:

> After the first demonstrations downtown, the regime launched massive attacks. The sit-in was broken on the first night. Then, we took refuge in our quarter. Each neighborhood became the main stage of the protest of Friday. But, quickly, it became impossible to move from one part to another. We knew from younger activists who knew how to use the internet that other parts of Syria were involved in the protest. They showed us on the computer other demonstrations, then from April 2011, Al-Jazeera started to use video documenting the uprising. This gave us some hope. But quickly, we lost electricity, connectivity and we were cut off from the world. From June 2011 until my departure in March 2012, it became really hard to know what was going on outside the neighborhood.[32]

Certainly, at the very beginning of the uprising, activists' initiatives helped to spread information and practical resources for organizing protests.[33] A few groups, such as three Free Students (Ṭulāb al-ḥūrrīn), played a particularly important role in urban areas and coordinated nationwide efforts.[34] However, all their activities and their results remained deeply dependent on the local situation on the ground and they failed to establish any kind of permanent structure to support the revolution. In fact, repression increased quickly and became more efficient by using the Internet.

As previously mentioned, the Internet in Syria was never free from strict government control. However, in contrast to the Tunisian and Egyptian cases, the regime was the first to allow access to Facebook, YouTube, and Twitter which suddenly became available in February 2011.[35] A new Internet utopia was born. As several activists have pointed out, contrary to common knowledge, they were unaware of these security procedures. They started to discuss, to exchange information, to express their anger or their joy through microblogging and YouTubing.

However, this new virtual space was usually being monitored by the regime. The mukhabarat's services deployed blanket rules to accumulate control and arrest the protestors. Locally and nationally, initiatives were taken to curb the use of the Internet as a means of protest.[36] This first stance of coercive practices combined standard torture and a campaign of arrests. The mukhabarat operated on two levels: on the national level, Iranians and head figures adopted practices used during the Iranian protest of 2009,[37] arresting key figures and using heavy torture was conceived as the best tool to stop the upheaval. Several young leaders disappeared. On the local stage, members of these services enjoyed relative autonomy. They did not target individuals, nor did they take into consideration electronic materials, which could constitute evidence. From this perspective, the dual strategy reflected the ambiguity of using the Internet to practice mass repression. It is not possible to label all the repressive tactics as public policy as they did not follow a common pattern. This was, however, true on the national level.

From April 2011, new strategies emerged, often after beating the "suspect" during the arrest they were brought to one of the branches of the services. Jail capacities increased quickly, using any available space to detain people, mostly underground. The new questions asked during the interrogation focused on electronic accounts as the services wanted to find out about the passwords that the activists used to access Skype or Facebook. Where were their cameras and their mobiles? Any photos and videos that were found constituted proof of plotting against the security of the state.[38] The first aim of this policy was to avoid any alternative symbolic order emerging from the opposition. If we follow Christina Fominaya's analysis, based on the work of Thomas Szasz, the Internet provides a useful tool for building a symbolic order to counter the dominant narrative.[39] Breaking the production and disturbing the producer can stop a revolutionary discourse from unifying. It reflected the national strategy to divide the country, in the virtual space.

This strategy of using basic tools and coercive apparatus marked the launch of the virtual fight in Syria. Certainly, I do not want to overestimate the role and the impact of the Internet in Syria. I assert that a small group of the activists was concerned by this method of fighting the regime. These groups received greater attention from the security apparatus in June and July 2011.[40] Indeed, a new initiative from the repressive forces targeted Internet traffic and its volume decreased several times in revolutionary neighborhoods. It was never switched off completely, as had been intended in Egypt and in Tunisia. This policy highlighted both the state of uncertainty towards the Internet between central and local commands, and also the multipolarity in the chain of command. After three months of demonstrations and clashes, the regime had mainly responded with repression but it still pretended to look for a political solution with a few reforms.

The first attack on Internet activity led activists from the Anonymous group to retaliate.[41] They focused largely on official websites, from ministries to local institutions such as the Chamber of Trade and Industry in Lattakia. They exposed the vulnerability of the system and showed that that it was possible to disseminate an alternative narrative. This damaged official propaganda. An understanding of the severity of the offense is linked to the nature of the government message: When the uprising broke out, the regime initially denied the events, claiming that nothing was going on. At the very least, it would concede that terrorist attacks were affecting the country. From this perspective, slogans that were being chanted shed light on the global strategy. While protesters chanted "God, Syria, Freedom—that's all", the partisans of the regime answered by organizing counter-demonstrations and shouting "God, Syria, Bashar—that's all." These techniques were aimed to confuse the general public's perception of what was happening on the ground.[42] Creating a common call against the repression threatened this strategy. In this context, attacks from Anonymous were immediately regarded as a substantial threat. Two different strategies were formulated to counter the threat. First, the repression targeted the cyber activists more precisely. Then, a new team of hackers was organized.

The Internet turned out to be a useful tool in order to track activists. Intelligence services followed new guidelines as they were unable to curb the protest despite a massive campaign of arrests. Consequently, informal groups who made up the resistance, such as *tansiqiyyat mahliyya* (local coordination), needed to recruit new members, as the older ones disappeared.[43] In addition, they had to become more cautious. As Evgeni Morozov argues, the Internet turned into "net delusion".[44] While most of the activists spoke about their activism and were able to exchange their views openly, they were being tracked on several forms of media. In addition to using physical torture to get information, intelligence services used digital media to deploy several nets of controls. For example, "men in the middle" were able to surveil two sides of a dialogue without the awareness of either side. Moreover, new procedures which employed viruses and worms permitted the services to spy on computers and increase mistrust.[45] Quickly, global networks countered the different methods used by the services. A specific group from Anonymous helped activists by deploying new secure means, such as Tor and VPN (Virtual Private Network) systems.[46] Communications improved but use of the Internet was no longer viewed as a discursive space in which the revolution could build an alternative voice.

The two sides pitted their respective strengths against each other, even though the regime could target the activists more precisely through carrying out mass arrests. Moreover, from February 2012, the regime launched the battle for the cities. In addition, bombing the neighborhood led to a collapse of the infrastructure. It was no longer a problem of deliberating and exchanging views; rather, it became a struggle to even secure access to electricity and Internet connectivity. The army entered the neighborhoods and then the intelligence services tracked the people down.[47] Several neighborhoods were cut off from the outside world. During this new stage of the uprising, the main task of the activists became being connected. At the same time, the regime turned the Internet into a useful way of tracking its opponents. Combining basic methods of repression with spying on the Internet permitted an extension to the scope of the repression. Therefore, the regime had almost monopolized the narrative built on the Internet, while the activists struggled to exist by spreading news, videos, and analyses through the media. As a consequence, using the Internet in Syria meant a national struggle to frame a new narrative. But the Internet also provided a useful tool to promote the regime's propaganda. From this perspective, it seems that the regime "learned" how to use the Internet to its best advantage.

In 2012, WikiLeaks revealed that at the beginning of the uprising, the president received advice on social media strategies from two young politicians from the same generation as the president, who were specially recruited to work in the electronic services.[48] Two years later, Guilia Prati shows that the presidency was still experiencing problems using Twitter. Bashar al-Assad (or those in charge of the presidential account) focused their actions on Syrian hours, meaning in the time zone of day-time Syria rather than the time zone in day-time Washington DC, depriving the services of the efficiency by disconnecting Twitter activities to the American public for example.[49] These two insights proved that the regime was relatively unspohisticated in its use of the Internet but it also highlights the very low level of institutionalizing. Assad's system mainly works on a network of personal relationships. At the beginning of the uprising, information services depended mostly on the departments in the company of Ramī Makhlūf. Therefore, the presidency could only employ a few specialists. The two managers of the presidency were from the same generation and background as Bashar al-Assad. They could not fulfill the technological gap. Similarly, even if the presidency adopted Facebook in 2007 and later Twitter, the regime could not make up for the vacuum of activity in public relations.

When the uprising broke out, some youths from the new generation who were well integrated within the regime took its side, and they committed themselves towards its struggle against the cyberactivists. They soon became labeled as the "Syrian Electronic Army" (SEA). In June 2011, Bashar al-Assad acknowledged its existence and publicly thanked "the brave fighters".[50] Later, they changed into an offensive group, targeting accounts and revealing secret passwords and IP addresses, which led to a new wave of arrests. The group crashed public websites, and surprisingly the majority of their targets were Israelis.[51] Israel kept a low profile in the Syrian struggle.[52] Tactics and goals highlighted the limitations of the group, but also its main constituencies. This informal group gathered in order to support the regime. It was not clearly organized or institutionalized.[53] Therefore, they supplied the regime with their services and this electronic army has to be viewed as a group more than a clearly defined state-run service.

With respect to its capabilities, the regime's electronic fight cannot be compared to that of Iran, Russia, or China. This is not to underestimate the capacities of Assad's regime, but the assessment of its practices proved that it was sparked by personal and informal motivations. It reflects a broader pattern of ruling and governing the country. This informal nature matches the contradictory nature of public policy implemented regarding the Internet. What characterized the regime was mainly a multipolarity of the decisions, the absence of coordination beyond a general framework, and general guidelines. From this perspective, Ian Kershaw's concept—"working towards the fuhrer"[54]—seems particularly relevant in this context. The general principle of the policy towards the Internet was based on a simple pattern: "working towards the fuhrer" means that the leader launches general trends which allow local actors to act in accordance to these considerations. Bashar al-Assad issued different general guidelines: curbing "terrorism" in the country; curbing dissidents' voices; and pretending that the population supported the regime and that it was under siege. Then, each department acted independently. Their abilities depended on their individual skills. Some services that were well connected with foreign partners such as Iranian ones were able to track opponents efficiently, while others conducted a massive campaign against all kinds of people. Then, the leader indicated what he viewed as the right policy but did not denounce the others.

To conclude, the Syrian case study provides insights on the idea of net delusion. I show how Internet repression dealt with public policies and reflects the political dynamics within the context of an authoritarian regime. Contrary to other studies, I analyze practices in the context of disturbances and upheaval. In most cases, scholars have brilliantly pinpointed how the regime reacts and provides special departments in order to use the Internet. In the Syrian case, the regime learned how to create electronic propaganda following the unrest. However, it was not able to systematize its treatment towards virtual spaces in Syria effectively. This explains why some areas which escaped Assad's control are still connected to the Internet. On the other hand, a systematic attack against cyberactivists was launched during the summer of 2011. Syrian practices against the free movement and the struggle for dignity were related directly to the nature of the regime. Its members who competed one against another tried to prove their high commitment by deploying a better repression. It remains highly repressive. Since 2015, this de facto decentralization has continued to grow as new providers appear by connecting neighboring areas with countries such as Turkey. This learning process explains, on the one hand, the high level of repression and, on the other hand, its contradictions.

NOTES

1. Interview with an activist in Damascus, August 2012.
2. On social media Arturo Escobar, "Welcome to Cyberia. Notes on the Anthropology of Cyberculture", *Current Anthropology* 35(1994): 211–231; Philip Howard and Malcolm Parks, "Social Media and Political Change: Capacity, Constraint, and Consequence," *Journal of Communication* 62(2012): 359–362; David Hakken, *Cyborgs@cyberspace? An Ethnographer Looks to the Future* (New York: Routledge, 1991); in the Arab word, Quitan Wiktorowicz, *Islamic Activism: A Social Movement Theory Approach* (Bloomington: Indiana University Press, 2004); Yves Gonzalez-Quijano, *Arabités numériques. Le printemps du Web arabe* (Paris: Acte Sud, 2012).

3. On an over-emphasized Walīd al-Ghonīm role, Elizabeth Thompson, *Justice Interrupted: The Struggle for Constitutional Movement in the Middle East* (New Haven, CT: Harvard University Press, 2013).

4. Farhad Khosrokhavar nuanced this approach with his concept of "demo-movement," Farhad Khosrokhavar, *The New Arab Revolution that Shook the World* (New York: Paradigm Publishers, 2012).

5. On the Syrian case, see the delightful paper, Delshād `Uthmān, "Al-Ittiṣālāt al-suriyya fī ḥāl ḥuṣūl al-darba al-`askariyya. Warqa `amal tadrusu al-ākhṭār allatī tuhaddidu al-khidma fī ḥāl al-darba awu fī ḥālā iyqāf al-khidma bi shakli maqṣūdi wa al-ḥulūl al-is`āfiyya allatī min al-mumkin tanfīdhha." (The Syrians Communications in case of military attack. Working papers studying the dangers which threaten the use of the communication in case of military attack or in case of suspending on purpose its use and the emergency solutions that can be implemented) Washington, September 1, 2013.

6. Eyal Ziyer, *Commanding Syria: Bashar al-Assad and the First Years of Power* (London: I.B. Tauris, 2007); David Lesch, *The New Lion of Damascus: Bashar al-Assad and Modern Syria* (New Haven: Yale University Press, 2005); Sylvia Chiffoleau, ed., "La Syrie au quotidien. Cultures et Pratiques du changement," *Revue des Mondes Méditerranéens et Musulmans* 115–116 (2006).

7. Chaymaa Hassabo, On revolutionary and institutional processes, "Trois ans de revolution," (paper presented at *Culture politique arabe* Seminar, Paris, 2012–2013).

8. Jean Pierre Filiu, *Le Nouveau Moyen Orient: les peuples à l'heure de la révolution syrienne* (Paris: Fayard, 2013); Matthieu Rey, "Syria: between revolution and repression, 2011–2013" (paper presented at *The Arab Uprising 2011–2014: Between Revolution and Authoritarianism*, Singapore, July 8, 2014).

9. This finding is based on Mary Douglas' argument that institutions are thinking. Mary Douglas, *Comment les Institutions pensent* (Paris: La découverte, 2004).

10. Erwin Goffman, *Frame Analysis: An Essay on the Organisation of Experience* (Boston, MA: Northeastern University Press, 1986).

11. Daniel Cefaï, "La construction des problèmes publics: Définitions de situations dans des arènes publiques," *Réseaux*, 14 (1996).

12. Hakken, *Cyborg@cyberspace: An Ethnographer Looks to the Future*, 20–23.

13. Mostly in the Iraqi case, Joseph Sassoon, *Saddam Hussein's Ba'th Party: Inside an Authoritarian Regime* (Cambridge: Cambridge University Press, 2011); Chris Kutchera, *Le Livre Noir de Saddam Hussein* (Paris: Oh! Edition, 2005).

14. The First circle refers to the close connected figures who rule Syria in cooperation with the President Bashar al-Assad, Hanna Batatu, *Syria's Peasantry, the Descendants of Its Lesser Rural Notables, and Their Politics* (Princeton: Princeton University Press, 1999).
15. Paul DiMaggio and Walter Powell, eds., *The New Institutionalism in Organizational Analysis* (Chicago: University of Chicago Press, 1991).
16. This company was first established by Basel al-Assad, older brother of Bashar al-Assad. He intended to promote the use of computers in Syria by attracting Syrian engineers who graduated from prestigious international universities. When he died in 1994, Bashar al-Assad inherited the project and improved the capacities of this society.
17. Lesch, *The New Lion of Damascus.*
18. "Internet Usage and Marketing Report: Syria," Internet World Stats, accessed February 1, 2016, http://www.internetworldstats.com/me/sy.htm.
19. For the data, "Syrie," Statistiques Mondiales, accessed February 1, 2016, http://www.statistiques-mondiales.com/syrie.htm; Barney Warf and Peter Vincent, " Multiples Geographies of the Arab Internet," *Area* 39(2007): 83–98.
20. `Uthmān, "Ittiṣālāt al-suriyya," 12.
21. Reporter Sans Frontière, "Syrie, ennemie d'internet," March 12, 2012, accessed February 2, 2016, http://fr.rsf.org/syrie-syrie-12-03-2012,42016.html.
22. Observation in Damascus and Aleppo (June 2010).
23. In the late 1990s, Syria was not equipped in IT nor was its mobile network well-developed. Implementing the new plan of computers and telephone and, then, improving them created a high level of growth. Ramy Makhluf through two companies has monopolized this market. Fred Lawson, *Demystifying Syria* (London: Saqi, 2009).
24. Interview with an activist (Damascus, June 2012).
25. Matthieu Rey, "2003, a new generation in Syria," in *Generations and Protests* ed. Ratiba el-Hajj et al. (London: Routledge).
26. `Uthmān, "Ittiṣālāt al-suriyya."
27. Baudoin Dupret, Zouhair Ghazzal and Youssef Courbage, *La Syrie au présent* (Paris: Acte Sud, 2006).
28. Interview with an activist (Gaziantep, October 2014).
29. Interview with an activist from Deraa in Damascus (June 2012).
30. Observation in Damascus (February 2012).
31. Matthieu Rey, "Body as a symbol of dignity, how Arabs mergered to defend the dignity," (paper presented at The Middle East in Revolt: the First Anniversary, Melbourne, Victoria, March 17–18, 2012).
32. Interview with an activist in Bekaa Valley (October 2014).

33. Céline Pigeot and Alexandre Durant, "'Nouvelles guerres de l'information': Le cas de la Syrie," *Note stratégiques CEIS*(2012), accessed March 30 , 2015, https://reflets.info/la-censure-du-net-en-syrie-mise-a-nu/.
34. Interviews with a Syrian activist (Gaziantep, October 2014).
35. Christophe Varin, "Le Web à l'épreuve de la 'cyberguerre' en Syrie," *Etudes* 417(2012).
36. Céline Pigeot and Alexandre Durant, "Nouvelles guerres de l'information"; Sophia Amine, et al., *Infowar in Syria*: the Web Between Liberation and Repression (Beirut: CEMAM, 2012); Margaret Weiss, "Assad's Secretive Cyber Forces," The Washington Institute, April 12, 2012.
37. Evgeny Morozov, *The Net Delusion*: *The Dark Side of Internet Freedom* (New York: Public Affairs, 2012).
38. Interviews in Damascus (June 2012).
39. Christina Fominaya, *Social Movements and Globalization: How Protests, Occupations and Uprisings are Changing the World*. Sociology for Globalizing Societies (London: Palgrave Macmillan, 2014), 121
40. The regime had no elaborate services specializing in the Internet, before 2010. Olivier Danino, *L'utilisation stratégique du cyber au Moyen Orient* (Paris: DAS, 2013).
41. Anonymous is an informal international network of activist and hacktivist entities. The group became known for a series of well-publicized publicity stunts and distributed denial-of-service (DDoS) attacks on government, religious, and corporate websites. During the Syrian uprising, two of them led the help towards the Syrians (Neumenn and Kheops).
42. Marc Gognon, "Graffitis et contre-manifestations volantes, des réponses du pouvoir à la contestation syrienne," in *Au Coeur des Révoltes Arabes: Devenir Révolutionnaires*, eds. Amin Allal and Thomas Pierret (Paris: Armand Colin, 2013).
43. Interviews with activists (Damascus-Hama, June 2012).
44. Morozov, *The Net Delusion*.
45. Helmi Norman, "The Emergence of Open and Organized Pro-Government Cyber Attacks in the Middle East: The Case of the Syrian Electronic Army," OpenNet Initiative, accessed February 1, 2016, https://opennet.net/emergence-open-and-organized-pro-government-cyber-attacks-middle-east-case-syrian-electronic-army.
46. Marc Gognon, "Les cyberactivistes ont besoin d'aide," *Œil sur la Syrie*, December 12, 2011.
47. Wladimir Glassman, "Les ressources sécuritaires du régime," in *Pas de Printemps pour la Syrie. Les clés pour comprendre les acteurs et les défis de la crise (2011–2013)*, eds. François Burgat and Bruno Paoli (Paris: la découverte, 2013).

48. Olivier Danino, "Le soulèvement syrien à la lumière du cyber," in *Les logiciels libres au Proche Orient. Société de l'information au Proche Orient*, ed. A. Nedelec (Paris, 2012).
49. Guilia Prati, "Between Propaganda and Public Relations: An Analysis of Bashar al-Assad's Digital Communications Campaign", *Journal of International Affairs*, March 9, 2015, accessed February 1, 2016, http://jia.sipa.columbia.edu/online-articles/propaganda-public-relations-analysis-bashar-al-assads-digital-communications-campaign/.
50. "Syrian Electronic Army: Disruptive Attacks and Hyped Targets," Information Warfare Monitor, June 25, 2011, accessed February 1, 2016, http://www.infowar-monitor.net/2011/06/syrian-electronic-army-disruptive-attacks-and-hyped-targets/.
51. Ibid.
52. Itamar Rabinovith, "New Israeli Policy Towards Syria: Should Israel Threaten to Intervene?," Brookings Blog, February 13, 2015, accessed February 1, 2016, http://www.brookings.edu/blogs/order-from-chaos/posts/2015/02/13-new-israeli-policy-on-syria-rabinovich.
53. Romain Renier, "Qui se cache derrière l'armée électronique syrienne?" *La Tribune*, September 2, 2013, accessed February 1, 2016, http://www.latribune.fr/technos-medias/20130902trib000782740/qui-se-cache-derriere-l-armee-electronique-syrienne-.html.
54. Ian Kershaw, *The Nazi Dictatorship: Problems and Perspectives of Interpretation* (London: Edward Arnold, 1985).

Bibliography

Batatu, Hanna. *Syria's Peasantry, the Descendants of Its Lesser Rural Notables, and Their Politics*. Princeton: Princeton University Press, 1999.

Cefaï, Daniel. "La construction des problèmes publics : Définitions de situations dans des arènes publiques." *Réseaux*, 14 (1996).

Chiffoleau, Sylvia, ed. "La Syrie au quotidien. Cultures et Pratiques du changement." *Revue des Mondes Méditerranéens et Musulmans* 115–116 (2006).

Douglas, Mary. *Comment les Institutions pensent*. Paris : La découverte, 2004.

Danino, Olivier. "Le soulèvement syrien à la lumière du cyber." In *Les logiciels libres au Proche Orient. Société de l'information au Proche Orient*, edited by A. Nedelec. Paris, 2012.

Danino, Olivier. *L'utilisation stratégique du cyber au Moyen Orient*. Paris : DAS, 2013.

DiMaggio, Paul, and Walter Powell, eds. *The New Institutionalism in Organizational Analysis*. Chicago: University of Chicago Press, 1991.

Dupret, Baudoin, Zouhair Ghazzal and Youssef Courbage. *La Syrie au présent*. Paris : Acte Sud, 2006.

El Amine, Sofia, Stéphane Bazan, Sabrine Saad, Addis Tesfa and Christophe Varin. *Infowar in Syria: the web between liberation and repression*. Beirut: CEMAM, 2012.

Escobar, Arturo. "Welcome to Cyberia. Notes on the Anthropology of Cyberculture." *Current Anthropology* 35 (1994): 211–231.

Filiu, Jean Pierre. *Le Nouveau Moyen Orient : les peuples à l'heure de la révolution syrienne*. Paris : Fayard, 2013.

Fominaya, Christina. *Social Movements and Globalization: How protests, occupations and uprisings are changing the world*. London: Palgrave Macmillan, 2014.

Glassman, Wladimir. "Les ressources sécuritaires du régime." In *Pas de Printemps pour la Syrie. Les clés pour comprendre les acteurs et les défis de la crise (2011–2013)*, edited by François Burgat and Bruno Paoli. Paris : la découverte, 2013.

Goffman, Erwin. *Frame Analysis: An Essay on the Organisation of Experience*. Boston: Northeastern University Press, 1986.

Gognon, Marc. *Les cyberactivistes ont besoin d'aide*." Œil sur la Syrie, December 12, 2011.

Gognon, Marc. "Graffitis et contre-manifestations volantes, des réponses du pouvoir à la contestation syrienne." In *Au Coeur des Révoltes Arabes: Devenir Révolutionnaires*, edited by Amin Allal and Thomas Pierret. Paris: Armand Colin, 2013.

Gonzalez-Quijano, Yves. *Arabités numériques: Le printemps du Web arabe*. Paris: Acte Sud, 2012.

Hakken, David. *Cyborgs@cyberspace? An Ethnographer Looks to the Future*. New York: Routledge, 1991.

Hassabo, Chaymaa. "Trois ans de revolution." Paper presented at Culture politique arabe Seminar, Paris, 2012–2013.

Howard, Philip, and Malcolm Parks. "Social Media and Political Change: Capacity, Constraint, and Consequence." *Journal of Communication* 62(2012): 359–362.

Information Warfare Monitor. "Syrian Electronic Army : Disruptive Attacks and Hyped Targets." June 25, 2011. Accessed February 1, 2016. http://www.infowar-monitor.net/2011/06/syrian-electronic-army-disruptive-attacks-and-hyped-targets/.

Internet World Stats. "Internet Usage and Marketing Report: Syria." Accessed February 1, 2016, http://www.internetworldstats.com/me/sy.htm.

Interviews with a Syrian activist. Gaziantep, October 2014.

Khosrokhavar, Farhad. *The New Arab Revolution that Shook the World*. New York: Paradigm Publishers, 2012.

Kutchera, Chris. *Le Livre Noir de Saddam Hussein*. Paris: Oh! Edition, 2005.

Lawson, Fred. *Demystifying Syria*. London: Saqi, 2009.

Lesch, David. *The New Lion of Damascus: Bashar al-Assad and Modern Syria.* New Haven : Yale University Press, 2005.

Morozov, Evgeny. *The Net Delusion: The Dark side of Internet Freedom.* New York: Public Affairs, 2012.

Norman, Helmi. "The Emergence of Open and Organized Pro-Government Cyber Attacks in the Middle East: The Case of the Syrian Electronic Army." *OpenNet Initiative.* Accessed February 1, 2016. https://opennet.net/emergence-open-and-organized-pro-government-cyber-attacks-middle-east-case-syrian-electronic-army.

Pigeot, Céline, and Alexandre Durant. ""Nouvelles guerres de l'information": Le cas de la Syrie." Note stratégiques CEIS (2012). Accessed March 30, 2015. https://reflets.info/la-censure-du-net-en-syrie-mise-a-nu/.

Prati, Guilia. "Between Propaganda and Public Relations: An Analysis of Bashar al-Assad's Digital Communications Campaign." *Journal of International Affairs* (2015). Accessed February 1, 2016, http://jia.sipa.columbia.edu/online-articles/propaganda-public-relations-analysis-bashar-al-assads-digital-communications-campaign/.

Rabinovith, Itamar. "New Israeli Policy towards Syria : Should Israel threaten to intervene ?" *Brookings Blog*, February 13, 2015. Accessed February 1, 2016, http://www.brookings.edu/blogs/order-from-chaos/posts/2015/02/13-new-israeli-policy-on-syria-rabinovich.

Renier, Romain. "Qui se cache derrière l'armée électronique syrienne ?" *La Tribune*, September 2, 2013. Accessed February 1, 2016. http://www.latribune.fr/technos-medias/20130902trib000782740/qui-se-cache-derriere-l-armee-electronique-syrienne-.html .

Reporter Sans Frontière. "Syrie, ennemie d'internet." March 12, 2012. Accessed February 2, 2016. http://fr.rsf.org/syrie-syrie-12–03-2012,42016.html.

Rey, Matthieu. "2003, a new generation in Syria." In *Generations and Protests*, edited by Ratiba el-Hajj, et al. London: Routledge, forthcoming.

Rey, Matthieu. "Body as a symbol of dignity, how Arabs merged to defend the dignity." Paper presented at The Middle East in Revolt: the First Anniversary, Melbourne, Victoria, March 17–18, 2012.

Rey, Matthieu. "Syria : between revolution and repression, 2011–2013." Paper presented at The Arab Uprising 2011-2014: Between Revolution and Authoritarianism conference, Middle East Institute, Singapore, July 8, 2014.

Sassoon, Joseph. *Saddam Hussein's Ba'th Party: Inside an Authoritarian Regime.* Cambridge: Cambridge University Press, 2011.

Statistiques Mondiales. "Syrie." Accessed February 1, 2016. http://www.statistiques-mondiales.com/syrie.htm.

Thompson, Elizabeth. *Justice interrupted: The Struggle for Constitutional Movement in the Middle East.* New Haven: Harvard University Press, 2013.

`Uthmān, Delshād. "Ittiṣālāt al-suriyyafīḥālḥuṣūl al-darba al-`askariyya. Warqa `amaltadrusu al-ākhṭāralatītuhaddidu al-khidmafīḥāl al-darbaawufīḥālātiyqāf al-khidmabishaklimaqṣūdiwa al-ḥulūlalis`āfiyyaalatī min al-mumkintanfīdhha." Paper presented, Washington, September 1, 2013.

Varin, Christophe. "Le Web à l'épreuve de la "cyberguerre" en Syrie." *Etudes* 417(2012).

Warf, Barney, and Peter Vincent. "Multiples Geographies of the Arab Internet." *Area 39* (2007): 83–98.

Weiss, Margaret. "Assad's Secretive Cyber Forces." *The Washington Institute*, April 12, 2012. Accessed February 20, 2016. http://www.washingtoninstitute.org/policy-analysis/view/assads-secretive-cyber-force.

Wiktorowicz, Quitan. *Islamic Activism: A Social Movement Theory Approach.* Bloomington: Indiana University Press, 2004.

Ziyer, Eyal. *Commanding Syria: Bashar al-Assad and the First Years of Power.* London: I.B. Tauris, 2007.

CHAPTER 6

Spectacles of Terror: Media and the Cultural Production of Terrorism

Suzi Mirgani

Ever since September 11, 2001, terrorism and the discourse of terrorism have been among the most prominent features of the first two decades of the twenty-first century. The Middle East has been defined, in particular, by extremist ideologies, with many countries falling victim to sustained terrorist attacks. In the age of globalization, and with the added dimension of digital media and global communication networks, these terrorist ideologies and activities have gained international momentum, and have been imported, exported, and home grown by sympathetic networks all over the world.

Terrorist attacks are essentially acts of political communication, and a means of partaking in a global discourse, no matter how rogue and alien the language of violence utilized. In many ways, "terrorism *is* communication and, as such, is really aimed at the people watching."[1] Since international terrorist networks, whether the Islamic State, al-Qaʿida, al-Shabaab, the Taliban, or Boko Haram, are not always well equipped or consistently funded, they often rely heavily on the persuasive abilities of a

S. Mirgani (✉)
Center for International and Regional Studies (CIRS), Georgetown
University in Qatar, Doha, Qatar

© The Author(s) 2017
N. Lenze et al. (eds.), *Media in the Middle East*,
DOI 10.1007/978-3-319-65771-4_6

powerful ideological message transmitted through cheap, instantaneous, and widely available communication platforms. In these ways, terrorist attacks often take on elements of the "global" and the "spectacular," achieved by dint of their high-profile attacks and expert utilization of global communication and media networks to publicize these atrocities. Thus, it is often the case that terrorists' "strength is judged not by their actual numbers or violent accomplishments, but by the effect these have on their audience."[2] This ability to shock and awe publics in the Middle East, and beyond, has only increased with the evolution of the concept of "global terrorism" facilitated by the development of international communication networks that see operations simultaneously ravaging multiple regions of the world, whether in Europe, the United States, Asia, or Australia.[3]

With the rise of digital global communication networks, the concept of "international terrorism" has risen to prominent notoriety, and its ideologies adopted by various terrorist groups all over the world. In the early 2000s, one of al-Qaʻida's commanders, al-Zawahiri, was quoted as saying that much of modern-day ideological conflict "is taking place in the battlefield of the media."[4] This statement becomes even more poignant in today's digital media saturated environment, where terrorist groups and their activities become no longer confined to any one nation or region of the world, but ricochet from continent to continent. Terrorist organizations are using digital media to internationalize themselves by forming global networks, and to justify their causes through a variety of publicized messages, including cyber *fatwas* that echo al-Zawahiri's sentiment by advocating that online "Jihad is not different from the armed one. In fact, it might be more important if you consider the global dimensions of the Internet. Whoever wins this war will become the strongest in the realm of information."[5]

This study examines the cultural production of terrorism by analyzing both terror and anti-terror campaigns. As with most ideological battles, narrative construction and opposition take center stage, with many of these struggles being acted out in a variety of available media, and, increasingly, taking place through the commodity form. The first part of this chapter examines the rise of international terrorist networks, and how these groups achieved their publicity goals by appealing to traditional corporate media channels. The essay then examines how terrorist organizations, with the aid of information and communication technologies, no longer have to court media networks, but publicize their own messages, resulting in the globalization of their ideologies and an increase in the quantity and quality of their cultural production. In a perverse reversal, corporate news networks, in their constant search for content, publicize terrorist activities, and sensationalize these stories as part of their profit-maximizing operations. The chapter concludes with some examples of how the spectacle of terrorism is used by both terror and anti-terror campaigns; there is an increasingly symbiotic relationship being created between seemingly disparate actors, including corporate news networks, terrorist networks, and the counter-terrorism security apparatus.

GLOBALIZATION OF TERRORISM IN THE AGE OF DIGITAL COMMUNICATION: GATEKEEPERS VS GATECRASHERS

In traditional mass media forms, such as television and newspapers, stories had to be verified and perspectives and ideologies aligned, with ultimate control in the hands of editors and network owners. Within these traditional media forms, "a terrorist's thirst for publicity was tempered by the 'selection threshold' of the media, who decided what stories and events were newsworthy, and most importantly how the story would be communicated to the public."[6]

Although al-Qaʿida enacted its own sustained communication efforts and cultural productions in the early 2000s, the terrorist group remained beholden to traditional and mainstream media for the global dissemination and recognition of its messages. It even resorted to faxing statements to newspapers, hoping that they would be picked up for increased publicity.[7] While some networks responded, of which a prime example is the Al Jazeera network, other, mostly Western, broadcasters simply ignored the extremist message, barring it from airplay. In one instance, a Peter Arnett, a CNN reporter, asked Bin Laden "'What are your future plans?' Bin Laden replied, 'You'll see them and hear about them in the media, God willing.'"[8] This statement of hope that the mainstream media would circulate news of al-Qaʿida's ideologies and atrocities was uttered prior to the widespread use of social media.

Today, those who use digital media platforms, whether terrorist or otherwise, can publicize their own news without waiting for the necessary permissions from networks and editors. For terrorists operating with the aid of information and communication technologies, "social media has changed the dynamic fundamentally. It has eliminated dependency on mainstream media, reversing the relationship by making mainstream media dependent on the jihadist-run social media."[9] In this sense, social media has challenged and changed the rules of media gatekeeping, and has afforded terrorists "direct control over the content of their messages by constructing and operating their own websites and online forums, effectively eliminating the 'selection threshold'."[10] Unofficial storytellers connect to global information networks, each with their own form of personal narrative and public testimony. For example, Musa Cerantonio, an Islamic State supporter, "was a televangelist on Iqraa TV in Cairo, but he left after the station objected to his frequent calls to establish a caliphate. Now [in 2015] he preaches on Facebook and Twitter,"[11] and reaches a more diverse audience all around the world.

Terrorist organizations no longer have to court corporate media networks in order to gain access to international audiences. Information and communication technologies are "designed to account for the entry of nonstate actors into the fields of war and diplomacy and to describe how information works as a weapon within this extensive field of combat."[12] Extremists have taken enthusiastically to the Internet not only to communicate, but also to build a knowledge cache and to educate and indoctrinate audiences into a particular mode of thought stemming from a particular ideological impetus. "The Internet contributes to several activities of terrorist groups, such as fundraising, networking, and coordination, as well as information gathering."[13] Since the Internet is difficult to police and regulate, it provides not only the necessary anonymity and decentralization needed for stealth communication, but also the mass exposure needed for global publicity.[14] The ability to operate multiple media platforms is not necessarily due to any form of extraordinary digital literacy, hacking, or subterfuge, but is simply a feature of contemporary social media platforms that allow for anyone with the means to operate multiple accounts with a high degree of anonymity.

In addition, terrorist organizations make maximum use of information and communication technologies to connect with each other, and with other international networks. Exemplifying the interconnected nature of contemporary terrorist groups, many have sought to create close ties with others, and, in recent years, smaller terrorist groups have pledged allegiance to more powerful ones, thereby creating an international network of similarly-minded organizations stretching all over the globe. While some of these complex partnerships have fizzled and failed, al-Shabaab has pledged allegiance to al-Qaʿida and, along with Boko

Haram, al-Qaʿida, and the Taliban, have made ideological commitments, at one point or another, to the Islamic State, the most popular terrorist network operating in the Middle East, and now being actively exported far beyond the region.[15]

With the expansion of globalization processes, and the proliferation of information and communication technologies, the reach of international terrorists extends into new parts of the world. "No longer geographically constrained within a particular territory, or politically or financially dependent on a particular state, they rely on technologically modern forms of communication."[16] This global agenda is communicated internationally through digital media and the Internet, and, importantly, increasingly in a variety of different languages, and in a sustained manner, whether emanating from a variety of disparate sources all over the world, or from more "official" centralized sources along a unified narrative trend. For example, "the full extent of Isis's [Islamic State in Iraq and Syria] media ambitions can be seen in the output of its 'Al Hayat Media Center' [which] is specifically aimed at non-Arabic speakers, particularly younger viewers, and its output is closer to mainstream broadcast standards than anything else Islamic extremism has yet produced."[17]

Al-Shabaab also has its own media production unit, Al Kataib Foundation,[18] which produces high-quality videos and documentaries, and the group regularly communicates with its audiences through a variety of media, including digital media platforms as well as a more traditional radio station, Radio Andalus, whose presenters speak with English and US accents. Betraying its desire to connect with, and appeal to, an international audience, and "to broadcast its message to the wider world,"[19] al-Qaʿida's affiliate in the Arabian Peninsula has produced an online magazine called *Inspire* which features such instructional articles as "Make a Bomb in the Kitchen of Your Mom,"[20] all published in the English language in an effort to attract a global readership. Many of the tweets emanating from al-Shabaab accounts during the 2013 attack on Nairobi's Westgate Mall were written using eloquent and sophisticated forms of the English language with tweets including the words "sheer fragility," "reap the bitter fruits of your harvest,"[21] and "#Westgate: a 14-hour standoff relayed in 1400 rounds of bullets and 140 characters of vengeance and still ongoing. Good morning Kenya!"[22] In similar fashion, much of the Taliban's online and social media activity is posted in English, and is therefore not meant for domestic consumption, but is squarely aimed at foreign occupiers and for global audiences.[23]

The Taliban operates online despite the fact that Internet penetration rates in Afghanistan are considered low in comparison with those found in other developing nations.[24] Thus, contemporary terrorist groups, and their international sympathizers, have taken a special interest in the communicative powers of digital media, and have gained expertise and access to these technologies that reach far beyond the realities of Internet penetration rates in many of the countries in which they were originally headquartered—Syria and Iraq for the Islamic State, Somalia for al-Shabaab, and Afghanistan and Pakistan for the Taliban.

TERRORISTS AND INFORMATION AND COMMUNICATION TECHNOLOGIES

The rise of online extremist activity can be mapped as increasing in direct correlation with the rise of digital network capabilities. In 1998, there were around fifteen terrorist organizations that had some kind of online presence, and this had increased to over 4000 extremist-related sites by 2005.[25] In 1998, for example, "less than half of the organizations designated as Foreign Terrorist Organizations by the US State Department maintained websites; by the end of 1999, nearly all these terrorist groups had established their presence on the Net. By now, all active terrorist groups have established at least one form of presence on the Internet."[26]

Many terrorist networks upload ideological propaganda and news of attacks to specific Internet forums and websites, but in the age of digital communication, it seems that even these new media methods have become stale. Social media channels, especially in the case of Twitter, means that extremist ideology and terrorist practices are now no longer just shared with like-minded people who visit specific clandestine websites, but are increasingly openly available in the public domain. By allowing the technology to do all the work, extremist "messages posted to social networking sites reach audiences immediately, and are extremely easy to access and redistribute, exponentially multiplying their audience."[27]

Among the most popular platforms used by extremists are Facebook, Instagram, Viber, WhatsApp, Ask.fm, JustPast.it, and Tumblr, as well as a variety of encryption software that is used to divert and disguise the origin of messages.[28] Twitter has proved to be by far the most popular and efficient application and is used by a variety of extremist networks.

"Specifically engineered for cellphones, it is easy and inexpensive to use. Posts (tweets) may contain images or text, links to other platforms can be embedded, and an incoming tweet can effortlessly be forwarded to everyone in an address list. Some types of social media require either 3G or wi-fi access but Twitter can be used in the absence of either."[29]

The evolution of social media dexterity reached a stage where the Islamic State could brazenly release an Arabic-language Twitter app by the name of *The Dawn of Glad Tidings* with the ability to channel "40,000 tweets in one day as ISIS marched into the northern Iraqi city of Mosul,"[30] making the story "trend" due to the large and sustained volume of online traffic. The app, which posted Islamic State tweets directly onto a user's personal account, was available for download from Google Play onto Android mobile phones,[31] and, as is the case with most apps downloaded online, it required that users give up some personal data and a certain degree of privacy.[32] The app has since been removed by Google.[33]

Twitter's appeal also stems from the fact that any time an account is shut down, the user can easily set up other alternative accounts.[34] For example, when al-Shabaab staged their 2013 attack on Westgate Mall in Nairobi, which ended with "65 civilians, six soldiers and police officers, and four terrorists among the dead,"[35] the group publicized its actions predominantly on Twitter using "five different Twitter handles as its account kept getting taken down."[36] In addition to easily and swiftly coming back online every time its accounts were targeted, al-Shabaab also understood the need to connect online media with traditional media forms, and to court established corporate news networks. During the attacks, "reporters received an email from the group's press office informing them that they could now follow the new handle @HSMPress, 'for the Mujahideen's take on the events in Somalia as well as current events in the wider global context.'"[37] In this instance, even though extremist communication channels are targeted and disrupted by authorities, journalists in mainstream media channels are often only too eager to capitalize upon such unique "scoops" and exclusive stories by closely following terrorist social media accounts, and directly engaging with the "public relations" units of terrorist networks.

In some other cases, authorities purposefully refrain from shutting down extremist accounts in order to monitor closely the messages uploaded to the feeds for purposes of gathering intelligence on the extremists, their actions, their locations, and their narratives.[38] In an interesting bind, anti-terror operators are, in fact, "liking," "friending," and "following" known terrorist Facebook and Twitter accounts and, in effect, boosting their audience numbers and followers. This interest in authorities becoming part of a terrorist group's audience has meant that, at one point, one of al-Shabaab's Twitter accounts had "more than 15,000 followers that has included a good number of journalists and terrorism analysts."[39]

DIGITAL MEDIA AND THE LIVE TRANSMISSION OF DEATH

Since anyone with access is able to partake in narrative creation in the age of digital communication, reporting on active events, such as "live tweeting" on Twitter, has become a common feature of daily online behavior. Like most other users of digital media, contemporary terrorists make use of the immediacy of microblogging in order to relay events in what is termed "real time." During Nairobi's Westgate Mall siege, for example, al-Shabaab live-tweeted their actions by sending 258 tweets over the course of the four-day attack,[40] marking this as "the first major terrorist attack in history in which the group that mounted the operation used Twitter to announce to the world it was responsible."[41] During the Westgate Mall siege, "the Shabaab's use of Twitter to provide nearly hourly updates on an ongoing attack represents an evolution from previous jihadi use of Twitter as a supplement to the still-dominant model of distributing media through established channels on moderated jihadi forums."[42]

Microblogging sites are becoming increasingly important forms of communication during extraordinary emergency situations. One thing that unites people in and around a terrorist attack, and indeed globally, including the attackers and their supporters, the victims and their families, the general public, the news media, government officials, and international audiences, is their use of social media, and especially Twitter, to relay messages from inside and outside an attack situation. Increasingly, Twitter is not only an optimal medium for reporting breaking news, but is growing to become the source of breaking news.

In the case of the Nairobi Westgate Mall attacks, Twitter proved to be the ideal social media accompaniment to the tragedy. It was the right kind of communication tool matched to the event, as it suited the needs of everyone involved, as well as of those seeking to become involved. "Twitter seems to have been the dominant social media platform used by the public and responding organizations,"[43] even though the Kenya Police and Kenya Military "joined Twitter less than ten days prior to the attack,"[44] and even though many of the various government offices were not following each other on the platform, leading the Ministry of Interior to publicly ask the Kenya Military account to follow it back.[45]

In keeping with the idea that social media channels allow for a faster and more immediate communication of news, citizens from outside and inside Westgate Mall were the first to alert the public about the sound of gunshots and explosions taking place—long before the Kenyan police and the news media became aware of the events. The first public news that something was amiss at Westgate Mall was relayed through Twitter by the "I Come from Somalia" account at 12:38 p.m.,[46] a few minutes after the attack commenced (around 12:30 p.m.).[47] The next tweet came from someone inside the mall at 12:40 p.m., and this was followed by a few more from citizens both inside and outside the mall.[48]

The first tweet to come from a government body, The National Disaster Operations Centre (NDOC Kenya), was at 13:05 p.m., and lagging behind by a full half an hour from the first message, "the first (local) media house to tweet about the incident was K24 TV at 1.11 p.m., 33 minutes and 17 seconds after the first tweet."[49] A local television station, Citizen TV, followed at 13:12 p.m., and then the first tweet by an international news organization, AP, was posted at 13:15 p.m.[50] From then on, those hiding in the mall, the terrorists inside the mall and their networks in Somalia, the news media, the government, the emergency responders, and the general public in Kenya and abroad, all used Twitter to ask for assistance, to ask for information, to give information—and misinformation, to sympathize, and to gloat.

Given the multiple voices, opinions, and claims of evidence being relayed via social media channels during any one event, it becomes increasingly important for authorities to maintain a coherent narrative. During the Westgate Mall attack, the Kenyan authorities made many futile attempts at controlling the flow of information, with the official communications channel of the Kenyan Government, PSCU Digital Kenya, tweeting: "We are appealing to Media to avoid showing photos of our @kdfinfo soldiers. Kindly, only tweet what you are absolutely sure about #Westgate." In another tweet, "the Kenya Police asked a Twitter user to delete a message that contained pictures of military helicopters preparing to launch an attack on the mall,"[51] and the Kenyan Disaster

Operation Center contacted a news channel asking them to delete a story.[52]

On the third day of the crisis, however, it was the Kenyan government that had to submit to the authority of a media corporation: "Twitter contacted the Kenyan government so that they could verify their accounts used to publish information on the Westgate attack."[53] Even though the Kenyan authorities attempted to control the narrative and to excise any instance of misinformation, they too were guilty of releasing a great deal of false information during the first few hours and days of the attack.[54]

Many of the news items released during the Westgate Mall attacks, even though false, proved to be simultaneously in the interest of publicizing the spectacle of terror that was produced, as well as in the interest of anti-terror authorities who used the attack to push for particular policy agendas related to the strengthening of the security apparatus both at home and abroad. In response to the attack, Interpol became involved, but, it too subsequently became embroiled in the circling of misinformation, and "issued an international arrest notice for Samantha Lewthwaite, a British woman who is the widow of one of four London suicide bombers who killed 56 people in 2005."[55] Other than the digital speculation of Lewthwaite's implication created through social media stories at the time, there is no evidence of her having any involvement in the Westgate Mall attacks. This story, even though false, was used to garner international sympathy and support from governments all over the world. When this news began doing the rounds on social media and on news networks, it was al-Shabaab who used social media to correct the false story, tweeting: "We have an adequate number of young men who are fully committed & we do not employ our sisters in such military operations #Westgate."[56]

DESERTS OF THE REAL: SOCIAL MEDIA AND VIRTUAL TERRORIST ATTACKS

Whether doing so knowingly or unknowingly, circulating false information is a central feature of social media, and conforms to the platforms' principal protocol of spreading information, generally without discrimination. This is, of course, unless the messages fall foul of the platform's terms of service, but, even then, social media platforms like Twitter are protective of their business model, and do not always react immediately to complaints. A variety of different types of information, regardless of their voracity, are taken up en masse and circulated and re-circulated by countless accounts. This is indicative of how false narratives come into existence and become part of social reality construction—at least within the realm of digital media, but can also often breach the media barrier.

Increasingly, because extremist organizations are so adept at treading the digital field, many are able to engineer terror scenarios by creating false and, sometimes, unverifiable threats. Since one of the goals of terrorist activities is to keep societies on edge and under threat, social media channels are the ideal conduit for waging a terror that cannot always be defined or identified. On September 11, 2014, for example, the Islamic State allegedly staged a spectacular attack on the Columbia Chemical plant in the US state of Louisiana, causing explosions and releasing toxic fumes throughout the St. Mary Parish area.[57] A series of text messages were sent to residents warning them to take shelter, and "the #ColumbianChemicals hashtag was full of eyewitness accounts of the horror."[58] The most spectacular part of this attack, however, was that it was a hoax. It was an elaborate fabrication designed to induce panic throughout the United States, and beyond, without members of Islamic State, allegedly responsible for the fake attack, having to actually enact the costly and dangerous execution of a full-scale operation.

Nevertheless, regardless of the story's authenticity, this was still a terrorist operation, whether enacted by Islamic State or by other international anti-US online trolls, and one that required meticulous planning and organization in order to create the reality of terror online. A variety of platforms were employed to break, circulate, and synchronize the story, including YouTube and Twitter, to give it extra cachet, and render it indelible—if not from social media, then from the minds of the panicked audiences. This form of digital terrorism,

> was a highly coordinated disinformation campaign, involving dozens of fake accounts that posted hundreds of tweets for hours, targeting a list of figures precisely chosen to generate maximum attention. The perpetrators didn't just doctor screenshots from CNN; they also created fully functional clones of the websites of Louisiana TV stations and newspapers [...] A Wikipedia page was even created for the Columbian Chemicals disaster, which cited the fake YouTube video. As the virtual assault unfolded, it was complemented by text messages to actual residents in St. Mary Parish. It

must have taken a team of programmers and content producers to pull off.[59]

Twitter did not immediately close down the accounts that spread the fake news, and, two months later, "many of the same Twitter accounts used to spread the Columbian Chemicals hoax began to post about an outbreak of Ebola in Atlanta. The campaign followed the same pattern of fake news reports and videos, this time under the hashtag #EbolaInAtlanta, which briefly trended in Atlanta."[60]

There are numerous other examples of cyberterrorist activity enacted by a variety of tech-savvy perpetrators, including the Syrian Electronic Army that has been tormenting authorities all over the world by temporarily taking over and posting critical messages on the official websites and social media pages of the US military's Central Command, the BBC, *The New York Times*, 60 Minutes, and the Associated Press sites, among others.[61]

Eschewing traditional editorial control, there is an increasing unverifiable barrage of real and imagined stories, images, and footage on social media platforms that, regardless of their veracity, speak the minds of those who create them. Online actors, whether authorities, terrorists, the media, or the public, all take part in the creation of social realities, and this is especially facilitated through the increasing infiltration of digital media and recording devices into public spaces and in everyday activities.

Corporate News Media and Terrorism Content

Such sensationalist stories, whether true or false, are eagerly circulated by corporate news media channels. Especially when traditional media becomes increasingly integrated with social media channels, this "presents a challenge, as censorship and regulation are alien to the nature of social media,"[62] and verification of stories and events becomes difficult. It is often the case that "media coverage regarding tragic events, such as mass shootings, is formulated to prolong the salience and news-worthiness of the event. This is done, in part, by frame-changing the evolving news story and by raising controversial issues."[63] Media scares are, after all, commodities,[64] and news media is a business.

What is more, in many instances, attempts to cover an active terrorist attack often "interfere with police operations,"[65] and may inadvertently aid terrorists in their operations. During the Westgate Mall attacks, there was very little control that could be exerted over the multiple stories and social media updates posted by the general public as well as by reporters. In many cases, details of the security operation were shared online, which "might have contributed to the prolonged siege, as the terrorists received live information detailing the armed response against them and were able to use this information to enhance their response."[66] A report released by the Media Council of Kenya criticized the ways in which journalists covered the Westgate events, arguing "that journalists, in their bid to report from the scene, breached the Code of Ethics by publishing graphic pictures of the dead and injured."[67]

Similarly, during the 2015 Hyper Cacher supermarket siege in Paris, a *Guardian* newspaper byline announced that the media is "accused of endangering lives of six people who hid in cold room by broadcasting their location live during siege."[68] Patrick Klugman, a lawyer for the six people suing French media channels, argued that "the working methods of media in real time in this type of situation were tantamount to goading someone to commit a crime."[69]

In many instances, the conditions in which news media and entertainment media operate are becoming increasingly similar, and it is often the case that the same parent corporation owns both news channels and entertainment channels, creating a vertical integration, and making their products similar in style and substance.[70] "The merging of the spectacle, terrorism, war, and politics (beginning with the September 11th terrorist attacks on the World Trade Center in New York City) suggests something unique about the deadly power and battle of images in contemporary global culture."[71] In the aftermath of terrorist attacks, the media often focus "on dramatic, most violent, bizarre, tantalising and brutal accounts of the attack magnifying the impact of their horrifying brutality."[72]

Writing in 2002, Ignacio Ramonet, editor of *Le Monde Diplomatique*, highlighted the increasingly fierce competition that was taking place at the time between corporate news networks as a result of the many commercial pressures they faced. He outlined the paradigmatic shift occurring as a result of the fact that "many top media executives today come from the corporate world, and no longer from the ranks of journalists. They are less sensitive to the quality and truthfulness of pictures. In their eyes, the market for information, the news business, is first and foremost a means of making profits."[73] These sentiments have only intensified over the past few years, and media competition has become an even more cut-throat business. In this increasingly profit-oriented paradigm:

> News organizations supply terrorists access to their audiences in exchange for the right to publish information about events that will entice consumers to purchase their products. For this reason, the relationship between terrorist organizations and the press is often described as one of mutual interest, since both terrorists and news organizations benefit when information about terrorist attacks is turned into the commodity of news.[74]

Adding to the media dominance and salaciousness of international terrorist attacks, news media networks compete against one another for audience share by delivering "scoops" and snippets of information, often unverified, regarding tragic events. For media networks, "as 'infotainment' on the nightly news, images of victims are commercialized; they are taken up into processes of global marketing and business competition."[75] In similar fashion to the visual culture of terrorism produced in the wake of 9/11, footage of contemporary terrorist attacks are repetitively circulated in a steady stream of images instantly consumed by audiences struggling to understand the sudden penetration of violence into everyday spaces.[76]

Corporate media channels, in turn, capitalize upon the violent acts as a steady stream of content for their networks. Terrorism, "war making and militarism is now presented by 'news' programs as an entertainment spectacle. News reporting on wars becomes indistinguishable from Hollywood film, video games, and reality television as the popular culture comes to normalize and glamorize militarization."[77] Especially with the advent of 24-hour news networks, the need for constant content is paramount.By appealing to the profit-maximizing corporate structure of news networks, "news formats, or the way of selecting, organizing, and presenting information, shape audience assumptions and preferences for certain kinds of information. The mass media are important in shaping public agendas by influencing what people think about and how events and issues are packaged and presented."[78] Since news networks are increasingly competing for audience share by broadcasting sensationalist content more in line with entertainment than education, terrorist acts provide some of the most newsworthy items that can also be reused as content in the entertainment industry.

THE CULTURAL PRODUCTION OF TERRORISM: REALITY TELEVISION, VIDEOGAMES, AND FILM

In a perverse paradigmatic shift in media content, atrocities and violence are increasingly aligning with notions of entertainment and film. For their part, during any major contemporary terror spectacle, news media networks provide all the hallmarks of a film production, and expertly provide and set up cameras, personnel, sets, newsrooms, editing suites, pundits, reviews, and audiences. In large part due to the availability of recording devices and the ease of distributing filmed material, there has been an increase in the volume of film footage uploaded to the Internet and shared via mobile phone applications regarding such public events. Many contemporary terrorist attacks are captured in "real time" on a multitude of recording devices, including CCTV cameras, mobile phones, and news cameras, all serving to fuel corporate media networks, feeding them with a steady stream of images, audiences, and advertising revenue.

With pervasive video surveillance and ubiquitous information and communication technologies, most contemporary terrorist attacks are recorded and digitally preserved. The ensuing action is presented on news and social media networks like a reality television show,[79] in which audiences all around the world are taken inside the event to watch "behind the scenes." With omnipresent CCTV security cameras all over contemporary urban spaces, not much can escape from being recorded. During the Nairobi Westgate Mall attacks, for example, footage was recorded by "more than 100 security cameras inside the mall, video from television crews and modest cellphones, as well as still photographs."[80] Increasingly, both the public and privatized spaces where terrorist attacks occur provide a camera-ready action set for the ensuing events. The mall, the street, and the cafe become microcosms for the recorded action viewed through the lenses of hundreds of cameras and beamed into the centralized command stations of remote security offices.

Audiences watching the tragic scenes unfold on the news become privy to footage from "inside" a terrorist attack. Dramatically, CCTV camera footage shows the precise moment when shoppers, diners, or concertgoers, in Westgate Mall, the cafés of Paris, or the Bataclan concert hall, who only a few minutes earlier were happy to sit, browse, or dance, are transformed into frightened captives attempting to escape from view, and from the attackers.[81] News networks release streams of video from the multiple security cameras that capture much of the rampage, including those victims fleeing or hiding in backroom areas reserved for staff and not normally visited by the public.

Similarly, in the style of a "behind the scenes" documentary, audiences also become privy to the movement of the terrorists in the days before and after an attack, as they plan their attacks or make their escape. With the increase in CCTV cameras on public streets and in private businesses, news networks screen the moments when the terrorists enter a bank to withdraw money ahead of an operation,[82] ride the metro,[83] or stop at a service station to get supplies after an attack.[84] Such documentation was especially rich in the case of Westgate Mall attack that took place over a sustained period of time in a confined space. Multiple cameras recorded the more private and quiet moments taking place backstage when the al-Shabaab attackers decided to no longer pursue any more victims, and to take refuge in the Nakumatt supermarket storeroom. The security cameras recorded several hours of the attackers' actions, including taking shelter and temporarily putting down their weapons, tending to their wounded colleague, drinking water, taking turns to pray on a mat on the ground, and, without CCTV audio capability, speechless hours in which the perpetrators idled the time waiting to be confronted by government forces.[85] As evidenced through the recorded footage, the terrorists were aware of the cameras, and, at one point, one of the perpetrators looks directly at the camera and is not perturbed by its presence.[86] The only time the al-Shabaab attackers actively divert a security camera's gaze is towards the end of the first day of the siege. From that moment on, it is difficult to ascertain the sequence of events, leading many to believe that the terrorists could have escaped via the supermarket's loading dock, which connected directly to the street outside.[87] There is, to date, no definitive evidence one way or another. Without a visual perspective from which to construct a narrative of events, what could not be seen on screen either did not exist as part of the narrative of the attacks, or could not be verified.

Such media blackouts, whether deliberate or accidental, are becoming less possible in the age of digital media and portable cameras that can capture action from a variety of different vantage points. Increasingly, attackers record themselves in the act and control the visuals from within an event. The seminal phrase coined by Jenkins in 1974 that "terrorism is theater" has never rung more true than in the contemporary media-saturated environment where the perpetrators are the stars of their own performances.[88] During the Westgate attacks, al-Shabaab said as much, tweeting: "The mesmeric performance by the #Westgate Warriors was undoubtedly gripping, but despair not folks, that was just the premiere of Act 1."[89]

As is the case with most social media users, terrorist organizations generate their own social realities through a variety of media campaigns and a multitude of visual narratives that can be controlled by the perpetrators themselves. Using social media, anyone "can directly share their positions—on their own terms and in their own words—to shape media coverage of their actions."[90] From the start of the Westgate Mall siege, al-Shabaab attempted to take control of the narrative of the attacks by placing themselves at the center of the story and live-tweeting the events taking place in the mall.[91] To act as a first-person narrator and central character in a story or event is to endow oneself with the status of a protagonist, imbuing self-made narrations with self-righteous justifications, with messages such as:

> The Mujahideen entered #Westgate Mall today at around noon and are still inside the mall, fighting the #Kenyan Kuffar inside their own turf. [92]

Al-Shabaab's use of the term "Mujahideen" (meaning holy warriors in Arabic) is a clear indication of the Westgate gunmen's status as heroes within the self-made narrative espoused by the terrorist group. In another tweet by al-Shabaab, the attackers were alliteratively hailed as "Westgate Warriors."[93]

Because of the pervasiveness of communication technologies, audiences are privy to seeing an event from a variety of different angles and vantage points. Increasingly, they can witness not only CCTV recordings from "within" a tragic event, but also footage that is delivered by the perpetrators themselves. French extremists Mehdi Nemmouche used a GoPro-style camera when he killed four people at the Brussels Jewish Museum, as did Mohamed Merah, who recorded "a series of attacks in which he killed seven people. Police described the footage as 'extremely explicit.'"[94] Following the trend, during the attack on the Hyper Cacher supermarket in Paris, Amédy Coulibaly wore a GoPro camera as he took hostages. Similarly placing himself at the center of the action, "Yassin Salhi, the French lorry driver who decapitated his boss before ramming a vehicle into a chemical plant near Lyon [...] sent a macabre selfie to a contact in Syria."[95]

In the age of information and communication technologies, it has thus become the norm for terrorists to record themselves before and during an attack in order to justify their actions and to leave behind a record or "*shahada*," meaning testament. Terrorists who use first-person camera angles act in the reality of their socially constructed world as the shooter of the gun and the shooter of the video, while the audience becomes the simulated shooter, and, remotely controlled to see what the attacker sees and do what the attacker does, becoming willingly or unwillingly part of the spectacle. Using first-person point of view footage similar to that utilized in videogames, with the use of first-person action cameras, the perpetrators transform themselves into protagonists in order to enact their own autobiographies, and to be the stars of their own films.

In the typical first-person-shooter videogame, the player learns to experience violence "from an embodied, subjective viewpoint, rather than from the detached overhead view that is common in other types of games. The simulation of embodiment connects players to a character and encourages them to identify with the character's experiences and motives."[96] In this way, virtual first-person violence has long been normalized through videogames that "work like advertisements for the military lifestyle, interpellating players into a military mind-set and turning them into 'virtual citizen-soldiers,' ready to accept the legitimacy of hard power and willing to apply it to virtually any social problem."[97]Videogame identification has also been used by nonstate actors in order to "construct alternative narratives of recent and ongoing conflicts in an attempt to influence audience perceptions of real events."[98] Hezbollah, for example, released two editions of the *Special Force* videogame in order to "allow players to become fighters in a virtual war against Israel, acting out real battles from recent conflicts in Lebanon."[99]

References to videogames, and comparisons between terrorist activities and videogame content have become a discursive and cultural norm. Abu Sumayyah Al-Britani, a British foreign fighter with Islamic State, describes the act of killing by noting: "It's actually quite fun, better than, what's that game called, Call of Duty? It's like that, but really, you know, 3D. You can see everything's happening in front of you."[100] In other instances, the structure of a videogame has been utilized in terrorist recruitment and training programs, whereby "recruits are passing through a series of tests in password protected websites and restricted chat rooms before being accepted and joining the terrorist group [...].

Tactics used includes the integration of terrorist acts in cartoons and music videos to attract the minors into terrorism. Also, video games that involve the acts of terrorism like mass suicide attack."[101] Islamic State media productions make full use of existing Western popular cultural artifacts, particularly content from high-grossing videogames and films. In order to recruit fighters to their cause, the terrorist organization systematically filch and modify existing content. One advertisement for the terrorist group is made up of an image taken from the popular *Grand Theft Auto* videogame overlaid with Islamic State branding and slogans.

Since waging war on the battlefield of the media has become a paramount concern for counter-insurgency operations, in direct response, the US State Department's Twitter site Think Again Turn Away "feebly parodies Isis's Grand Theft Auto video" with the message "'Grand Theft Innocence—don't let Isis be your controller!'" In a bizarre online dialogue, "Isis supporters have parodied Think AgainTurn Away's parodies. It becomes a hall of mirrors."[102] Many government efforts have been directed at online message battles and promote a direct counter-narrative to extremist ideologies—in many cases showcasing terrorist violence as a deterrent. The US State Department, for example, often takes extremist footage, and edits it with its own anti-terror messages and depictions of extremist violence.[103] However, this strategy only helps strengthen the position of the terrorists who encourage the screening of violent episodes. John Rosenthal, an Al-Monitor contributor, "points to the State Department's habit of illustrating al-Qaeda's brutality with gruesome images of beheadings and executions. 'Jihadist online propaganda is itself full of such images. For the jihadists, these are selling points.'"[104]

Authorities, international news media networks, and the entertainment industry have become increasingly embroiled, in one complex way or another, in the cultural production of terrorism. "The war on terror has been mediated through an overwhelming array of visual forms and media, including photography, sculpture, painting, film, television, advertisements, cartoons, graphic novels, video games, and the Internet."[105] During any particular conflict, the state is in need of the expertise and persuasive skills of the entertainment industry, and their interests are often aligned. Especially since World War II, there has been a concerted and deliberate synchronizing of propaganda interests between the military and the entertainment industry, resulting in a more palatable cultural production of ideological messages. During these early years in the US context, Hollywood was in service of "the government and injected a sense of drama into documentary formats. The Why We Fight series, in particular, is well known for its rousing tone, appeals to the emotions, and, above all, its Walt Disney animation sequences."[106] Such ideological dovetailing between the state and cultural industries can be read most acutely during times of conflict, when it is especially pertinent to construct particular ideological allegiances and to counter others, and where it "normalizes and aestheticizes the militarization of culture and everyday life."[107]

The alignment between the militarization of popular cultural texts, terrorism, and the anti-terror effort is betrayed in the common initial reaction to comprehending the brutal images and footage emanating from terrorist attacks, which is to associate them with the fiction of film.[108] Nowhere was the conflation of popular culture and terrorism more symbolically manifest than in the spectacle of terror produced on September 11, 2001, which, as has been mentioned countless times, "looked like a disaster film."[109] The initial spectacular terror attack is subsequently subject to circulation, adaptation, modification, and recirculation in other forms of cultural text by international media industries.

In many ways, Western corporate and popular cultural content provide "raw material for Isis's image library. Hollywood has even been accused of setting the tone, with its dark, doomsday scenarios, not to mention its own expensive recruitment films, from Top Gun to Transformers, made with the cooperation (and conditional approval) of the US military."[110] Terrorist narrative creations are similarly channeled through a multitude of different media texts, including self-produced films, social media campaigns, digital applications, and videogames. Despite extremists' outspoken disavowal of the corruptions of Western culture, the connection between popular cultural artifacts and terrorist activity can be read in many of these productions. For one al-Qaʿida supporter, Younis Tsouli, this involves giving himself the codename "Irhabi007,"[111] which means Terrorist 007 in Arabic, in his attempt to embody elements of spy thrillers and popular movie culture. Many examples of extremist video footage are expertly acted in, filmed, edited, and distributed, and show a sophisticated relationship to the medium of film, including dramatic license as well as impactful synchronization of music and image. The Islamic State "is in competition with western news channels, Hollywood movies, reality shows, even music video, and it has adopted their vocabulary."[112]

Extremists release a variety of visual footage that is fluent in the language of professionally-produced media texts. Especially in the case of the Islamic State, media productions are often technically sophisticated, and bear the hallmarks of professional filmmaking. "In the beheading videos, 'Jihadi John' and his masked kidnappers indicate their next victim at the end, as if enticing viewers to stay tuned, in the manner of a reality TV show. Why do this? Isis is trying to make its hostage videos look more professional, more *entertaining*, even."[113] In many of the extremist-produced cultural material, "explosions are lingered over in super slow motion... Transitions between clips are sheets of flame and blinding flashes. Graphics fly across the screen. Sonorous, auto-tuned chanting and cacophonous gun-fire reverberate on the soundtrack. The Isis regime might have outlawed music, singing, smoking and drinking alcohol, but it clearly embraces Final Cut Pro."[114]

Ultimately, such terrorist-produced media texts are not only consumed by those with a taste for extremist ideology, but also educational to authorities and other investigators and researchers seeking clues by watching, analyzing, and reporting on the media productions. In counter-terror operations, footage recorded by terrorists "is immensely useful to intelligence agencies' experts tasked with developing an understanding of technical procedures employed by terrorist groups."[115] In the same way that terrorists pay close attention to corporate and popular cultural texts, and use and reuse them in their own adapted productions, anti-terror investigators and authorities have become a primary audience for terrorist-produced cultural texts. In a complex bind, each learns from the other, even as they attempt to disavow and negate the other.

Many of the well-known international extremist networks, including the Islamic State, al-Qaʿida, Boko Haram, and al-Shabaab, attempt to present themselves as an identifiable organization by engaging in organized and consistent forms of branding and self-promotion through concerted and sustained advertising and promotional activities, primarily disseminated through the media. So far, the Islamic State leads the way in terrorist organizational branding strategies, with its dedicated Al-Hayat media center, which is "like a conventional broadcaster, it has its own glossy ident, not dissimilar to that of Al-Jazeera: a teardrop-shaped logo of Arabic script materialising from a digital cascade of water. Its broadcasts invariably feature this logo or a fluttering black-and-white Isis flag in the top corner of the screen."[116]

The black and white Islamic State logo has become one of the most recognizable terrorist brands, not only because of the fear or reverence it induces, but also because the logo has been franchised to other extremist outfits, and adopted by other terrorist organizations, such as Boko Haram and factions of the Taliban, who extend the reach of the brand into new markets.[117] The Islamic State logo is not only advertised by those pledging allegiance to the extremist ideology, but is also given airtime and circulated by those most vehemently opposing it. In a paradoxical bind, to oppose terrorism is to engage with it, and the black and white Islamic State logo has been circulated widely in the media by journalists, researchers, and counter-terrorism organizations.

Along with the strategic international solidarities between the Islamic State and other terrorist organizations, there has been a visible increase in the quantity and quality of these groups' cultural productions. Before Boko Haram publically announced its formal affiliation with the Islamic State, its "early videos were of low quality and were disseminated haphazardly."[118] After the partnership, however, the group "created its own media outlet and opened its first Twitter account."[119] The marked increase in the quality of Boko Haram's media output has been attributed to the Islamic State sharing its media expertise and knowledge with other international extremists.

CONCLUSION: THE SYMBIOTIC COMMODIFICATION OF TERROR

The discourse of terrorism, and the associated cultural production, is propagated by multiple players, including: the terrorists who enact violence in public space; the authorities who respond in counter-violence; the corporate news networks that circulate and sensationalize; the international security apparatus that capitalizes on terrorism for the creation of policy and deployment of retaliatory action at home and abroad; and corporate industries that profit from acts of terror by commodifying the anti-terror response.

In the wake of contemporary terrorist attacks, the conflation of terrorism, international media networks, and a profit-oriented capitalist response is most visible in the commodification of terror. In the immediate aftermath of many terrorist attacks, there is a rush to condemn the events by producing and distributing a multitude of symbols and signals, turning the violent act into a further spectacle to be viewed and commodity to be consumed. After the Charlie Hebdo offices were attacked in Paris in 2015, one of the popular responses was the mass production, distribution, and consumption of the "Je suis Charlie" slogan, which was emblazoned on a variety of products, including bracelets, pendants, T-shirts, and mugs, among a variety of other paraphernalia.[120] One form of solidarity against terrorism is being embodied visibly in the purchase of product.

In a world that is increasingly defined by ideologies of globalized economic liberalization, marketization, and commodification, these become the ideational forces that shape overall value systems and extend "beyond the commercial realm into other spheres of human society."[121] The discourse of terrorism is no exception. Spectacular international terrorist activities, as well as highly visual and publicized responses, elicit the attention of corporate and social media channels, and are instantly produced, circulated, and consumed all over the world. The commodification of media affects the Middle East in the same ways that it does other regions that are increasingly subjected to these globalizing neoliberal forces. Operating within an overarching and penetrative liberalized global economic system, an increasingly entangled and complementary relationship is developing between the military, the media, and terrorists, resulting in a symbiosis of cultural production.[122]

Notes

1. Cristina Archetti, *Understanding Terrorism in the Age of Global Media: A Communication Approach* (London: Palgrave Macmillan, 2013), 2.
2. Brian M. Jenkins, "International Terrorism: A New Kind of Warfare." *The Rand Paper Series* (1974): 4.
3. Gabriel Weimann, "Cyber-Fatwas and Terrorism.," *Studies in Conflict & Terrorism* 34 (2011): 768. For some examples of recent global terrorist attacks, see Alan Cowell, "Subway and Bus Blasts in London Kill at Least 37." *The New York Times,* July 8, 2005, accessed January 28, 2016, http://www.nytimes.com/2005/07/08/world/europe/subway-and-bus-blasts-in-london-kill-at-least-37.html; Victoria Burnett, "7 Are Acquitted in Madrid Bombings." *New York Times,* November 1, 2007, accessed January 28, 2016, http://www.nytimes.com/2007/11/01/world/europe/01spain.html?_r=0; James Glanz, Sebastian Rotella, and David E. Sanger, "In 2008 Mumbai Attacks, Piles of Spy Data, but an Uncompleted Puzzle." *The New York Times,* December 21, 2014, accessed January 28, 2016, http://www.nytimes.com/2014/12/22/world/asia/in-2008-mumbai-attacks-piles-of-spy-data-but-an-uncompleted-puzzle.

html; "Tunisia attack on Sousse beach 'kills 39," *BBC News*, June 27, 2015, accessed January 28, 2016, http://www.bbc.com/news/world-africa-33287978; Lars Eriksen, Robert Booth, Mark Townsend and Warren Murray, "Copenhagen shootings suspect was 'known to police'," *The Guardian*, February 15, 2015, accessed January 28, 2016, http://www.theguardian.com/world/2015/feb/14/copenhagen-cartoonist-charlie-hebdo-style-attack; "Sydney siege: Hostages held in Lindt café," *BBC News*, December 15, 2014, accessed January 28, 2016, http://www.bbc.com/news/world-australia-30473983; "Charlie Hebdo attack: Three days of terror," *BBC News*, January 14, 2015, http://www.bbc.com/news/world-europe-30708237.

4. Donald Rumsfeld, "Speech," US Department of Defense, November 9, 2006, accessed January 28, 2016, https://web.archive.org/web/20141216060320/http://www.defense.gov/Speeches/Speech.aspx?SpeechID=1060.

5. Weimann, "Cyber-Fatwas and Terrorism," 773.

6. Bruno Nordeste and David Carment, "A Framework for Understanding Terrorist Use of the Internet." *Trends in Terrorism Series* 2 (2006): 6.

7. Weimann, "Cyber-Fatwas and Terrorism," 768. Weimann writes that one of the *fatwas* was titled, "Declaration of War against the Americans Occupying the Land of the Two Holy Places."

8. Graeme Wood, "What ISIS Really Wants." *The Atlantic*, March 2015, accessed January 28, 2016, http://www.theatlantic.com/features/archive/2015/02/what-isis-really-wants/384980/.

9. Jytte Klausen, "Tweeting the Jihad: Social Media Networks of Western Foreign Fighters in Syria and Iraq," *Studies in Conflict & Terrorism* 38 (2015): 4.

10. Nordeste and Carment, "A Framework for Understanding Terrorist Use of the Internet," 6.

11. Wood, "What ISIS Really Wants."

12. Stacy Takacs, "Real War News, Real War Games: The Hekmati Case and the Problems of Soft Power." *American Quarterly* 65 (2013): 180.

13. Archetti, *Understanding Terrorism in the Age of Global Media*, 41.

14. Gabriel Weimann, "Terror on Facebook, Twitter, and Youtube." *Brown Journal of World Affairs* 16 (2010): 45.

15. Caroline Hellyer, "ISIL courts al-Shabab as al-Qaeda ties fade away," *Al Jazeera*, March 23, 2015, accessed January 28, 2016, http://www.aljazeera.com/indepth/features/2015/03/isil-eyes-east-africa-foments-division-150322130940108.html.

16. Weimann, "Terror on Facebook, Twitter, and Youtube," 45.

17. Steve Rose, "The Isis propaganda war: a hi-tech media jihad," *The Guardian*, October 7, 2014, accessed January 28, 2016,

http://www.theguardian.com/world/2014/oct/07/ isis-media-machine-propaganda-war.
18. Nel Hodge, "How Somalia's al-Shabab militants hone their image," *BBC News*, June 5, 2014, accessed January 28, 2016, http://www.bbc. com/news/world-africa-27633367.
19. Jastinder Khera, "Authorities and militants take Nairobi battle to Twitter," September 24, 2013, *BBC News*, accessed January 28, 2016, http://www.bbc.com/news/world-africa-24218276.
20. John Curtis Amble, "Combating Terrorism in the New Media Environment." *Studies in Conflict & Terrorism* 35 (2012): 343.
21. Harriet Alexander, "Tweeting terrorism: How al Shabaab live blogged the Nairobi attacks," *The Telegraph*, September 22, 2103, accessed January 28, 2016, http://www.telegraph.co.uk/news/worldnews/ africaandindianocean/kenya/10326863/Tweeting-terrorism-How-al-ShabaabAl-Shabaab-live-blogged-the-Nairobi-attacks.html.
22. Ibid.
23. Vincent Bernatis, "The Taliban and Twitter: Tactical Reporting and Strategic Messaging." *Perspectives on Terrorism* 8 (2014): 25.
24. Ibid.
25. Amble, "Combating Terrorism in the New Media Environment," 341.
26. Weimann, "Cyber-Fatwas and Terrorism," 769.
27. "The Westgate Attack: A New Trend in al-Qaeda Communication Strategies," SITE Intelligence Group, January 15, 2014, accessed January 28, 2016, https://news.siteintelgroup.com/Articles-Analysis/ the-westgate-attack-a-new-trend-in-al-qaeda-communication-strategies. html.
28. Klausen, "Tweeting the Jihad," 1.
29. Ibid.
30. J.M. Berger, "How ISIS Games Twitter," *The Atlantic*, June 16, 2014, accessed January 28, 2016, http://www.theatlantic.com/international/ archive/2014/06/isis-iraq-twitter-social-media-strategy/372856/.
31. Ibid.
32. Ibid.
33. "Google removes Isis app from Play store," *ITV News*, July 18, 2014, accessed January 28, 2016, http://www.itv.com/news/ story/2014-06-18/google-play-store-isis-app/.
34. Alexander, "Tweeting terrorism."
35. United States Department of State, "Country Reports on Terrorism 2013," April 2014, accessed January 28, 2016, http://www.state.gov/ documents/organization/225886.pdf.

36. Peter Bergen, "Are Mass Murderers Using Twitter as a Tool?" CNN, September 27, 2013, accessed January 28, 2016, http://www.cnn.com/2013/09/26/opinion/bergen-twitter-terrorism/.
37. Alexander, "Tweeting Terrorism."
38. Alex Altman, "Why Terrorists Love Twitter." *Time*, September 11, 2014, accessed January 28, 2016, http://time.com/3319278/isis-isil-twitter/.
39. Bergen, "Are Mass Murderers Using Twitter as a Tool?"
40. Tomer Simon, Avishay Goldberg, Limor Aharonson-Daniel, Dmitry Leykin, and Bruria Adini, "Twitter in the Cross Fire—The Use of Social Media in the Westgate Mall Terror Attack in Kenya," *PLoS* One 9 (2014): 6.
41. Bergen, "Are Mass Murderers Using Twitter as a Tool?"
42. "The Westgate Attack," SITE Intelligence Group.
43. Simon et al., "Twitter in the Cross Fire," 4.
44. Ibid., 5.
45. "Kenyan Ministry of Interior," Twitter, accessed January 29, 2016, https://twitter.com/InteriorKE/status/381960772420923392.
46. Nanjira Sambuli, "How Useful is a Tweet? A Review of the First Tweets from the Westgate Mall Attack," Ihub Research, October 3, 2013, accessed January 29, 2016, http://www.ihub.co.ke/blogs/16012.
47. Daniel Howden, "Terror in Westgate Mall: the Full Story of the Attacks That Devastated Kenya," *The Guardian*, October 4, 2013, accessed January 29, 2016, http://www.theguardian.com/world/interactive/2013/oct/04/westgate-mall-attacks-kenya-terror.
48. Sambuli, "How Useful is a Tweet?"
49. Ibid.
50. Ibid.
51. Simon et al., "Twitter in the Cross Fire," 8.
52. Ibid.
53. Ibid.
54. Dennis Okari, "Kenya's Westgate Attack: Unanswered Questions One Year On," *BBC News*, September 21, 2014, accessed January 29, 2016, http://www.bbc.com/news/world-africa-29282045.
55. Heidi Vogt and Patrick Mcgroarty, "Before Kenya Attack, a Warning on Terrorism," *The Wall Street Journal*, September 30, 2013, accessed January 29, 2016, http://www.wsj.com/articles/SB10001424052702303643304579105222268968650.
56. Richard Lough and Abdi Sheikh, "UPDATE 3-Kenya launches probe as Shabaab leader confirms mall attack," *Reuters*, September 25, 2013, accessed January 29, 2016, http://www.reuters.com/article/2013/09/25/kenya-attack-idUSL5N0HL0MS20130925.

57. Adrian Chen, "The Agency." *New York Times*, June 2, 2015, accessed January 29, 2016, http://www.nytimes.com/2015/06/07/magazine/the-agency.html.
58. Ibid.
59. Ibid.
60. Ibid.
61. Ian Stewart, Scott Sweeney, "Twitter Terrorism: Criminals Choose the Hack Attack," Wilson Elser, July 7, 2015, accessed January 29, 2016, http://www.jdsupra.com/legalnews/twitter-terrorism-criminals-choose-the-22378/.
62. Simon et al., "Twitter in the Cross Fire," 9.
63. James M. Shultz et al., "Multiple Vantage Points on the Mental Health Effects of Mass Shootings." *Current Psychiatry Reports* 16 (2014): 4, DOI 10.1007/s11920-014-0469-5.
64. Liane Tanguay, *Hijacking History: American Culture and the War on Terror* (Montreal: McGill-Queen's University Press, 2013), 116.
65. Archetti, *Understanding Terrorism in the Age of Global Media*, 38.
66. Simon et al., "Twitter in the Cross Fire," 9.
67. Aggrey Mutambo, "Bodies of Westgate Terrorists 'Are With the FBI', says KDF Chief Julius Karangi," *Daily Nation*, February 7, 2014, accessed January 29, 2016, http://mobile.nation.co.ke/news/Julius-Karangi-Kenya-Defence-Forces-Westgate-Attack/-/1950946/2196566/-/format/xhtml/-/r6oqhdz/-/index.html.
68. "Paris Supermarket Siege Survivors Sue Media over 'Dangerous' Coverage," *The Guardian*, April 3, 2015, accessed January 29, 2016, http://www.theguardian.com/world/2015/apr/03/paris-supermarket-siege-survivors-sue-media.
69. Ibid.
70. Archetti, *Understanding Terrorism in the Age of Global Media*, 141; Dwayne Winseck, "The Political Economies of Media and the Transformation of the Global Media Industries," in *The Political Economies of Media: The Transformation of the Global Media Industries*, eds. Dwayne Winseck and Dal Yong Jin (London: Bloomsbury, 2011), 16.
71. Henry A. Giroux, "Beyond the Spectacle of Terrorism: Rethinking Politics in the Society of the Image," *Situations: Project of the Radical Imagination* 2 (2007): 19.
72. Jerry Abuga, "Media Council Tables Findings on Westgate Coverage," Media Council of Kenya, February 10, 2014, accessed January 29, 2016, http://www.mediacouncil.or.ke/en/mck/index.php/news/101-media-council-tables-findings-on-westgate-coverage. In the aftermath of the attacks, Linus Gitahi, the Chief Executive Officer of the Nation Media Group and a representative of the Media Owners

Association said: "Overall, we are delighted with the coverage. We are delighted that we were as close as possible to the issues. It was not all gloom. There were many things that were done well," Mutambo, "Bodies of Westgate Terrorists 'Are With the FBI'."

73. Ignacio Ramonet, "The Power of Television Pictures." *Points of View*, February 20, 2002, accessed January 29, 2016, http://www.unesco.org/webworld/points_of_views/200202_ramonet.shtml.

74. Aaron M. Hoffman, Dwaine H.A. Jengelley, Natasha T. Duncan, Melissa Buehler, and Meredith L. Rees, "How Does the Business of News Influence Terrorism Coverage? Evidence From *The Washington Post* and *USA Today*." *Terrorism and Political Violence* 22 (2010): 576.

75. Arthur Kleinman and Joan Kleinman, "Cultural Appropriations of Suffering," in *Cultures of Fear: A Critical Reader*, eds. Danielle Taana Smith and Uli Linke (London: Pluto Press, 2009), 288.

76. Jeffory A. Clymer, *America's Culture of Terrorism: Violence, Capitalism, and the Written Word* (Chapel Hill: University of North Carolina Press, 2003), 215.

77. Willian I. Robinson, *Global Capitalism and the Crisis of Humanity* (New York: Cambridge University Press, 2014), 211.

78. David L. Altheide, "Terrorism and the Politics of Fear," in *Cultures of Fear: A Critical Reader*, eds. Danielle Taana Smith and Uli Linke (London: Pluto Press, 2009), 57.

79. Mutambo, "Bodies of Westgate Terrorists 'Are With the FBI'."

80. Nicholas Kulish, "In this Horror Film, Blood is All Too Real: 'Terror at the Mall' on HBO Documents an Attack in Kenya," *New York Times*, September 14, 2014, accessed January 29, 2016, http://www.nytimes.com/2014/09/15/arts/television/terror-at-the-mall-on-hbo-documents-an-attack-in-kenya.html?_r=0.

81. "'Terror at the Mall,' Documentary on Siege of Westgate Mall in Nairobi, Kenya, Coming to HBO," Press Release, September 2, 2014, accessed January 29, 2016, http://blogs.indiewire.com/shadowandact/terror-at-the-mall-an-inside-look-at-the-siege-of-westgate-mall-in-nairobi-kenya-debuts-sept-15-on-hbo-20140902.

82. Rukmini Callimachi, "Police Detail Car Used by Radical Militants in Brutal Kenyan Mall Attack," *NBC News*, October 6, 2013, accessed January 29, 2016, http://www.nbcnews.com/news/other/police-detail-car-used-radical-militants-brutal-kenyan-mall-attack-f8C11345670.

83. Paul Dallison, "Paris Attacks Leader Captured on CCTV Minutes After Massacre," *Politico*, January 10, 2016, accessed January 29, 2016, http://www.politico.eu/article/paris-attacks-leader-cctv-minutes-camera-abdeslam-abaaoud/.

84. "Paris Attacks Suspect Abdeslam 'Caught on CCTV' in French Petrol Station," *BBC News*, January 11, 2016, accessed January 29, 2016, http://www.bbc.com/news/world-europe-35286647.
85. *Terror at the Mall*, directed by Dan Reed (2014; London; Amos Pictures).
86. Ibid.
87. Ibid.
88. Jenkins, "International Terrorism," 4.
89. Vogt and Mcgroarty, "Before Kenya Attack, a Warning on Terrorism."
90. "The Westgate Attack," SITE Intelligence Group.
91. Laura Petrecca, "39 Die in Kenya Mall Siege; Hostages Still Held," *USA Today*, September 21, 2013, accessed January 29, 2016,http://www.usatoday.com/story/news/world/2013/09/21/witness-kenya-mall-attackers-target-non-muslims/2846319/.
92. Alexander, "Tweeting Terrorism."
93. Vogt and Mcgroarty, "Before Kenya Attack, a Warning on Terrorism."
94. Jason Burke, "Paris Shootings: Investigation Launched Into Where Gunmen got GoPro Cameras," *The Guardian*, January 12, 2015, accessed January 29, 2016, http://www.theguardian.com/world/2015/jan/12/paris-shootings-cameras-kouachi-brothers-amedy-coulibaly.
95. Angelique Chrisafis, "French Terror Suspect Sent Macabre Selfie to Contact in Syria," *The Guardian*, June 29, 2015, accessed January 29, 2016, http://www.theguardian.com/world/2015/jun/29/french-terror-suspect-sent-macabre-selfie-to-contact-in-syria.
96. Marcus Schulzke, "Simulating Terrorism and Insurgency: Video Games in the War of Ideas." *Cambridge Review of International Affairs* 27 (2014): 632.
97. Takacs, "Real War News, Real War Games," 177–178.
98. Schulzke, "Simulating Terrorism and Insurgency," 628.
99. Ibid., 627–628.
100. John Plunkett, "BBC Radio 1 criticised for airing 'Call of Duty' interview with Isis Briton," *The Guardian*, November 10, 2014, accessed January 29, 2016, http://www.theguardian.com/media/2014/nov/10/bbc-radio-1-criticised-british-isis-militant-interview.
101. Amble, "Combating Terrorism in the New Media Environment," 343.
102. In this chapter, I refer to the terrorist group as Islamic State (IS), which can also be known as Islamic State in Syria (ISIS) and Islamic State in Syria and the Levant (ISIL); Rose, "The Isis Propaganda War."
103. Ibid. This is the work of the Center for Strategic Counterterrorism Communications (CSCC), which is described as an experimental unit of the State Department established to counter extremist online propaganda.

104. Raf Sanchez, "Tweeting at Terrorists: Inside America's Social Media Battle with Online Jihad." *The Telegraph*, May 21, 2014, accessed January 29, 2016, http://www.telegraph.co.uk/news/worldnews/al-qaeda/10829355/Tweeting-at-terrorists-inside-Americas-social-media-battle-with-online-jihad.html.

105. Matt Delmont, "Visual Culture and the War on Terror." *American Quarterly* 65 (2013): 157.

106. Claudia Springer, "Military Propaganda: Defense Department Films from World War II and Vietnam." *Cultural Critique* 3 (1986): 151.

107. Robinson, *Global Capitalism and the Crisis of Humanity*, 212.

108. Kulish, "In This Horror Film, Blood Is All Too Real."

109. Douglas Kellner, "September 11, Spectacles of Terror, and Media Manipulation: A Critique of Jihadist and Bush Media Politics." *Logos* 2 (2003): 87.

110. Rose, "The Isis Propaganda War."

111. Weimann, "Terror on Facebook, Twitter, and Youtube," 46.

112. Rose, "The Isis Propaganda War."

113. Ibid.

114. Ibid.; Final Cut Pro is a professional film editing software program.

115. Amble, "Combating Terrorism in the New Media Environment." 348.

116. Rose, "The Isis Propaganda War."

117. Sarah Almukhtar, "How Boko Haram Courted and Joined the Islamic State," *The New York Times*, June 10, 2015, accessed January 29, 2016, http://www.nytimes.com/interactive/2015/06/11/world/africa/boko-haram-isis-propaganda-video-nigeria.html.

118. Ibid.

119. Ibid.

120. Vanessa Friedman, "After a Tragedy, the Memorabilia," *The New York Times*, January 21, 2015, accessed January 29, 2015, http://www.nytimes.com/2015/01/22/fashion/after-a-tragedy-like-the-charlie-hebdo-shooting-come-the-products.html.

121. Mona Moufahim and Michael Humphreys, "Marketing an Extremist Ideology: The Vlaams Belang's Nationalist Discourse," in *The Routledge Companion to Ethics, Politics and Organizations*, eds. Alison Pullen and Carl Rhodes. Oxon: Routledge, 2015, 85.

122. Archetti, *Understanding Terrorism in the Age of Global Media*, 38.

BIBLIOGRAPHY

Abuga, Jerry. "Media Council Tables Findings on Westgate Coverage." Media Council of Kenya. February 10, 2014. Accessed January 29, 2016, http://www.mediacouncil.or.ke/en/mck/index.php/news/101-media-council-tables-findings-on-westgate-coverage.

Alexander, Harriet. "Tweeting Terrorism: How al Shabaab Live Blogged the Nairobi Attacks." *The Telegraph*, September 22, 2013. Accessed January 28, 2016, http://www.telegraph.co.uk/news/worldnews/africaandindianocean/kenya/10326863/Tweeting-terrorism-How-al-Shabaab-live-blogged-the-Nairobi-attacks.html.

Almukhtar, Sarah. "How Boko Haram Courted and Joined the Islamic State." *The New York Times*, June 10, 2015. Accessed January 29, 2016, http://www.nytimes.com/interactive/2015/06/11/world/africa/boko-haram-isis-propaganda-video-nigeria.html.

Altheide, David L. "Terrorism and the Politics of Fear." In *Cultures of Fear: A Critical Reader*, eds. Danielle Taana Smith and Uli Linke, 54–69. London: Pluto Press, 2009.

Altman, Alex. "Why Terrorists Love Twitter," *Time*, September 11, 2014. Accessed January 28, 2016, http://time.com/3319278/isis-isil-twitter.

Amble, John Curtis. "Combating Terrorism in the New Media Environment." *Studies in Conflict & Terrorism* 35 (2012): 339–353.

Archetti, Cristina. *Understanding Terrorism in the Age of Global Media: A Communication Approach*. London: Palgrave Macmillan, 2013.

BBC News. "Charlie Hebdo Attack: Three Days of Terror." January 14, 2015. Accessed January 28, 2016, http://www.bbc.com/news/world-europe-30708237.

BBC News. "Paris Attacks Suspect Abdeslam 'caught on CCTV' in French Petrol Station." January 11, 2016. Accessed January 29, 2016, http://www.bbc.com/news/world-europe-35286647.

BBC News. "Sydney Siege: Hostages Held in Lindt café." December 15, 2014. Accessed January 28, 2016, http://www.bbc.com/news/world-australia-30473983.

BBC News. "Tunisia Attack on Sousse Beach 'kills 39." June 27, 2015. Accessed January 28, 2016, http://www.bbc.com/news/world-africa-33287978.

Bergen, Peter. "Are Mass Murderers using Twitter as a tool?" *CNN*, September 27, 2013. Accessed January 28, 2016, http://www.cnn.com/2013/09/26/opinion/bergen-twitter-terrorism/.

Berger, J. M. "How ISIS Games Twitter." *The Atlantic*, June 16, 2014. Accessed January 28, 2016, http://www.theatlantic.com/international/archive/2014/06/isis-iraq-twitter-social-media-strategy/372856/.

Bernatis, Vincent. "The Taliban and Twitter: Tactical Reporting and Strategic Messaging." *Perspectives on Terrorism* 8, no. 6 (2014). Accessed January 28, 2016, http://www.terrorismanalysts.com/pt/index.php/pot/article/view/389/html.

Burke, Jason. "Paris Shootings: Investigation Launched into Where Gunmen Got GoPro Cameras." *The Guardian,* January 12, 2015. Accessed January 29, 2016, http://www.theguardian.com/world/2015/jan/12/paris-shootings-cameras-kouachi-brothers-amedy-coulibaly.

Burnett, Victoria. "7 Are Acquitted in Madrid Bombings." *New York Times,* November 1, 2007. Accessed January 28, 2016, http://www.nytimes.com/2007/11/01/world/europe/01spain.html?_r=0.

Callimachi, Rukmini. "Police Detail Car Used by Radical Militants in Brutal Kenyan Mall Attack." NBC News, October 6, 2013. Accessed January 29, 2016, http://www.nbcnews.com/news/other/police-detail-car-used-radical-militants-brutal-kenyan-mall-attack-f8C11345670.

Chen, Adrian. "The Agency." *New York Times,* June 2, 2015. Accessed January 29, 2016, http://www.nytimes.com/2015/06/07/magazine/the-agency.html.

Chrisafis, Angelique. "French Terror Suspect Sent Macabre Selfie to Contact in Syria." *The Guardian,* June 29, 2015. Accessed January 29, 2016, http://www.theguardian.com/world/2015/jun/29/french-terror-suspect-sent-macabre-selfie-to-contact-in-syria.

Clymer, Jeffory A. *America's Culture of Terrorism: Violence, Capitalism, and the Written Word.* Chapel Hill: University of North Carolina Press, 2003.

Cowell, Alan. "Subway and Bus Blasts in London Kill at Least 37." *The New York Times,* July 8, 2005. Accessed January 28, 2016, http://www.nytimes.com/2005/07/08/world/europe/subway-and-bus-blasts-in-london-kill-at-least-37.html.

Dallison, Paul. "Paris Attacks Leader Captured on CCTV Minutes after Massacre." *Politico,* January 10, 2016. Accessed January 29, 2016, http://www.politico.eu/article/paris-attacks-leader-cctv-minutes-camera-abdeslam-abaaoud.

Delmont, Matt. "Visual Culture and the War on Terror," *American Quarterly* 65 (2013): 157–160.

Eriksen, Lars, Robert Booth, Mark Townsend, and Warren Murray, "Copenhagen shootings suspect was 'known to police'." *The Guardian,* February 15, 2015. Accessed January 28, 2016, http://www.theguardian.com/world/2015/feb/14/copenhagen-cartoonist-charlie-hebdo-style-attack.

Friedman, Vanessa. "After a Tragedy, the Memorabilia." *The New York Times,* January 21, 2015. Accessed January 29, 2015, http://www.nytimes.com/2015/01/22/fashion/after-a-tragedy-like-the-charlie-hebdo-shooting-come-the-products.html.

Giroux, Henry A. "Beyond the Spectacle of Terrorism: Rethinking Politics in the Society of the Image." *Situations: Project of the Radical Imagination* 2 (2007): 17–52.

Glanz, James, Sebastian Rotella, and David E. Sanger, "In 2008 Mumbai Attacks, Piles of Spy Data, but an Uncompleted Puzzle." *The New York Times*, December 21, 2014. Accessed January 28, 2016, http://www.nytimes. com/2014/12/22/world/asia/in-2008-mumbai-attacks-piles-of-spy-data-but-an-uncompleted-puzzle.html.

Hellyer, Caroline. "ISIL Courts al-Shabab as al-Qaeda Ties Fade Away." *Al Jazeera*, March 23, 2015. Accessed January 28, 2016, http://www.aljazeera.com/indepth/features/2015/03/isil-eyes-east-africa-foments-division-150322130940108.html.

Hodge, Nel. "How Somalia's al-Shabab Militants Hone Their Image." *BBC News*, June 5, 2014. Accessed January 28, 2016, http://www.bbc.com/news/world-africa-27633367.

Hoffman, Aaron M., Dwaine H. A. Jengelley, Natasha T. Duncan, Melissa Buehler, and Meredith L. Rees. "How Does the Business of News Influence Terrorism Coverage? Evidence From *The Washington Post* and *USA Today*." *Terrorism and Political Violence* 22 (2010): 559–580.

Howden, Daniel. "Terror in Westgate Mall: The Full Story of the Attacks That Devastated Kenya." *The Guardian*, October 4, 2013. Accessed January 29, 2016, http://www.theguardian.com/world/interactive/2013/oct/04/westgate-mall-attacks-kenya-terror.

Indiewire. "Terror at the Mall,' Documentary on Siege of Westgate Mall in Nairobi, Kenya, Coming to HBO." Press Release, September 2, 2014. Accessed January 29, 2016, http://blogs.indiewire.com/shadowandact/terror-at-the-mall-an-inside-look-at-the-siege-of-westgate-mall-in-nairobi-kenya-debuts-sept-15-on-hbo-20140902.

ITV News. "Google Removes Isis App from Play Store." July 18, 2014. Accessed January 28, 2016, http://www.itv.com/news/story/2014-06-18/google-play-store-isis-app/.

Jenkins, Brian M. "International Terrorism: A New Kind of Warfare," *The Rand Paper Series* (1974).

Kellner, Douglas. "September 11, Spectacles of Terror, and Media Manipulation: A Critique of Jihadist and Bush Media Politics." *Logos* 2, no.1 (2003): 86–102.

Khera, Jastinder. "Authorities and Militants Take Nairobi Battle to Twitter." *BBC News*, September 24, 2013. Accessed January 28, 2016, http://www.bbc.com/news/world-africa-24218276.

Klausen, Jytte. "Tweeting the Jihad: Social Media Networks of Western Foreign Fighters in Syria and Iraq." *Studies in Conflict & Terrorism* 38 (2015): 1–22.

Kleinman, Arthur, and Joan Kleinman. "Cultural Appropriations of Suffering." In *Cultures of Fear: A Critical Reader*, eds. Danielle Taana Smith and Uli Linke, 288–303. London: Pluto Press, 2009.

Kulish, Nicholas. "In this Horror Film, Blood is All Too Real: 'Terror at the Mall' on HBO Documents an Attack in Kenya." *New York Times*, September 14, 2014. Accessed January 29, 2016, http://www.nytimes.com/2014/09/15/arts/television/terror-at-the-mall-on-hbo-documents-an-attack-in-kenya.html?_r=0.

Lough, Richard, and Abdi Sheikh. "UPDATE 3-Kenya Launches Probe as Shabaab Leader Confirms Mall Attack." *Reuters*, September 25, 2013. Accessed January 29, 2016, http://www.reuters.com/article/2013/09/25/kenya-attack-idUSL5N0HL0MS20130925.

Moufahim, Mona, and Michael Humphreys. "Marketing an Extremist Ideology: The Vlaams Belang's Nationalist Discourse." In *The Routledge Companion to Ethics, Politics and Organizations*, eds. Alison Pullen and Carl Rhodes, 85–99. Oxon: Routledge, 2015.

Mutambo, Aggrey. "Bodies of Westgate Terrorists 'Are With the FBI', says KDF Chief Julius Karangi." *Daily Nation*, February 7, 2014. Accessed January 29, 2016, http://mobile.nation.co.ke/news/Julius-Karangi-Kenya-Defence-Forces-Westgate-Attack/-/1950946/2196566/-/format/xhtml/-/r6oqhdz/-/index.html.

Nordeste, Bruno, and David Carment, "A Framework for Understanding Terrorist Use of the Internet," ITAC CIEM *Trends in Terrorism Series* 2 (2006). Accessed January 28, 2016, http://www4.carleton.ca/cifp/app/serve.php/1121.pdf.

Okari, Dennis. "Kenya's Westgate Attack: Unanswered Questions One Year On." *BBC News*, September 21, 2014. Accessed January 29, 2016, http://www.bbc.com/news/world-africa-29282045.

Petrecca, Laura. "39 Die in Kenya Mall Siege; Hostages Still Held." *USA Today*, September 21, 2013. Accessed January 29, 2016, http://www.usatoday.com/story/news/world/2013/09/21/witness-kenya-mall-attackers-target-non-muslims/2846319/.

Plunkett, John. "BBC Radio 1 Criticised for Airing 'Call of Duty' Interview with Isis Briton." *The Guardian*, November 10, 2014. Accessed January 29, 2016, http://www.theguardian.com/media/2014/nov/10/bbc-radio-1-criticised-british-isis-militant-interview.

Ramonet, Ignacio. "The Power of Television Pictures." *Points of View*. February 20, 2002. Accessed January 29, 2016, http://www.unesco.org/webworld/points_of_views/200202_ramonet.shtml.

Reed, Dan. *Terror at the Mall*, documentary. London: Amos Pictures, 2014.

Robinson, Willian I. *Global Capitalism and the Crisis of Humanity*. New York: Cambridge University Press, 2014.

Rose, Steve. "The Isis Propaganda War: a Hi-tech Media Jihad." *The Guardian*, October 7, 2014. Accessed January 28, 2016, http://www.theguardian. com/world/2014/oct/07/isis-media-machine-propaganda-war.

Rotella, Sebastian, and David E. Sanger. "In 2008 Mumbai Attacks, Piles of Spy Data, but an Uncompleted Puzzle." *The New York Times*, December 21, 2014. Accessed January 28, 2016, http://www.nytimes.com/2014/12/22/world/asia/in-2008-mumbai-attacks-piles-of-spy-data-but-an-uncompleted-puzzle.html.

Rumsfeld, Donald. "Speech." U.S. Department of Defense, November 9, 2006. Accessed January 28, 2016, https://web.archive.org/web/20141216060320/http://www.defense.gov/Speeches/Speech.aspx?SpeechID=1060.

Sambuli, Nanjira. "How Useful is a Tweet? A Review of the First Tweets from the Westgate Mall Attack," Ihub Research, October 3, 2013. Accessed January 29, 2016, http://www.ihub.co.ke/blogs/16012.

Sanchez, Raf. "Tweeting at Terrorists: Inside America's Social Media Battle with Online Jihad." *The Telegraph*, May 21, 2014. Accessed January 29, 2016, http://www.telegraph.co.uk/news/worldnews/al-qaeda/10829355/Tweeting-at-terrorists-inside-Americas-social-media-battle-with-online-jihad.html.

Schulzke, Marcus. "Simulating Terrorism and Insurgency: Video Games in the War of Ideas." *Cambridge Review of International Affairs* 27 (2014): 627–643.

Shultz, James M. et al. "Multiple Vantage Points on the Mental Health Effects of Mass Shootings." *Current Psychiatry Reports* 16 (2014). Accessed January 28, 2016, doi 10.1007/s11920-014-0469-5.

Simon, Tomer, Avishay Goldberg, Limor Aharonson-Daniel, Dmitry Leykin, and Bruria Adini. "Twitter in the Cross Fire—The Use of Social Media in the Westgate Mall Terror Attack in Kenya." *PLoS* One 9, no. 8 (2014). Accessed January 29, 2016, http://dx.doi.org/10.1371/journal.pone.0104136.

SITE Intelligence Group. "The Westgate Attack: A New Trend in al-Qaeda Communication Strategies." January 15, 2014. Accessed January 28, 2016, https://news.siteintelgroup.com/Articles-Analysis/the-westgate-attack-a-new-trend-in-al-qaeda-communication-strategies.html.

Springer, Claudia. "Military Propaganda: Defense Department Films from World War II and Vietnam." *Cultural Critique* 3 (1986): 151–167.

Stewart, Ian, and Scott Sweeney. "Twitter Terrorism: Criminals Choose the Hack Attack." Wilson Elser, July 7, 2015. Accessed January 29, 2016, http://www.jdsupra.com/legalnews/twitter-terrorism-criminals-choose-the-22378/.

Takacs, Stacy. "Real War News, Real War Games: The Hekmati Case and the Problems of Soft Power." *American Quarterly* 65 (2013): 177–184.

Tanguay, Liane. *Hijacking History: American Culture and the War on Terror*. Montreal: McGill-Queen's University Press, 2013.

The Guardian. "Paris Supermarket Siege Survivors Sue Media over 'Dangerous' Coverage." April 3, 2015. Accessed January 29, 2016, http://www.theguardian.com/world/2015/apr/03/paris-supermarket-siege-survivors-sue-media.

Twitter. "Kenyan Ministry of Interior." September 22, 2013. Accessed January 29, 2016, https://twitter.com/InteriorKE/status/381960772420923392.

United States Department of State. "Country Reports on Terrorism 2013." April 2014. Accessed January 28, 2016, http://www.state.gov/documents/organization/225886.pdf.

Vogt, Heidi, and Patrick Mcgroarty. "Before Kenya Attack, a Warning on Terrorism." *The Wall Street Journal*, September 30, 2013. Accessed January 29, 2016, http://www.wsj.com/articles/SB10001424052702303643304579105222268968650.

Winseck, Dwayne. "The Political Economies of Media and the Transformation of the Global Media Industries." In *The Political Economies of Media: The Transformation of the Global Media Industries*, eds. Dwayne Winseck and Dal Yong Jin, 3–48. London: Bloomsbury, 2011.

Weimann, Gabriel. "Terror on Facebook, Twitter, and Youtube." *Brown Journal of World Affairs* 16, no. 2 (2010): 45–54.

Weimann, Gabriel. "Cyber-Fatwas and Terrorism," *Studies in Conflict & Terrorism* 34 (2011): 765–781.

Wood, Graeme. "What ISIS Really Wants." *The Atlantic*, March 2015. Accessed January 28, 2016, http://www.theatlantic.com/features/archive/2015/02/what-isis-really-wants/384980/.

PART III

Media, Culture and Language in the Middle East

Winning Hearts and Minds through Soft Power: The Case of Turkish Soap Operas in the Middle East

Jana Jabbour

Introduction

While soap operas are popular all around the world, they have a particular strategic significance and unique importance in the context of the Middle East region. Indeed, television series (*musalsalat*) are a key component of Arab modern culture and represent a social phenomenon and a societal trend: women, men, young or old people, the majority of Arab viewers watch at least one *musalsal*, individually or with friends and family, in the comfort of a living room or in a coffee shop with a giant screen, during day-time and in the evening, or even after *iftar* (meal that breaks the fast) in the holy month of *ramadan*. Therefore, given the pervasiveness of TV series in the Arab World, whoever is able to dominate

J. Jabbour (✉)
CERI (Center for International Research), Sciences Po, Paris, France

© The Author(s) 2017
N. Lenze et al. (eds.), *Media in the Middle East*,
DOI 10.1007/978-3-319-65771-4_7

the soap opera industry and to export its own "*musalsalat*" to the region can—at least to a certain extent—spread its worldview, values, and ideas to Arab populations, and build cultural prestige in the region.

For decades, the soap opera industry in the Middle East has been controlled by Egypt (since the 1950s) and by Syria (since the 1980s). Yet the twenty-first century marks Turkey's entry into the Arab film and television market. In recent years, Turkish soap operas (*diziler*) managed to dethrone their Syrian and Egyptian counterparts and to compete with Mexican and Venezuelan *telenovelas* which have long experienced glory and fame on Middle Eastern markets.[1]

This chapter examines the dynamics behind Turkey's export of soap operas to the wider Middle East region. Soap operas are considered to be an important vehicle for the exercise of soft power, emphasizing the importance of exporting soap operas as a high-stakes activity. First put forward by the American political scientist Joseph Nye, the concept of soft power refers to a country's ability "to get what it wants through attraction rather than coercion" (Nye 2005: 5). In that sense, Turkish soap operas have a strategic significance as they contribute to Turkey's soft power capacity: by disseminating Turkey's values and appealing to the populations of the Middle East, they can help Turkey rise to the status of a regional power.

The first part of the chapter looks at the theoretical foundations that underlie Turkey's projection of soft power in direction of the Middle East. In particular, the chapter explores the so-called "Davutoğlu doctrine" of "strategic depth" (*stratejik derinlik*) and its impact in terms of paving the way for Turkey's rapprochement with the Middle East. The second part examines Turkish soap operas as vectors of soft power: it analyses the popularity of these *diziler* in light of the narrative they convey and the symbols they disseminate. The third part assesses the impact of Turkish soap operas in the Middle East.

---

[1] In the 1990s, Mexican series like *Rosalita* or *Maria Mercedes*, dubbed in classical Arabic language, were very popular in the Middle East.

TURKEY'S RE-ENGAGEMENT WITH THE ARAB WORLD AND THE SHIFT FROM HARD POWER TO SOFT POWER

"My country is your faithful ally and friend".[2] This statement, made by then-rime minister of Turkey, Recep Tayyip Erdoğan, and addressed to the Arab people in March 2003, marks a turning point in the history of Turkish–Arab relations. In fact, since the establishment of the Turkish Republic by Mustafa Kemal Atatürk in October 1923, Turkey's foreign policy and strategic thinking were best illustrated by the motto "There is no friend for a Turk other than a Turk". In particular, according to the founder of the Turkish Republic, the Middle East was seen as a region characterized by backwardness and underdevelopment, and as a source of threat and danger for the nascent Turkey. Turks' mistrust of Arabs,[3] coupled with the numerous territorial disputes with Arab states,[4] pushed Turkey to turn its back on the Middle East. In that sense, the securitization of the Middle East region for much of the twentieth century meant that the interaction between Turkey and the Middle East was either non-existent or, where it was present, entirely based on hard power and the threat of use of military force.[5]

However, with the Justice and Development Party (AKP)'s ascent to power in November 2002, Turkey's foreign policy and strategic thinking have undergone a major paradigm shift (Sözen 2010). As of 2002, Turkey's public discourse and conduct of foreign policy reflect a desecuritization of the Middle East and a push away from hard power. In fact, in the 2000s, and for the first time since the establishment of the Turkish Republic, Turkey has asserted itself as a central actor and a regional power in the Middle East.

---

[2] Recep Tayyip Erdogan, "My Country is Your Faithful Ally and Friend," *The Wall Street Journal*, 30 March 2003, http://online.wsj.com/news/articles/SB104907941058746300.

[3] According to Kemalist Turkish historiography, Arabs were seen as the "enemies of the interior", and were accused of accelerating the collapse of the Ottoman Empire because they orchestrated the "Arab revolt".

[4] With Syria over the Hatay province, and with Iraq over Mosul.

[5] For example, Turkey and Syria had arrived to the brink of war in 1999 because Syria was hosting the Kurdish PKK leader Abdullah Öcalan.

Turkey's rapprochement with the Middle East must mainly be understood in light of the vision of Ahmet Davutoğlu, the architect of Turkish foreign policy, who is nicknamed "Turkey's Kissinger". In 2001, Ahmet Davutoğlu, then professor of International Relations at Boğazıçı University, published a book titled *Stratejik Derinlik: Türkiye'nin Uluslararası Konumu* [*Strategic Depth: Turkey's International Position*], in which he articulated a new strategic vision for Turkey (Davutoğlu 2001). In this seminal work, Davutoğlu assessed the strengths and weaknesses of Turkey in the twenty-first century and suggested ways in which Turkey could become a global power.

Davutoğlu's main argument is straightforward: in the post-Cold War order, a country's significance and power on the world stage depended on its "strategic depth" (Jabbour 2011). For a country to be a "central state" (*merke ülke*) and a leading actor in international relations, it must possess "geographical depth"—meaning an exceptional geopolitical location—and "historical depth", meaning a rich cultural and historical background (Davutoğlu 2001: 87). Considering the Turkish case, Davutoğlu states that his country is uniquely endowed to be a central state. In fact, with regard to geographical depth, Turkey is strategically positioned at the confluence of East and West, at the intersection of the Middle East, the Balkans, the Caucasus, Central Asia, and Europe. Its exceptional location on the Rimland belt grants it the natural ability to influence the regional and international geopolitical balances. With regard to historical depth, Turkey has a rich historical and cultural legacy as heir to the Ottoman Empire. Therefore, based on the cultural and historical ties it has with the former Ottoman territories, Turkey must be able to increase its influence and power in neighbouring regions. In the words of Davutoğlu:

> Turkey enjoys multiple regional identities and thus has the capability as well as the responsibility to follow an integrated and multidimensional foreign policy. The unique combination of our history and geography brings with it a sense of responsibility. To contribute actively towards conflict resolution and international peace and security in all these areas is a call of duty arising from the depths of a multidimensional history of Turkey. (Davutoğlu 2001: 142)

Yet, while all neighbouring regions are seen as important, Davutoğlu considers the Middle East to be of the utmost significance and value for Turkey. Reviving the geopolitics theories developed by Halford Mackinder and Nicholas Spykman, Davutoğlu asserts that the Middle East region is located in the heart of Eurasia, and is therefore "key to strategic balances" (Davutoğlu 2001: 357). Whoever is able to control this area will be able to greatly influence regional and international power configurations (Davutoğlu 2001: 146). Therefore, according to the professor-turned-politician, Turkey should increase its influence in the Middle East so as to create a regional "hinterland", necessary for Ankara's rise in the international arena (Davutoğlu 2001: 155).

After stating the importance of the Middle East, Davutoğlu suggests means to increase Turkey's power in this region. The author insists that Turks must first reconcile with their Muslim identity and their Ottoman past, that they must "overcome psychological barriers", so that they can genuinely use Turkey's historical and identity ties with the Arabs in order to facilitate interaction with the Middle East and therefore to increase Ankara's regional leverage. Furthermore, in order to help Turkey rise to the status of regional power, Davutoğlu emphasizes the necessity of making his country culturally attractive and appealing to Arab populations (Davutoğlu 2001: 615). Hence, soft power—as conceptualized by Joseph Nye—is clearly incorporated in Davutoğlu's thinking. It is noteworthy that in his book, Davutoğlu draws a very positive image of the Ottoman past, and ignores the "dark side" of the Empire: in particular, he makes no mention of the negative perception the Arab populations have of the Ottoman Empire. In fact, for most of the twentieth century, Arab historiography associated the empire with the memory of oppression and domination.

Ahmet Davutoğlu's vision could have remained just ink on paper. However, the ascent to power of the AKP party in 2002 played in his favour. In fact, being a "nascent" party with no foreign policy experience, AKP searched for experts to advise the government on foreign policy and diplomacy issues. Thus, Davutoğlu was appointed advisor to Prime Minister Erdogan in 2013, before becoming minister of foreign affairs in 2009, and prime minister from 2014 to 2016. He became the third intellectual—after Zbigniew Brzezinski and Henry Kissinger— to be nominated for a state position and to be offered the opportunity to put his theory into practice. Hence, as of 2003 and the nomination of Davutoğlu, the conceptual framework advanced by the latter has structured and guided Turkey's diplomatic action in the regional and international arenas. In particular, a new policy of rapprochement with the Middle East has been set in motion, with constant use of soft power—as imagined by Davutoğlu. In fact, throughout the 2000s, Turkey has been culturally present in the Middle East, particularly through soft power and soap operas.[6]

TURKEY'S EXPORT OF SOAP OPERAS OR THE POWER TO SEDUCE ARAB POPULATIONS THROUGH POPULAR CULTURE

One of the reasons that account for Turkey's relatively quick rise to cultural prestige and attractiveness as well as power in the Middle East in the 2000s is closely associated with the massive export of soap operas.

From the outset, it is important to note that the production and export of television series to the Middle East has been done by non-governmental/private companies, independently of official circles in Ankara. These private companies produced TV series essentially for a local Turkish public and with the sole objective of doing business and making profit; however, as the first series were exported to the Arab world and became popular in this region, they have contributed to Turkey's soft power, something that the cultural entrepreneurs were neither intending nor expecting. And while the Turkish government did not provide any public support for these cultural entrepreneurs, it nevertheless capitalized on the success of these series to increase Ankara's prestige in the Middle East.

It is possible to identify three different categories of Turkish soap operas that have been exported to the Middle East (Gonzales-Quijano 2011): romantic, historical, and political thriller/action soap operas. Each of these categories promote a certain image or "brand" of Turkey. The first "conquest" of the Middle East by Turkish soap operas began in 2008 with the export of the romantic soap opera *Gümüş* [Silver] which, with its 85 million Arab viewers, represented a genuine success story in the Middle East. While the series was popular in other regions, such as the Balkans and Central Europe, it achieved its highest audience ratings in the Arab world (Rotivel 2011). *Gümüş*

---

[6] Soap operas are not the only *soft power* tool used by Turkey. Other elements of Turkey's *soft power* in the Middle East include: the launching of an Arabic-speaking TV channel (*TRT Al Arabiyya*); the establishment of Turkish cultural centers in Arab countries (known as *Yunus Emre centers*); and the offer of scholarships to Arab students through a program known as *Turkiye Burslari*.

displayed the story of a wealthy, handsome gentleman—Mehmet (Kıvanç Tatlıtuğ)—who is forced by his grandfather to marry his cousin—Gümüş (Songül Öden)—a young lady with a conservative background born and raised in a traditional village of Anatolia. Beyond the love story that eventually unfolds between Gümüş and Mehmet and that mesmerizes the Arab public, the series became attractive in the region as it portrayed Turkey as a country where people have a modern, yet Muslim-compatible lifestyle: in fact, the characters drink alcohol, dance in nightclubs, kiss in public, yet they often pray, and they respect the patriarchal model of their family by listening to the elders[7] and living with their parents. Moreover, throughout the series, the viewers witness the emancipation and empowerment of the female character—Gümüş: with the strong support of her husband Mehmet, Gümüş becomes a successful businesswoman and a renowned fashion designer; she therefore personifies the ideal of a Muslim lady who perfectly succeeds in both business duties and household responsibilities.

In Egypt, Syria, Lebanon, Morocco, Qatar, and Saudi Arabia, the series created a phenomenon of *Gümüş-mania*. Ladies rushed to buy T-shirts and posters with photos of their favourite character; new-born babies were named after the actors; and divorce cases were recorded due to the fact that Arab wives were no longer content with their husbands and demanded that the latter be as romantic as the character "Mehmet" (Buccianti 2010). While the series was first aired on the Saudi Arabian satellite channel MBC in the daytime slot (2 p.m.), its high audience ratings pushed the managers of MBC to broadcast it in evening prime time (9.30 p.m.) (Buccianti 2010).

Being a success story in the Arab world, the series *Gümüş* paved the way for the export of other Turkish romantic soap operas such as *Aşk ve Ceza, Öyle Bir Gece Zaman Ki, Aşk-i Memnu, Asi,* and *Fatmagülün Suçu Ne?*, all of which have achieved high audience ratings in the region.[8] Our interviews in Turkey show that Turkish producers originally created their series exclusively for a local Turkish audience. However, the popularity that *Gümüş* acquired in the Arab world alerted them to the potential

---

[7] Personified here by Mehmet's mother and grandfather.

[8] According to a survey by the Turkish think tank TESEV, 78% of Arab populations watch at least one romantic Turkish soap opera. "The perception of Turkey in the Middle East", *TESEV*, 2010, 16.

and opportunities offered by the Middle East market. Motivated by economic and financial gains, they have, since then, attempted to export their series to the Arab World.

The plots of the romantic soap operas exported to the Middle East market often have striking similarities: almost all the stories revolve around a conservative family who moves from Anatolia to engage in business in Istanbul, and who succeeds in business without compromising their religious values and Muslim traditions. The importance and significance of these soap operas in terms of cultural power and social attractiveness lies in the fact that they promote an image of Turkey as an ideal society where Islam coexists with modernity, where men and women are equal, and where capitalism and consumerism do not erode traditional social and religious values. This is precisely the ideal-type of society that Muslims and Arabs are longing for, but which they cannot find in their own countries. In that sense, Turkish romantic soap operas are—for the Arab populations—a means to escape their grim reality; they offer them the possibility to imagine themselves living in a better world. In other words, Turkish *diziler* act like a mirror that reflects what Arab viewers dream of: embracing modernity without compromising their religious values and social traditions. Therefore, by conveying images and representations that appeal to the Arab public, Turkish romantic soaps contribute to the idea of "winning hearts and minds", and to making Turkey attractive in the imaginary of Arab viewers.

The second category of Turkish soap operas are the historical series, exemplified by *Muhteşem Yüzyıl* [Magnificent Century], a hit-series in the Middle East. Based on the life of Sultan Suleiman the Magnificent—the longest-reigning Sultan of the Ottoman Empire, and his wife Hürrem, the soap opera glorifies the Ottoman past and revives Turkish history in the minds of Turks and Arabs. What is of major importance in our analysis is the political message indirectly conveyed to the Arab and Muslim audience through this soap opera: an in-depth analysis of the script shows that *Muhteşem Yüzyıl* portrays the Ottoman Empire—and, by inference, Turkey—as a legitimate power and a perfect representative of the interests of Arabs and Muslims worldwide. Throughout the series, we note 765 occurrences of the terms "Islam", "Muslim", and "Jihad", and a repetition of several statements that convey the message that the past rulers of this country (the Sultan-Caliphs) ruled "with the Koran and the Sharia" and "protected Islam and Muslims against infidels and heretics". For instance, we note statements such as: "I want to combat for the cause of Allah, for it is a sacred duty"; "Our mission is to spread the light of Islam; May Allah be with us."[9] Furthermore, the series implicitly reminds the Middle Eastern populations of their historical ties with Turkey. For example, we note significant statements by Suleiman the Magnificent, such as: "I am the Sultan of Anatolia, Diyarbakır, Kurdistan, Azerbaidjan, Damascus, Aleppo, Egypt, Mecca, Jerusalem, and Yemen. I am the Sultan of Arab territories which my ancestors had conquered;" "I rule over the Safavids, the Mameluks of Egypt, the Abbasids, Syria, Palestine, Hijaz, and the Silk Road."[10]

Hence, by emphasizing the historical ties between Turks and Arabs under the Ottoman Empire, and by portraying Turkey as heir to the Caliphate—an institution that defended Muslims and spread the word of Islam, *Muhteşem Yüzyıl* attempts to appeal to Muslims in the Arab world, who have long suffered from a lack of credible leadership. It is noteworthy that the series underlines the positive side of the Ottoman past, and ignores its "dark side" and the oppression the Sultan-Caliphs practiced over Arab territories. In this regard, the series in itself is a work of historiography—in the sense that it promotes one vision and one interpretation of Ottoman history. As to Arab Christian viewers who follow this series, our interviews and research show that *Muhteşem Yüzyıl* attracts them for a different reason: rather than being fascinated by the *musalsal*'s Muslim connotations and the invocation of the Caliphal epoch—which they do not relate to, Christian viewers are mesmerized by the costumes and accessories that the characters wear, the attractive theme songs, as well as the beauty of the actors and actresses, in particular Meryem Uzerli playing the role of Hürrem. Therefore, the series is liked regardless of religious or political sentiments, although for different reasons.

Here again, it is interesting to note that the production of a historical series was not politically motivated, but based solely on economic and financial incentives. In an interview we made with Timur Savcı, producer of *Muhteşem Yüzyıl*, the latter asserted that "his main objective when producing this series was to sell a story [and a product] which everybody, in Turkey and in neighbouring regions, would relate to".[11] Creating a series based on the life of Suleiman the Magnificent and the history of

---

[9] Season 2, episode 35.

[10] Season 1, episode 48.

[11] Interview in Istanbul, April 2014.

the Ottoman Empire was a rational choice, according to Savcı: Turks would be attracted by the rediscovery of their past; Muslim and Turkmen populations in the Arab world, in Central Asia, and in the Balkans would identify with the story as they share the same identity, history, and values as Turkey, while other minorities in the neighbourhood will at least be attracted by the setting, the sound and light effects, and the expensive costumes and accessories (a budget of $70 million).

Finally, the third category of soap operas exported to the Middle East are the political action/thriller series as exemplified by *Kurtlar Vadısı* [Valley of the Wolves], which have promoted an image of Turkey as a powerful country able to confront the West and to defy Israel and the United States in particular. In fact, in *Kurtlar Vadısı*, the plot revolves around the Turkish intelligence agent Polent Alemdar (the actor Necati Şaşmaz) who is sent to the Palestinian territories to defend Palestinians. The series is built around a manichean vision of the world in which Israelis are portrayed as Evil, "the bad guys", "the barbarians", while the Turkish characters are represented as "the good guys", the "benevolent forces", and the big brothers and godfathers of the oppressed Palestinian population. One statement in the script is particularly symbolic: in a scene where Polent Alemdar meets an Israeli agent who asks him why he came to Israel, Alemdar answers "I did not come to Israel, I came to Palestine". And when the Israeli character warns him in an aggressive way saying "You know you won't make it out of our promised land", Alemdar defies him by answering "I don't know what part of this land has been promised to you".[12] The message conveyed is clear: Turkey has the political courage to challenge Israel and to defend the interests of Arabs and Palestinians. In another scene, Polent Alemdar makes a strong statement: "All those who had ruled this region in the past oppressed local populations, except our ancestors. Our ancestors taught us to fight against injustice, colonization, and imperialism."[13] In that sense, Turkey is implicitly portrayed as a benign power, which does not seek to dominate other countries. Hence, through sseducing image, the Middle Eastern audience is encouraged to view Turkey as a good leader at the regional and international level, and as a legitimate and credible representative of the Arab and Palestinian cause.

---

[12] See images in the Appendix.

[13] Season 1, Episode 10.

Beyond the representations and the images that Turkish soap operas transmit and that appeal to Arab populations, the success of the *diziler* lies in other elements: in particular, their quality of production on the one hand and the structure and nature of the export market (the Arab market) on the other. In terms of production, the Turkish soap opera industry is highly developed: benefitting from a good economic situation in their country, production companies devote huge budgets to produce high-standard series that can compete with international and American hit-series. The quality of the image and the sound, the professional performance and the charisma of the actors, the realistic scenario, and the beauty of the picturesque shots (at the Bosphorus, in luxurious villas), have all participated in making these series appealing for a wide public. Moreover, the format used contributed to making the series competitive: the majority of the *diziler* are made up of two to four seasons, composed each of 30 episodes of 90 minutes. This makes them price-competitive: broadcasters and TV channels buy long episodes that can fill up lengthy airing time. Hence, the success of Turkish soap operas lies in part in their production strategies.

Additionally, it is the export strategies that account for their popularity in the Arab world. While Latin American *telenovelas* that dominated the Middle East market in the 1990s were dubbed in literary/classical Arabic,[14] Turkish *diziler* are dubbed in dialectal Arabic, the language that people use in their daily life. Through the use of a dialect and an easy language to which people can connect, these series easily penetrate the minds of the Arab public and allow the viewers to identify with the characters and accept the message that is indirectly conveyed in the scenario. The dialect, in this sense, creates an awareness of proximity between the Arab viewer and the soap opera on the one hand, and between Turkish and Arab societies on the other hand. In particular, dubbing was made in Syrian dialect rather than Egyptian: this choice is intriguing given that Egyptian soap operas have dominated the Arab media scene for decades, and that Egypt is the biggest consumption market in the Middle East—with a population of 94 million.[15] The Syrian dialect was privileged over the Egyptian one due to political factors. In

---

[14] Mainly Mexican and Venezuelan series like *Cassandra* and *Maria Mercedes*.

[15] Egypt State Information Service: http://www.sis.gov.eg/Ar/Templates/Articles/tmpArticles.aspx?ArtID=9.

fact, when *Gümüş* was first aired on Arab TV channels in 2008, Syria and Turkey enjoyed excellent diplomatic, economic and social relations. Erdoğan and Bashar el-Assad had become close friends, Ankara and Damascus had signed a free trade agreement and were considering the removal of visas, diplomatic visits were common between the two countries, and Turkey was mediating between Syria and Israel. The soap opera industry has therefore benefitted from the Turkish–Syrian honeymoon: it is indeed highly probable that dubbing in the Syrian dialect was made possible by the political rapprochement between Damascus and Ankara. The author's research shows, in fact, that all Turkish *diziler* were translated into Arabic in Damascus, by three Syrian production companies—Sama Art Production, Firdaws Art Production, and ABC Damascus—and were dubbed by Syrian actors. By contrast, Turkey's relations with Egypt were not as warm: Cairo was suspicious and wary of Ankara's regional ambitions and Mubarak sought to keep some distance from Erdoğan. Moreover, had Turkish series been dubbed in Egyptian, this would have probably offended the Egyptian soap opera industry which, in contrast to its Syrian counterpart, draws on a rich tradition and takes pride in its century-long achievements.

In addition to dubbing, the names of the characters and the title of the soaps were adapted to the Arab context: in *Gümüş*, for example, the name of the main character "Mehmet" becomes "Mouhannad" in the Arabic-dubbed version of the series; similarly, "Gümüş" becomes "Nour", a common female Arabic name. Very amusingly, the title of the series *Muhteşem Yüzyıl*—which literally means "Magnificent Century"—was translated in Arabic into a very different name: "Harim El Sultan"—which means "The Sultan's Harem". In fact, the expression "Sultan's Harem" speaks to the imaginary of Arab viewers for whom the harem is the object of various phantasms and reflects an exotic world in which all desires are fulfilled. Therefore, the title in itself made the series very appealing for the Arab public.

The success of Turkish soap operas in the Middle East is not only based on their dubbing language and their adaptation to the Arab context, but also on the nature and structure of their "export market"—that is, the Arab drama industry. In terms of content, while Arab soap operas generally display an unrealistic scenario and do not touch upon "sensitive" topics encountered in daily life (such as love, betrayal, abortion, premarital sex, women's emancipation), Turkish soap operas—by contrast—deal with these "real" issues, which are seen by the Arab public as relevant and attractive. In terms of format, Arab soap operas are usually produced with very low budgets, which impacts negatively on their quality (image and sound, actors' performance, communication strategies, etc.). These shortcomings of the Arab media have therefore left a room for the Turkish *diziler* to take hold in Middle East societies.

The author's interviews show that the projection of soft power through Turkish soap operas is the result of private/non-governmental actors. It is important here to consider the interaction between these actors and the Turkish government, and to study the role—if any— played by the latter. Our field research and interviews with Turkish producers show clearly that production companies did not receive any kind of material or non-material support from political actors and governmental circles. The producer of *Muhteşem Yüzyıl*, Timur Savcı, even told us that when his production team asked for the authorization to film some shots in Topkapı palace, the government only accepted to grant them this permission for a few days, and the team later had to create its own palace-like setting as it was not allowed to make use of Topkapı.

However, we notice that while the government did not contribute to the production of Turkish soap operas, it nevertheless sought to "surf" on their popularity and success in order to increase Ankara's influence and prestige in the region, and to build a regional power. Two anecdotes provide concrete illustrations. In an interview with a diplomat in Ankara,[16] we were told that President Abdullah Gül, during a visit to the United Arab Emirates in 2010, and in order to "break the ice" with the Gulf rulers, started his official meeting by talking about the latest episode of the series *Fatmagül'ün Suçu Ne* ("Fatma" in the Arabic-dubbed version), which was very popular in the Gulf and was watched even by the royal family! Another anecdote relates to the series *Muhteşem Yüzyıl*: in late 2012, Erdoğan called for prosecutors to ban this soap opera accusing the story of distorting historical facts. In particular, Erdoğan claimed that the series misrepresented Suleiman the Magnificent by portraying him as an emotional man spending more time in the harem than in conquests. The series was in fact taken off TV channels and Turkish airlines flights for over a week. During that time, we had the chance to meet with the consul of Turkey in Dubai, who told us that "it is highly doubtful that this ban will continue, as Erdoğan knows that the series

---

[16] Off-the-record interview, January 2014.

is very popular all over the Arab world; therefore, he will soon put it back on the screens, as it serves our soft power in the region."[17] Indeed, all claims against *Muhteşem Yüzyıl* were quickly dismissed, and the series was broadcasted again. This clearly shows that even when the Turkish government has negative views of the soap operas, it has nevertheless capitalized on them to increase Ankara's attractiveness in the Middle East, and has instrumentalised their popularity to win prestige in the region.

ASSESSING THE REAL IMPACT OF TURKISH SOAP OPERAS

The projection of soft power through soap operas had an economic and a political impact on Turkey. At the economic level, with its 350 million consumers, the Arab market has become the number one export market for Turkish soap operas, accounting for two-thirds of Turkey's overall soap operas exports. The sale of Turkish soap operas in the Middle East generated a profit of 50 million euros in 2012. In addition, the export of soap operas contributed to boosting Arab tourism in Turkey. According to the Turkish official statistics agency (Türkstat), while in 2005–2006 the number of Arab tourists in Turkey did not exceed 800,000, it reached two million in 2009–2010.[18] While it would be naive to explain this evolution solely by the attraction that Turkish soap operas have had on the audience, it would nevertheless be wrong to completely exclude this variable from the analysis. In fact, the majority of Arab tourists in Turkey visit the locations of their favorite soap operas: for instance, the luxurious villa where *Gümüş* was filmed, on the Bosphorus, has become a major tourist attraction, with Arab tourists queuing to buy their entrance tickets and visit the house of their favorite actors. Travel agencies in the Middle East now include tours of this villa and the location where *Mühteşem Yüzyıl* was shot.

While the economic gains from soap operas are tangible, the political gains are more diffuse. In fact, the political impact of Turkey's soft power in the Middle East is subject to controversy: while some analysts consider that Turkey has won the hearts and minds of Arabs and Muslims through its soft power (Kalin 2011), others argue that Turkey's soft power has

---

[17] November 2012, Dubai.

[18] Turkish Statistical Institute, www.turkstat.gov.tr.

produced limited positive effects (Benli 2011). We support the view that Turkey's soft power has produced highly mitigated effects, and that its shortcomings outweigh its achievements.

On the positive side, a poll the author conducted in the Middle East shows clearly that soap operas have had a positive influence on Arab populations' perceptions of Turkey. The poll was conducted between 2012 and 2013, on a sample of 1000 persons in Egypt, Lebanon, Iraq, and Qatar, chosen randomly.[19] It shows that 77% of the polled watched a Turkish soap opera. Furthermore, it demonstrated that the regular consumption of Turkish soap operas increased the probability of viewers having a good perception of Turkey: among those people who watched one or two Turkish soap operas, 54% had a favourable view of Turkey; among those who watched more than two soap operas, 82% had a positive perception of Turkey. By contrast, among the people who did not watch any Turkish soap opera, only 41% had a favourable view of Turkey.[20] Moreover, field research and interviews conducted in the region show clearly that soft power actions reinforce each other and create a "virtuous circle": the more one watches a soap opera, the more he/she is willing to visit Turkey for tourism, the more he/she is tempted to enrol in a Turkish cultural centre to learn the Turkish language, the more he/she is tempted to apply to the scholarship program offered by Turkey (*Türkiye Bursları*) to get the opportunity to study in Istanbul; and vice versa. Therefore, it is clear that Turkey's cultural presence in the Middle East has made Arab populations curious to discover or rediscover Turkey, as well as having had an economic impact (more Arab tourism in Turkey). Consequently, Turkish soap operas clearly had a concrete effect in terms of winning the hearts and minds of Arab populations and boosting Turkey's popularity and prestige in the Middle East.

Yet this argument should be nuanced. In fact, while soap operas have increased Turkey's cultural popularity in the region and promoted a "Turkish way of life", they did not empower Turkey politically. For, being culturally attracted to Turkey does not lead Arab populations to take a political stance with Turkey; cultural power is not fungible into political power. For instance, while many people in the Middle East currently condemn Turkey's Syria policy, they continue to watch Turkish

---

[19] The poll has a margin of error of +/− 3.5%.

[20] Poll conducted in the framework of a Ph.D. thesis at Sciences Po Paris; unpublished.

soap operas. Therefore, if Turkey's soft power aims at increasing the country's political capacity in the region—especially when Turkish interests are threatened, it has—thus far—failed to produce the desired outcome (i.e., making Arab people side politically with Ankara and defend Turkey's interests in the Middle East).

Furthermore, when a political dispute erupts between Turkey and an Arab state, the effect of soft power becomes null. One example provides an excellent illustration of this phenomenon: when the Syrian revolution started and Turkey took a stance against Bashar al-Assad, the latter prohibited Syrian companies from dubbing Turkish soap operas. As a result, the entire Middle East market was deprived of Turkish soap operas, as all the dubbing activities were done in Syria. Similarly, following Turkey's alignment with Mohammad Morsi against the current Egyptian president Abdelfattah al-Sissi, the latter banned the broadcast of Turkish soap operas on Egyptian TV channels. Hence, any return to a hard power behaviour automatically nullifies the effectiveness of soft power.

Moreover, while Turkey's strong cultural presence in the Middle East through soap operas may have appealed to some Arab populations, it has also created negative reactions and feelings in certain segments of Arab societies. In fact, our interviews in Cairo, Beirut, Doha, and Erbil show that while soap operas are popular among the "masses" and the general public, they are nevertheless negatively perceived by the intelligentsia and the elite who see them as a "cultural invasion" or as "cultural imperialism".[21] Also, given the religious and cultural diversity of the Middle East populations, soap operas have failed to please everybody; while *Muhteşem Yüzyıl*, for instance, was generally popular, it nevertheless was subject to much criticism from certain conservative segments of the Sunni Arab community, because of the portrayal of Sultan Suleiman as a libertine who devotes much of his time for love adventures. Similarly, the soap opera *Gümüş* drew much criticism from religious circles for whom *Gümüş* exhibited a liberal lifestyle that might "corrupt the Muslim conservative values of Arab youth".[22] A Saudi sheikh went as far as to offer a pilgrimage to the hajj for all those who boycott Turkish soap operas, and

---

[21] For example, in a TV interview, a Lebanese scriptwriter, Claudia Marchalian, denounced Turkish soap operas as "a sign of Turkey's return to its imperialist ambitions".

[22] See fatwa by Sheikh AbdelazizAbdallah Al Sheikh: "Jugée « subversive » et « anti-islamique » : « Noor » s'attire les foudres des muftis saoudiens," Oumma, 14 September 2014, http://oumma.com/Jugee-subversive-et-anti-islamique.

a Syrian sheikh ruled that the picture of the Turkish character Mehmet on one's T-shirt invalidates his/her prayers (Buccianti 2010).

CONCLUSION

While Turkish soap operas have won the hearts and minds of Arab viewers, they have failed to increase Turkey's actual power capacity in the region. Yet the real relevance of these soap operas lies in their capacity to make Turkey highly present in the minds and imagination of Arab populations and to raise a debate in the Middle East around the so-called "Turkish model".[23] In fact, Turkey's soft power through soap operas, combined with the country's economic success and active foreign policy, made Turkey a hotly-debated subject in the region. Here is the true success of Turkey's soft power: the cultural presence of Turkey in the Middle East has drawn the attention of Arab populations to this country, and stirred their curiosity to understand the Turkish experience, or the so-called "Turkish model". In that sense, Turkish soap operas are a tool of foreign policy insofar as they have built a certain "brand" image of Turkey in the Middle East, thus paving the way for the country's political rapprochement with the region.

Finally, it is questionable whether Turkey's soft power would allow the country to have a sustainable and long-lasting presence in the Middle East. In this context, it is legitimate today to wonder whether Turkey has truly acquired a "place in the sun" in the region, or has simply achieved "fifteen minutes of fame" (Ülgen 2010).

---

[23] For analyses and studies on the so-called "Turkish model" and its relevance to the Arab world, see: Meliha Benli Altunışık (2011) "La question du 'modèle turc' ou le soft power de la Turquie au Moyen-Orient," in Dorothée Schmid, *La Turquie au Moyen-Orient: Le retour d'une puissance régionale?*, Paris, CNRS; Kemal Kirişci (2011), "Turkey's 'Demonstrative Effect' and the Transformation of the Middle East," *Insight Turkey*, Vol. 13, No. 2, 33–55; Emre İşeri and A. Oğuz Dilek (2012), "Beyond a Turkish Model in Transforming the Penetrated Middle East: The Nexus of Domestic Authority and International Prestige," *Ortadoğu Etütleri*, Vol. 3, No. 2, 119–142.

BIBLIOGRAPHY

Al Sheikh, Sheikh Abdelaziz Abdallah. "Jugée « subversive » et « anti-islamique » : « Noor » s'attire les foudres des muftis saoudiens." *Oumma*, 14 September 2014, http://oumma.com/Jugee-subversive-et-anti-islamique.

Altınay, Hakan. "Turkey's Soft Power: An Unpolished Gem or an Elusive Mirage?" *Insight Turkey* 10 No. 2 (2008), 55–66.

Benli Altunışık, Meliha. "Challenges to Turkey's Soft Power in the Middle East." *TESEV Policy Brief*, 2011. http://www.tesev.org.tr/assets/publications/file/21102013113608.pdf.

Benli Altunışık, Meliha. "La question du 'modèle turc' ou le soft power de la Turquie au Moyen-Orient." In Dorothée Schmid, *La Turquie au Moyen-Orient: Le retour d'une puissance régionale?*. Paris: CNRS, 2011.

Buccianti, Alexandra. "Dubbed Turkish soap operas conquering the Arab world: Social liberation or cultural alienation?" *Arab Media & Society*, 1. http://www.arabmediasociety.com/?article=735.

Burdy, Jean-Paul. "Retour sur le 'discours du balcon' et sur la victoire d'un nouveau leader régional." *OVIPOT*, 2011. http://ovipot.hypotheses.org/5873.

Davutoğlu, Ahmet. *Stratejik Derinlik: Türkiye'nin Uluslararası Konumu*. Istanbul: Küre Yayinlari, 2001. [Note that we are using the Arabic translation published by Al Jazeera Center for Studies in 2010].

Erdogan, Recep Tayyib. "My Country is Your Faithful Ally and Friend." *The Wall Street Journal*, 30 March 2003. http://online.wsj.com/news/articles/SB104907941058746300.

Grigoriadis, Ioannis. "The Davutoğlu Doctrine and Turkish Foreign Policy." *Hellenic Foundation for European and Foreign Policy (ELIAMEP)*, Working Paper 8, 2010.

Gonzales-Quijano, Yves. "L'attraction de la modernité "à la turque" dans le monde arabeà travers les productions audiovisuelles." In Schmidt, Dorothée (ed.) *La Turquie au Moyen-Orient: le retour d'une puissance régionale?*, 115–126. Paris: CNRS Editions, 2011.

Hale, William. *Turkish Foreign Policy Since 1774*. London: Routledge, 2002.

Handy, Nathaniel. "Turkey's shifting relations with its Middle East neighbors during the Davutoğlu era: History, power and policy." *Bilgi University Journal*, Special Issue 23 (2011), 61–85.

İşeri, Emre and Oğuz Dilek, A. "Beyond a Turkish Model in Transforming the Penetrated Middle East: The Nexus of Domestic Authority and International Prestige." *Ortadoğu Etütleri*, 3, No. 2 (2012), 119–142.

Jabbour, Jana. "Le monde selon Ankara." *Telos*, November 2011, http://www.telos-eu.com/fr/globalisation/politique-internationale/le-monde-selon-ankara.html.

Kalın, Ibrahim. "Soft Power and Public Diplomacy in Turkey", *Perceptions* 16 No. 3 (2011), 5–23. http://sam.gov.tr/wp-content/uploads/2012/01/ibrahim_kalin.pdf.

Kirişci, Kemal. "Turkey's 'Demonstrative Effect' and the Transformation of the Middle East." *Insight Turkey*, 13, No. 2 (2011), 33–55.

Kutlay, Mustafa and Dincer Bahadir, Osman. "Turkey's power capacity in the Middle East: Limits of the possible." *USAK Report* 12, No. 4 (2012). http://www.usak.org.tr/dosyalar/rapor/ctZTC1gAenLx7HaF8Gi7oip-20CoDVX.pdf.

Nye, Joseph. *Soft Power: The Means to Success in World Politics*. New York: Public Affairs, 2005.

Öner, Selcen. "Soft Power in Turkish Foreign Policy: New Instruments and Challenges." *Euxeinos* 10 (2013), 7–15. http://acturca.info/2013/05/27/soft-power-in-turkish-foreign-policy-new-instruments-and-challenges/.

Rotivel, Agnès. "Les novelas turques, un modèle qui s'exporte", *La Croix*, 2011. http://www.la-croix.com/Actualite/Monde/Les-novelas-turques-un-modele-qui-s-exporte-_NG_-2011-06-06-622207.

Sözen, Ahmet. "A Paradigm Shift in Turkish Foreign Policy: Transition and Challenges", *Turkish Studies* 11, No. 1, (2010): 103–123. http://psi305.cankaya.edu.tr/uploads/files/Shift%20in%20TFP.pdf.

Telhami, Shibley. "The 2011 Arab Public Opinion Poll." *Brookings*, 2011. http://www.brookings.edu/research/reports/2011/11/21-arab-public-opinion-telhami.

Today's Zaman. "Turkey's Soft Power on the Rise Despite Challenges." 2013. http://www.todayszaman.com/newsDetail_openPrintPage.action?newsId=311464.

Turkish Statistical Institute. www.turkstat.gov.tr.

Ülgen, Sinan. "A place in the sun or fifteen minutes of fame? Understanding Turkey's new foreign policy", *Carnegie Papers*, 2010. http://carnegieendowment.org/files/turkey_new_foreign_policy.pdf.

CHAPTER 8

Locating Emirati Filmmaking within Globalizing Media Ecologies

Dale Hudson

A few Kuwaiti feature films appeared in international film festivals during the 1970s; a few Bahraini ones during the 1990s. It was not until the past decade, however, that the Arab Gulf would again register to international audiences—not through feature films but through international film festivals held in Dubai, Doha, and Abu Dhabi that attracted top talent from around the world, offered generous prizes, and sometimes disappeared as suddenly as they appeared. While sensationalized stories attracted foreign media attention, the festivals provide much-needed development and financial support to filmmakers, recognizing and amplifying perspectives often excluded from festivals elsewhere, as well as prominent venues for their exhibition. Filmmaking in Kuwait, Bahrain, the United Arab Emirates (UAE), and Qatar share common Khaleeji ("from the Gulf") experiences that differ from those experienced elsewhere in the Middle East—yet also differ amongst themselves in terms of constructing, consolidating, and contesting national identities and of

D. Hudson (✉)
New York University Abu Dhabi, New York, NY, USA

© The Author(s) 2017
N. Lenze et al. (eds.), *Media in the Middle East*,
DOI 10.1007/978-3-319-65771-4_8

developing institutions for exhibition of domestically produced films and for active film cultures to sustain production.

Emirati filmmaking develops within very different global conditions than ones that shaped national (e.g., French or Japanese), regional (e.g., African or Latin American), and ethnic (e.g., African American or Arab) frameworks for conceptualizing filmmaking. Over the past quarter-century, globalized neoliberalism has shifted the terms by which all states, regardless of their size or power, define themselves at home and to the world. Since the particularities of Emirati filmmaking do not always register under extant frameworks, Emirati filmmaking provides an important site for critical inquiry that generate new questions within larger fields, such as film studies or Arab media studies. It contributes to the devising of new frameworks to address unacknowledged biases and oversights in current frameworks, not only limiting frameworks of national cinema, genre, and authorship that have been depoliticized by festivals and marketing, but also the persistence of colonial-era expectations of cultural verisimilitude in so-called nonwestern media that reject the nuances of non-Western modernities.[1]

This chapter situates the question of *locating* Emirati filmmaking within the context of competing expectations about film's audience and purpose within a relatively small, yet affluent place. Unlike most formerly colonized places, the UAE did not undergo the kinds of violent anticolonial struggles elsewhere. It came into its petroleum revenue at a time when oil-producing states were better equipped to contest the unfair concessions to foreign companies that had delayed and prevented postindependence development in other states. At the same time, Emiratis are a numerical minority of about ten percent of the overall UAE population. The UAE witnessed larger influxes of foreigners after independence rather than during colonialism. Emirati filmmaking, thus, negotiates different challenges and opportunities. Despite a series of setbacks,

---

[1] Historical examples of such denials of non-Western modernities include mid-twentieth-century misperceptions that the early narrative films of Satyajit Ray and Ousmane Sembène were documentaries. See, for example, Chandak Sengoopta, "'The Universal Film for All of Us, Everywhere in the World': Satyajit Ray's *Pather Panchali* (1955) and the Shadow of Robert Flaherty," *Historical Journal of Film, Radio and Television* 29.3 (September 2009) 277–293 and essays in *Ousmane Sembène: Dialogue with Critics and Writers*, eds. Samba Gadjigo, Ralph Faulkingham, Thomas Cassirer, and Reinhard Sander (Amherst: University of Massachusetts Press, 1993).

uncertainties, and controversies around its major film festivals, grassroots and state agencies in the UAE have created spaces for a new generation of Emirati feature filmmakers who began by making short films, supported by less internationally visible institutions, such as Emirates Film Competition (EFC) from 2001 until 2014, Gulf Film Festival (GFF) from 2007 to 2013, and GCC Film Festival's 2012 edition in Doha and 2016 edition in Abu Dhabi. Hundreds of short films have been produced, ranging from first-time films by students to award-winning films by established filmmakers. The topics range from satirical examinations of cultural norms and political critiques of social conventions to documentaries and dramas on everyday life.

Emirati filmmakers have produced more than forty narrative and documentary features since Ali Al Abdul's *Abr Sabeel/The Wayfarer* (UAE 1988), which is generally considered to be the first Emirati-produced feature film. Often exhibited only at festivals, the theatrical exhibition of Emirati films has increased gradually since Hani Al Shaibani's *Al Hilm/A Dream* (UAE 2004), which became the first Emirati film to screen theatrically in 2005. Previously, Emiratis only saw images of the UAE in foreign films, primarily Bollywood ones, which often use Dubai as a stand-in for an Indian city. A little more than a decade later, three features screened at the same time in commercial theaters in October 2016. This output and visibility is prolific for a place without the conventional infrastructure established to nurture an active film culture, such as a cinémathèque or film journal where serious debates can take place—or even a film school for technical training at the graduate level. A common frustration among Emirati filmmakers is the perceived willingness of Emirati audiences to consume Emirati television shows at home but not to attend commercial screenings of Emirati films in theaters. In part, the situation extends ones throughout the Arabian Peninsula, where popular Egyptian films have been screened privately for decades. Emirati filmmakers struggle to convene audiences who will arrive at cinemas with an enthusiasm comparable to the existing enthusiasm for the latest Bollywood release. While such a situation is hardly unique, the context of the UAE is particular.

Misunderstood as "peripheral" to history—or dismissed as a "cultural desert" with occasional "cultural oases," the UAE offers perspectives that reveal deep historical connections across the Indian Ocean and into the Red Sea and the Mediterranean Sea, so that identity and culture unfold "at large," to borrow Arjun Appadurai's term for modernity, rather than according to the territorially or ethnically/racially bounded national, regional, and global configurations often used to locate cultural production.[2] Emirati—and more broadly Khaleeji—perspectives challenge assumptions about the Middle East as a place defined by civil wars, religious fundamentalisms, failed states, neocolonial dictators, mass poverty, displaced refugees, foreign occupations, and oppression of women. They signal other aspects of life, including controversies and aspirations amongst a demographically young population.

Convening Popular and Academic Audiences for Gulf Filmmaking

English-language books on Arab, Middle Eastern, or Middle Eastern and North African (MENA) filmmaking often foreground conflict and violence as defining the region. As such, they have not widely considered Emirati films since most concern other topics that do not conform to this preconception.[3] Emirati feature films have infrequently screened at the region's oldest and most prestigious festivals, where critics and audiences share common concerns and promote Arab and Muslim perspectives not widely included in festivals in Berlin, Busan, Cannes, Toronto, or Venice. Unlike the pan-Arab/pan-African ambition of Les Journées Cinématographiques de Carthage (JCC aka Carthage Film Festival) and the commercial ambition for Arabic-language films of the Cairo

---

[2] Arjun Appadurai, *Modernity at Large: Cultural Dimensions of Globalization* (Minneapolis: University of Minnesota Press, 1995).

[3] Viola Shafik, *Arab Cinema: History and Cultural Identity* (1998/2007), revised edition (New York: Oxford University Press, 2016); *Companion Encyclopedia of Middle Eastern and North African Film*, ed. Oliver Leaman (London: Routledge, 2001); Roy Armes, *Postcolonial Images: Studies in North African Film* (Bloomington: Indiana University Press, 2005); *The Cinema of North Africa and the Middle East*, ed. Gönül Dönmez-Colin (London: Wallflower, 2007); Lina Khatib, *Filming the Modern Middle East: Politics in the Cinemas of Hollywood and the Arab World* (London: I.B. Tauris, 2009); *Film in the Middle East and North Africa: Creative Dissidence*, ed. Josef Gugler (Austin: University of Texas Press, 2011); Gayatri Devi, *Humor in Middle Eastern Cinema* (Detroit: Wayne State University Press, 2014); Roy Armes, *New Voices in Arab Cinema* (Bloomington: Indiana University Press, 2015); *Ten Arab Filmmakers: Political Dissent and Social Critique*, ed. Josef Gugler (Austin: University of Texas Press, 2015); Kamran Rastegar, *Surviving Images: Cinema, War, and Cultural Memory in the Middle East* (Oxford: Oxford University Press, 2015).

International Film Festival (CIFF), the festivals in Dubai, Doha, and Abu Dhabi—Dubai International Film Festival (DIFF), Doha Tribeca Film Festival (DTFF), and Abu Dhabi Film Festival (ADFF)—emerged alongside strategic planning for twenty-first–century post-oil economies in the Dubai Strategic Plan, Qatar National Vision 2030, and Abu Dhabi Vision 2030. The festivals and the films, thus, signal a different moment in the history of the Middle East, one that claims its right to determine its own articulation of modernity within the current flows and networks of globalization.

Such strategic plans extend earlier state initiatives and individual commitments. Qatar's commitment to the arts, sciences, and education is articulated through the Qatar Foundation, launched in 1995 and establishing Education City in 1997; the television network Al Jazeera, launched in 1996; Qatar Museums, launched in 2005 to oversee the Museum of Islamic Art, Mathaf: the Arab Museum of Art, and other museums, including one dedicated to slavery in the region; and the 2010 opening of Katara, the cultural village foundation, which houses the Doha Film Institute (DFI) and hosted the DTFF from 2009 to 2012 and now hosts the Ajyal Youth Film Festival and Qumra Film Festival. In the UAE, the two largest festivals (ADFF and DIFF) were primarily supported by agencies in the emirates of Abu Dhabi and Dubai to manage culture and heritage, tourism, and business.[4] The UAE had already figured prominently in the art world through the Sharjah Biennale since 1993 and the Sharjah Art Foundation since 2009. In Abu Dhabi, Michele Bambling and Safiya Al Maskari's *Lest We Forget* initiative transforms private photographs and family heirlooms into books and installations on cultural heritage, recently exhibited at Warehouse 421, a renovated industrial space at the port, comparable to spaces in Dubai's Alserkal Avenue. Major projects in development include branches of the Louvre and Guggenheim museums in Abu Dhabi and the Art Jameel complex in Dubai, along with an acquisition fund for the Metropolitan Museum of New York. Initiatives to develop an arts culture, which have included productive discussions on topics ranging from censorship to cultural imperialism anticipate the development a film culture to guide future directions for Emirati filmmaking.

---

[4] ADFF was initially branded as the Middle East International Film Festival (MEIFF).

It seems improbable that Emirati filmmaking can follow the "build it and they will come" model of aspirational planning that made Dubai famous for its free port and free zones. Many of the strongest foundations for Emirati filmmaking and film culture have been initiated by individuals, working both with and without state agencies. Filmmaking ultimately bears the responsibility of convening its own audiences and developing its own active film culture through grassroots initiatives such as the EFC, which was conceived by Ali Al Jabri, Nawaf Al Janahi, and Masoud Amralla Al Ali, then integrated into ADFF years later. EFC screenings foreground indigenous (rather than international film festival) concerns. Launched in 2013, the Emirati Cinema Campaign (ECC) is another effort that involves taking to the streets on bicycles to raise awareness about Emirati filmmaking and its cultural importance. Emirati short or feature films are programmed in festivals outside the region, particularly Arab diasporas. Emirati short films are also programmed at screenings hosted by academic organizations, such as the Middle East Studies Association (MESA) and the Association for Arabian Gulf and Peninsula Studies (AGAPS). Short films are sometimes included in programs of foreign films hosted by foreign cultural agencies, such as the Alliance Française and the Goethe-Institut. Others are occasionally included as in-flight entertainment along with content about the UAE targeted at tourists and business travelers. Due to the politics of festival premieres, only twice have Emirati features actually opened Emirati festivals: Ali F. Mostafa's self-funded *City of Life* (UAE 2009) opened DIFF and his state-supported *From A to B* (UAE 2014) opened ADFF. Most Emirati films are exhibited at non-theatrical venues, including cultural centers, schools, pop-up cinemas, and online platforms, such as iTunes and YouTube. Both features and shorts, however, have received little commercial theatrical exhibition within the UAE until recently (Fig. 8.1).

Film clubs offer a locally oriented venue for nurturing film cultures. Unlike Kuwait, where film clubs continue from the pre-independence period, film clubs in the UAE have been launched and discontinued, contingent upon the resources and dedication of individuals. Recent examples include Nayla Al Khaja's Scene Film Club in Dubai (2007–present) and Aflam Film Club in Abu Dhabi (2012–2014), Anasy Media's Documentary Film Club in Abu Dhabi (2011–2012), and Butheina Kazim's Cinema Akil in Dubai (2014–present), which will soon become a cinémathèque in Alserkal Avenue. In Abu Dhabi, Mohammad

Fig. 8.1 A screening by Cinema Akil, Dubai. Image credit: Cinema Akil

Khawaja programs pop-up screenings for Cinema Space. The Abu Dhabi International Book Fair hosts a Black Box Cinema with shorts and features from the MENA region. The Sharjah Art Foundation hosts screenings, and the Abu Dhabi Media Zone Authority (MZA)'s production unit, twofour54, continued SANAD ("support" in Arabic) Fund, which offered pre- and post-production support from 2010 until a year after cancelling ADFF, which premièred SANAD-funded films. One of the most productive grassroots institutions is the Zayed University Middle East Film Festival (ZUMEFF), established in 2010 as a senior project by two students, AlYazyah Al Falasi and Reema Majed, under the direction of their professor, Alia Yunis. The festival involves students in all aspects of the festival. Other universities, including New York University Abu Dhabi (NYUAD), sponsor public screenings of Emirati features.[5] More

---

[5]ADFF and the NYUAD Institute collaborated on six film series between 2011 and 2014. The NYUADI regularly screens an Emirati feature during the first month of its annual program.

commercially, Bollywood Parks Dubai has augmented cinephilia for Mumbai's film industry amongst residents and tourists alike.

The permanent postponement of GFF in 2013 and the abrupt cancellation of ADFF and EFC in 2015 foreclosed three of the most important venues for filmmaking from and about the UAE and reduced both the number and quality of public spaces for local perspectives on the Gulf. The decision to end ADFF initially attracted negative international attention, particularly amongst Arab filmmakers, producers, and audiences, regarding the MZA's business model of "nurturing local talent" via massive tax incentives for foreign productions.[6] Although the number of Hollywood productions in the UAE has increased, purportedly offering professional opportunities (i.e., mentoring and apprenticeship) to Emiratis, Hollywood's long history of profiting and propagating anti-Arab and anti-Islam sentiments raises concerns that such an alliance might have unanticipated consequences. Although Hollywood accepted the risk to produce numerous so-called Judeo-christian biblical epics, it was unwilling to support Mustafa Akkad's cinematic adaptation of the Qar'anic narrative of the Prophet Mohammad's life in *Al-Risala/The Message* (Lebanon–Libya–Kuwait–Morocco–UK 1976), which was eventually supported in part by Libyan dictator Muammar Gaddafi. Hollywood typically depicts Gulf Arabs as "oil-rich" buffoons or as "veiled" women whose only agency comes through shopping, in films sometimes banned from UAE cinemas, yet always readily available on download, DVD, or BluRay. Hollywood films enjoy a cultural power unknown to some of the earliest features produced by Khaleeji filmmakers, such as Khaled Al Siddiq in Kuwait and Khalifa Shaheen in Bahrain, which are not readily available today. Collaboration, however, might reduce Hollywood antipathy towards Arabs and Muslims through the soft power of film production and, more significantly, film financing.

Optimistic recent developments include Cinema Akil's programs, notably "Meet the New Generation" programmed by Özge Calafato on new filmmaking in the Middle East that includes the UAE. Another

---

[6]For examples of such responses, see: Nadeem Hanif, "Abu Dhabi Film Festival Closure Met with Shock," *The National* (07 May 2015): http://www.thenational.ae/uae/abu-dhabi-film-festival-closure-met-with-shock; Nick Vivarelli, "Abu Dhabi Film Festival Scrapped After Eight Editions," *Variety* (07 May 2015): http://variety.com/2015/film/festivals/abu-dhabi-film-festival-scrapped-after-eight-editions-1201489683/.

is the launch of Minaa, a public-engagement and distribution scheme, founded by Creative Documentary Platform (Jordan) and MAD Solutions (Egypt). Minaa VOD (video-on-demand) specializes in "creative docs from the Arab world, of different lengths, genres and styles," including *As One: The Autism Project* (UAE 2014; dir. Hana Makki), produced by Image Nation Abu Dhabi.[7] Another recent online initiative is a collaboration between DIFF and Image Nation Abu Dhabi in the Support Arab Cinema campaign, which solicits individuals to support theatrical exhibition of Arab films and filmmakers, actors, and other film professionals to become "ambassadors" for Arab film.[8] For several years, Dubai-based crowd-funding platform Aflamnah ("our films" in Arabic) offered alternatives and supplements to other financing sources.[9] Also encouraging, Dhabi Gulf Films has produced three feature films—*Mazraat Yado/Grandmother's Farm* (UAE 2013; dir. Ahmed Zain), *Mazraat Yado 2/Grandmother's Farm 2* (UAE 2015; dir. Ahmed Zain), and *Hajwala* (UAE 2016; dir. Alin Bin Matar and Ibrahim Bin Mohammad)—that have screened commercially and attracted large audiences. The films foreground Emirati culture as modern rather than "exotic" or "traditional." The first films focus on horror and mystery during a weekend holiday, the third focuses on drift racing (*hajwala* in Arabic). Such initiatives define a wide array of Emirati filmmaking from commercial genre films to art-house fare to documentary (Fig. 8.2).

For people living outside the UAE, such initiatives might not register. A consequence of the limited theatrical visibility of Emirati perspectives on a regular basis to counter the historical visibility of foreign film production—mostly Egyptian and Indian, though more visibly Hollywood—allows foreign assumptions and suspicions to frame perceptions about the UAE, often based on ones about neighboring Saudi Arabia and Iran. In this regard, education—beyond technical training and professional tutelage opportunities—is critical, so that aspiring filmmakers can communicate their stories not only to fellow Emiratis but also to the world. A danger in not controlling the narrative through

---

[7] "A Word about Minaa," *Minaa* website (n.d.; accessed 06 June 2016): http://minaa.org/about/.

[8] Homepage, *Support Arab Cinema* website (n.d.; accessed 06 June 2016): http://supportarabcinema.com/en/.

[9] Homepage, *Aflamnah* website (n.d.; accessed 06 June 2016): https://www.aflamnah.com/.

Fig. 8.2 An outdoor screening at Cinema Akil, Alserkal Avenue, Dubai. Image credit: Cinema Akil

media production by training aspiring filmmakers in critical thinking about film styles and history has been international attention to what is framed as excessive luxury and exploitative labor policies. Criticism about possible human rights violations, which peaked in 2006, surged again in relation to the large-scale construction projects, such as the stadiums for the 2022 World Cup in Doha and the museums on Abu Dhabi's cultural district on Saadiyat Island. Prices paid at auction for the purchase of art and the amount of awards the film festivals are easy targets for ridicule based on misperceptions, such as a story that Islamic law required Pablo Picasso's *Les Femmes d'Alger (Version O)/Women of Algiers* (1955) to be hidden from public view in Qatar due to the partial nudity of its abstracted subject.

Such media attention obscures populations of middle-class Emiratis, who do not keep "exotic" animals as pets or drive gold-plated sports cars with special-number plates, as well as large middle-class South Asian communities who have lived in the Gulf for generations. Such stereotypes are often inserted into foreign films as markers of authenticity, much like camels walking on highways. Foreign media attention a limited number of realities erases indigenous methods that operate in more discreet and culturally aware ways to address social inequities and human rights.[10] Foreign assumptions take a shallow view on history of the Trucial States. Many institutions governing labor, including the *kafala* (sponsorship) system, extend colonial and imperial structures, such as temporary and conditional legal status under British Empire/British Commonwealth immigration policies and racially segregated housing and racially hierarchical wages from US company towns. The system has been occasionally exploited and unevenly regulated. Although Gulf states only achieved formal independence four or five decades ago, their high gross national income (GNI) tends to reinforce assumptions that change should be more than incremental; that is, accelerated development is expected to include accelerated changes to inherited systems.[11] Limited media attention also tends to obscure the historical presence of South Asians, Iranians, and Africans, and other Arabs, particularly Yemenis, whose children and grandchildren now have Emirati citizenship, by assuming the western fantasy of historically homogeneous nation-states—something that erupted into violent white nationalism during recent elections and referendums in northwestern Europe—can be used to map and define the UAE.[12] Social differences within and between the seven emirates of the UAE can also be substantial.

Locating Emirati filmmaking, then, opens discussion to consider different configurations of variables (e.g., economic power, media infrastructure) that organize critical inquiry. Whether Emirati filmmaking will address itself primarily to residents, to both citizens (nationals) and expatriates (foreigners), or to a broader audience—whether pan-Arab,

---

[10] Protests by the artist/activist collective Gulf Labor over the living and working conditions for migrant laborers on the future construction of a Guggenheim Museum are organized around reorienting neoliberal discourses of branding to counter neoliberal practices of flexible labor. Andrew Ross describes the tactical maneuvers the Gulf Labor Coalition in "Leveraging the Brand: A History of Gulf Labor," in his edited volume *The Gulf: High Culture/Hard Labor* (New York: OR Books, 2015): 11–35.

[11] According to the World Bank, Qatar ranks number one in terms of GNI according to the purchasing power parity (PPP) method in 2014; Kuwait, six; UAE, eight; and Bahrain, 39. For comparison, the United States ranks 16; Russia, 63; China (exclusive of Macau and Hong Kong), 105; and India, 148.

[12] Citizenship is granted automatically to children with Emirati or stateless fathers. Children with Emirati mothers can apply for citizenship at majority.

pan-Gulf, or international—remains to be determined, as does the question of whether the UAE will break with some of the dominant models for film production in the regions that converge around the Arab Gulf: (1) Egyptian, Indian, Iranian, and Turkish commercial film production, which generally prioritizes entertainment value and thus typically normalizes conservative politics and social hierarchies based on sex, gender, class, caste, race/ethnicity, and religion and conditional inclusion of minoritized groups within national debates; (2) Arab, Iranian, Kurdish, and Turkish art films, which counter narratives of commercial cinema yet are often restrained by dependency on European funding that can involve censorship, self-censorship, or "pandering"; (3) Israeli art films, which are heavily supported by state funding for production, distribution, and exhibition at international festivals, often as *hasbara* (state propaganda) around selective inclusivity of LBGTQ perspectives (e.g., "pink-washing" the occupation of Palestine) and alleged democratic exceptionalism despite Israel's recent classification by the United Nations as an apartheid state; (4) Indian art films, funded by both state and private financing that extend a tradition of criticism of state and society, including religious majorities, that dates to the 1950s; (5) monetization of Tunisia, Jordan, and Morocco as locations for foreign films—along with Israel as a stand-in for sovereign Arab states—without regard to content and potential for collateral damage to international reputation; (6) Arab films produced for domestic audiences only, often in Arabic dialects that do not travel as easily as Cairene or Modern Standard Arabic, such as Moroccan films in Darija (Moroccan Arabic) funded by the state through presale for television; and (7) emerging commercial filmmaking in East Africa modeled after Bollywood and Nollywood, such as "Swahiliwood" in Kenya, "Somaliwood" in the Somali diaspora, and "Gulfiwood" between the Gulf and Kerala.

In light of the UAE's very different historical, cultural, and financial context from these other states, regions, or ethnicities/race, it seems unlikely that any extant model would attract sustainable audiences without modifications.[13] Emiratis may be a numerical minority in the UAE, but they exercise economic and cultural power at home and abroad.

---

[13] In *World Politics Since 1945*, 9th edition (London: Routledge, 2013), Peter Calvocoressi defines OPEC states as a "Fourth World" insofar as "wealth distinguishes them dramatically from the world's poor" yet "solidarity enabled them to play a forceful role in international affairs" (781) through oil pricing during the 1970s.

Emirati filmmaking, thus, takes the form of financing Arab films that may have little to do with the UAE. Emerging models within the Gulf include the financial support of festivals and institutes, including the DFI's Grants Programme, SANAD Fund under ADFF and Enjaaz Fund under DIFF. Established in 2007, the Dubai Film Market (DFM) has supported more than 270 projects primarily by Arab filmmakers but also by non-Arab filmmakers "from the Middle East, Asia, and Africa." In terms of film festivals for exhibition and development of an active and critical film culture, the historical models for the MENA region—JCC since 1966 and CIFF since 1976—have been less significant in the conceptualization of DIFF and ADFF. Although situated in very different historical and economic moments, the EFC and GFF were efforts to convene some of the dynamic debates and discussion about art and politics of the JCC.

For this reason, locating Emirati filmmaking involves looking to established and emerging models of both film production and exhibition that have not widely been considered in relation to the Gulf emirates due to assumptions about its geographical location within the Middle East.[14] Locating Emirati filmmaking can involve looking to policies in Singapore and New Zealand, indigenous media practices throughout Latin America and Asia Pacific, alternative commercial models after media convergence in Nigeria's Nollywood and South Korea's Hallyuwood and K-dramas, and exhibition venues that allow indigenous and commercial media to share a single festival in México's Morelia Film Festival. Emirati filmmaking complicates extant models, thereby prompting us to look beyond concepts from the last century that prioritized Hollywood commercial and European art cinemas as so-called global models.[15] With digital media convergence that destabilizes strict definitions of film and television, models for filmmaking emerge in non-theatrical narrative media, including soap operas and television serials from Egypt, Pakistan, Turkey,

---

[14] The Abu Dhabi Tourism and Culture Authority (TCA) announced geographical rebranding from "Middle East" to "Arabian Peninsula," seen as more attractive in customer surveys. Craig Platt, "Abu Dhabi Tourism: Tourism Body No Longer Wants to be Associated with 'Middle East'," *Traveller* (08 September 2016): http://www.traveller. com.au/abu-dhabi-tourism-tourism-body-no-longer-wants-to-be-associated-with-middle-east-grbsvl#ixzz4Kis2CkaW.

[15] See: Stephen Crofts, "Reconceptualizing National Cinema/s," *Quarterly Review of Film and Video* 14.3 (1993): 49–67.

and Syria, as well as web series, which have become important cultural productions in places without established practices for cinema-going, notably Saudi Arabia, by reworking on television formats from the United States and Egypt.

So-called South-to-South (S2S) models of cultural transmissions are increasingly significant despite Hollywood efforts to dominate global media through the auspices of the World Trade Organization (WTO). Emirati filmmaking might turn to K-dramas and Nollywood in much the same way that Nigerian and Pakistani filmmakers turned to Bollywood mediated through local television practices as an *alternative* to Hollywood—producing representational strategies that might be influenced by Hollywood but draw significantly upon indigenous cultural frameworks to convey the particularities of alternative modernities.[16] Indeed, Mostafa's *City of Life* emerged from an idea of making a film about a Bollywood superstar Shahrukh Khan lookalike. It actually challenges the colonial arrogance of the British press coverage of Dubai as seeming like Disneyland or Second Life by adopting conventions from Bollywood, suggesting that Indian models are typically more culturally relevant than British ones. Majid Abdulrazak produced multiple language versions (e.g., Arabic, Farsi, and Urdu) of his second feature, *Eqaab* (UAE 2006), in an effort to gain theatrical exhibition in Pakistan, whose cinematic links to the Arab Gulf date to the super-hit *Dubai Chalo/Let's Go to Dubai* (Pakistan 1979; dir. Haider Chaudhry). Orientation, then, is not always directed towards Hollywood/Europe. Like audiences in Nigeria and Pakistan, ones in the UAE and broader Arab Gulf can turn to films and series to ease anxieties over accelerated changes initiated by neoliberalism and other aspects of globalization, as Madhava Prasad described among Indian audiences during the last century, and as young Saudi audiences turn to narrowcasting on YouTube from startups like Creative Culture Catalyst (3C) and Talfaz11. tv rather than broadcasting on television from corporate giant Rotana as an alternative to Saudi state television.[17] The recent *Barakah Yoqabil*

---

[16]Shahnaz Khan, "Consumer Citizens and Troubling Desires: Reading Hindi Cinema in Pakistan," *Studies in South Asian Film & Media* 3.2 (November 2012): 66. Khan draws upon Brian Larkin's work on Bollywood's popularity with Nigerian audiences, as well as Arjun Appadurai and Carol Breckenridge's work on modernities.

[17]Madhava Prasad, *Ideology of the Hindi Film: A Historical Construction* (New Delhi: Oxford University Press, 1998).

Barakah/Barakah Meets Barakah (Saudi Arabia 2016; dir. Mahmoud Sabbagh) experiments with extending situation comedy into a feature-length romantic comedy, starring Hisham Fegeeh known widely around the Gulf for his role on the web series *La Yakthar/Zip It* (Saudi Arabia 2010–present).[18]

COUNTERING FOREIGN ASSUMPTIONS AND CULTIVATING CRITICAL SELF-REPRESENTATIONS

Reconfiguring frameworks allows for an opening of assumptions that come to bear on thinking about media and the UAE. International film festivals historically capitalized on art films from the MENA region that are critical of *particular* circumstances but may easily confused by foreign audiences under *generalized* assumptions, including white-savior myths that Muslim women do, in fact, need saving *from* Islam.[19] In so doing, international festivals exclude other stories, such as ones about families, friendship, and work. Foreign perceptions within film and media studies also tend to subsume Emirati filmmaking under assumptions and expectations around issues that gain international visibility through news media. They reproduce narratives that deny nonwestern modernities to necessitate Western interventions, whether economic or military. The hyper-visibility of such a narrow set of topics reproduce assumptions that women's lives are determined solely by the presence or absence of "the veil," for example, or that religious leaders and non-elected political leaders are despots by definition. They look for conflict as endemic to the region whose history was often centered upon religious and cultural tolerance before the advent of European colonialism. The preference by programmers and distributors of art-house films comparably ignores forms of polity and agency for women through practices of Islam and/or hijab along with forms of patriarchy that have less to do with clothing or religion than with culture and custom.

---

[18] For a discussion of Saudi web series, see: Dale Hudson and Patricia R. Zimmermann, *Thinking through Digital Media: Transnational Environments and Locative Places* (New York: Palgrave Macmillan, 2015), 156–160.

[19] Lila Abu-Lughod, *Do Muslim Women Need Saving?* (Cambridge, MA: Harvard University Press, 2013).

Orientalisms continue to frame expectations about the Arab Gulf, through some have been appropriated and reconfigured in ways that reinforce the relevance of Edward Said's landmark trilogy on the topic.[20] Postcolonial and transnational feminist scholarship points to how earlier models of area studies also obscures critical inquiry in what Ella Shohat describes as a "discursive quarantine of fields of inquiry" that hinder rather than facilitate knowledge production.[21] Collaborations with Hollywood can be incrementally helpful in terms of industry professionalism yet also damaging. Foreign misrepresentations of Gulf Arabs are transformed for profit, exemplified in Hollywood films such as *Syriana* (USA 2005; dir. Stephen Gaghan) and *The Kingdom* (USA–Germany 2007; dir. Peter Berg), which offer more nuanced representations of diverse political positions within the region but nonetheless trade in negative stereotypes and reduce the region to a zone of irreconcilable and timeless conflict.

The potentially damaging effects of such films increase as anti-Arab and anti-Muslim stereotypes have proliferated on US television. The popular and acclaimed cable series *Homeland* (USA 2011–present; cr. Gideon Raff), for example, is a Hollywood adaptation of *Hatufim/ Prisoners of War* (Israel 2010–2012; cr. Gideon Raff) that mobilizes US national exceptionalism mediated by white feminism (albeit with a critique of abilism) to normalize reactionary agendas that often appear to reinforce Israeli state interests more than US ones.[22] Israeli military interests become confused with US ones over Hezbollah; the hostage crisis in Tehran (1979–1980) is restaged to encourage opposition to normalized US–Iranian diplomatic relations, which Israel's government opposed; and fears over attacks in European cities by Daesh

---

[20] *Orientalism* (New York: Pantheon, 1978); *The Question of Palestine* (New York: Vintage, 1979/1992); *Covering Islam: How the Media and the Experts Determine How We See the Rest of the World* (New York: Pantheon, 1981/1997).

[21] Ella Shohat, "Area Studies, Transnationalism, and the Feminist Production of Knowledge," *Signs* 26:4 (2001): 1270.

[22] In the context of the United States, "white feminism" refers to non-intersectional feminism that universalizes the experiences of white, straight, cisgender females over the experiences of women of color and queer women, thus rejecting or overlooking the significance of intersectionality. The term joins comparable ones—mainstream feminism, first-wave feminism—yet marks the racial dimension of white privilege that allows white women to benefited disproportionately from Affirmative Action policies. In a transnational context, white feminism can be linked to global capitalism and cultural imperialism.

are all rendered in a television narrative with high production values. The use of downtown Ouarzazate and the UNESCO World Heritage Site of Aït Benhaddou (an Amazigh or "Berber" village) in Morocco as downtown Abu Dhabi suggest an unwillingness to acknowledge Emirati modernization. Since such orientalisms continue to frame Khaleejis as indistinguishable from other Arabs for many international audiences, it is unlikely that they will also distinguish the UAE from Saudi Arabia or Iran any more than many *Homeland* fans could distinguish Hamra Street in Ras Beirut, where episodes of the series were set and which is known for its trendy shops and hipster cafés, from the back alleys of Jaffa in Israel, where these episodes were filmed. Although *24* (USA 2001–2014; cr. Joel Surnow and Robert Cochran) had previously stood as the benchmark for Islamophobic US television, *Homeland* appears eager to overtake it.

During the 1970s oil embargo, when the Organization of the Petroleum Exporting Countries (OPEC) regulated oil supply to critique Western imperialism, Hollywood orientalism refigured its classical stereotype of avaricious and lascivious "sheiks" (rather than *sheikhs*) as Gulf Arabs. More recently, Hollywood writers and producers added financially liberated "veiled" women to accompany their covetous "sheik" stereotypes, most visibly in *Sex and the City 2* (USA 2010; dir. Michael Patrick King), set in Abu Dhabi yet shot in Morocco. The film did not receive approval for theatrical exhibition in the UAE. Film scholars cite it as an example of Hollywood filmmaking that profited handsomely despite US critics largely panning its racism and misogyny.[23] In addition to its flagrant orientalism, Liza Minnelli's musical performance of Beyoncé's "Single Ladies" literally whitewashes an anthem that anticipates the African American singer's defiant racial consciousness in her later *Lemonade* album, into what becomes a celebration of queer and queer-friendly white-national exceptionalism, that is, what Jasbir Puar labels "homonationalism."[24] The film's financial and popular success with US and other foreign audiences suggests a willingness to overlook Hollywood's racism and sexism, particularly the homoerotics

---

[23] The film is cited as an example of one that did well at the box office despite negative reviews in Glyn Davis, Kay Dickinson, Lisa Patti, and Amy Villarejo, *Film Studies: A Global Introduction* (New York: Routledge, 2015): 356–357.

[24] Jasbir K. Puar, *Terrorist Assemblages: Homonationalism in Queer Times* (Durham: Duke University Press, 2007).

of orientalism, when it is distanced from the United States and reenergized by antiquated white-feminist and white-queer pleasures from the 1970s.[25] In fact, the narrative celebrates its rejection of cultural difference with a fireworks display as its oldest and most materialist protagonist, Samantha (Kim Cattrall), rejects the allure of so-called petrodollars for the presumed liberty and freedom to have sex on the beach in the Hamptons. Like the series before it, the film identifies a space for white, middle-class, cisgender, queer-friendly, secular women that seldom allows for other perspectives apart from politely phrased condescension. The UAE is merely an exotic and backwards setting for over-privileged, queer-friendly yet racially insensitive, white women to "discover" themselves.

At the same time, local film production cannot merely invert foreign negative stereotypes into positive ones or filling in the gaps of foreign erasures of local cultures with uncritical representations.[26] Marketing campaigns to "sell back orientalism" to the orientalists, needs to be considered for possible long-term effects.[27] Revivals of heritage can have adverse effects on women and other minoritized groups.[28] Historians and anthropologists correct misconceptions about the isolation of Gulf Arabs by pointing to historical connections between the Gulf and South Asia and East Africa that predate the more divisive moments of European colonialism and US imperialism when notions of a so-called pure and authentic Arab culture (*asala*) emerged.[29] In additional to patriarchy, ethnocentric nationalisms risk unwittingly reproducing some of the

---

[25] For a historical analysis of homoerotic orientalism that informs the queered and feminist orientations of the film, see: Joseph Allen Boone, *The Homoerotics of Orientalism* (New York: Columbia University Press, 2014).

[26] For an analysis of the limiting vision of positive images, see Ella Shohat/Robert Stam, *Unthinking Eurocentrism: Multiculturalism and the Media* (1994; New York: Routledge, 2014), 178–219.

[27] The notion of "selling back orientalism" is developed in the documentary *Mariano Fortuny y la lámpara maravillosa/Fortuny and the Magic Lantern* (Spain 2010; dir. Claudio Zulian) in relation to the use of Fortuny's orientalist lamps in Indian restaurants, catering to European tourists and expatriates, in Dubai.

[28] Rajeswari Sunder Rajan and You-me Park, "Postcolonial Feminism/Postcolonialism and Feminism," in Henry Schwartz and Sangeeta Ray (eds.), *A Companion to Postcolonial Studies* (Malden, MA: Blackwell, 2000), 63–64.

[29] Examples of such academic studies include: Christopher Davidson, *Abu Dhabi: Oil and Beyond* (New York: Columbia University Press, 2009); Ahmed Kanna, *Dubai: The City as Corporation* (Minnesota: University of Minnesota Press, 2011); and Neha Vora, *Impossible Citizens: Dubai's Indian Diaspora* (Durham: Duke University Press, 2013).

discourses of tourism that erase contributions by expatriates, including South Asians before the days of the Trucial States, Arabs from Egypt, Jordan, Iraq, Palestine, and Syria since the 1970s and 1980s, followed by increased recruitment of South Asians and Southeast Asians after the Gulf War in 1990 and of Africans after the Arab Spring in 2011.

The tourism campaign of "travellers welcome" emphasizes the UAE as a territorial crossroads for Arab and European travelers and deemphasizes its more significant history as maritime entrepôt for South Asian, Iranian, and East African traders. Representations by foreigners sometimes frame British interventions as primarily altruistic, akin to the "they gave us roads and Shakespeare" apologies articulated elsewhere in the former British Empire. Multicultural discourses, with their acknowledgement of multidirectional assimilation, are sidelined for hierarchical notions of cosmopolitanism. Diversity trumps inclusion and equity. Nonetheless, marginalization of non-Arab histories informs social taboos about discussing slavery and social stigmas in being "half Emirati." Citizens with South Asian, Southeast Asian, European, or non-Emirati Arab parents, particularly fathers, often feel excluded from the national stories told in feature films. Discourses of *asala* also risk inadvertently reinforcing the orientalism that fuels Islamophobia across the North Atlantic by essentializing cultures in ways that play into clash-of-cultures paranoia, notably Bernard Lewis's invention of "Muslim rage."[30]

The UAE is culturally diverse in terms of multiple tribes, ethnicities, and nationalities. It is linguistically diverse, with Arabic, Hindi, English, Malayalam, and Urdu generally considered the most widely spoken languages but also large populations of Bengali, Indonesian, Sinhala, Somali, Tagalog, and Tamil speakers. Ramsa (Emirati Arabic) includes different expressions and accentuations than other Arabic dialects. Emirati filmmaking cannot rely on a majority national audience like most states. Critical self-representation by Gulf filmmakers that question *asala* and cosmopolitanism, thus, is important both at home and abroad as a corrective to misrepresentations and erasures. By countering and ignoring foreign stereotypes, Emirati filmmaking contributes to the everyday practices of constructing and consolidating national identity, as well as ongoing contestations over national identity in light of: (1) the relatively recent unification of distinct tribes and families into a single state in

---

[30] Bernard Lewis, "The Roots of Muslim Rage," *The Atlantic Monthly* (1990): 47–60.

1971; (2) historical marginalization of the Gulf emirates within Arab and Muslim cultures; (3) centuries-old cultural and economic ties to South Asia, Iran, and East Africa; and (4) cultural submersion by a majority expatriate population, including middle-class families and migrant "bachelors" (men whose families are not permitted residency under their work visas) from South Asia that constitute a substantial percentage of the overall population, but also significant African, Arab, and Southeast Asian professionals and domestic workers.[31] Emirati filmmaking can inject counter-narratives to the so-called universal stories on offer at multiplexes and stand-alone theaters that are produced in Cairo, Chennai, Mumbai, and Los Angeles—all of whom have profited from negative stereotypes of Gulf Arabs as backwards and greedy and of the Gulf emirates as safe havens for pirates, smugglers, and terrorists.

Negotiating Culture and Finance Among "Small Nations"

Newer concepts within film and media studies offer ways to locate Emirati filmmaking without forcing it to conform to models for Arab, Middle Eastern, or MENA cinema. Mette Hjort and Duncan Petrie's "the cinema of small nations" grapples with various definitions of smallness, including film production, population, and gross national product, to recuperate kinds of knowledge that are lost when we focus only on the prolific, big, and powerful.[32] As a concept, cinema of small nations challenges the top-down frameworks of so-called national, regional, and ethnic cinemas with a middle-outward (rather than bottom-up) framework. Among their case studies, the most relevant to a discussion of Emirati filmmaking are studies on Singapore, whose cinema has "simultaneously local, national, and transnational dimensions, similar to the country's multiracial, multicultural, multi-religious, and multi-linguistic environments," and on New Zealand, whose efforts to negotiate a "creative industries agenda" and a "more overly market-driven conception of the

---

[31] The UAE National Bureau of Statistics does not publish census data by nationality. For 2015 population statistics, see: "UAE's Population—by Nationality," *bq magazine* (12 April 2015): http://www.bqdoha.com/2015/04/uae-population-by-nationality.

[32] Mette Hjort and Duncan Petrie, "Introduction," in Hjort and Petrie (eds.), *The Cinema of Small Nations* (Indianapolis: Indiana University Press, 2007), 1–19.

value of cultural activity," which has often resulted in "a vigorous and explicit marketing of a 'national brand', yoking the creative industries to tourism in the process."[33]

With regard to Singapore, See Kim Tan and Jeremy Fernando describe the logic of its former prime minister Goh Chok Tong (1999–2004) as producing two mutually exclusive categories: "cosmopolitan" Singaporeans, who speak English and work in professional sectors of the economy, and "heartlanders," who speak Singlish and work in shops or factories or emigrate to the United States to live in Chinatowns where they open Chinese restaurants.[34] They point to Singapore's *de-emphasis* of cultural nationalism, which is typically a priority under rubrics of national or ethnic cinemas, and *emphasis* on technocratic nationalism, that is, "the idea that Singapore is first and foremost a globally connected market place of ideas and commodities" that dates to its historical status as an entrepôt like many cities of the Arab Gulf.[35] Their critique of cosmopolitanism's allure within globalization's highly uneven and unequal relationships underscores the intellectual negotiations that scholars have sometimes undertaken to redeem the term *cosmopolitan* from ancient Greece's misogyny and slavery.[36]

Unsurprisingly, the term is well suited for branding the city for tourism and business. Cosmopolitanism aligns neatly with the processes of capitalist exploitation, revealing an irony in Singapore's disappointment

---

[33] See Kim Tan and Jeremy Fernando, "Singapore," and Duncan Petrie, "New Zealand," in Hjort and Petrie (eds.), *The Cinema of Small Nations* (Indianapolis: Indiana University Press, 2007), 127, 168. On Singapore, also see David Birch, "Film and Cinema in Singapore: Cultural Policy as Control," in Albert Moran (ed.), *Film Policy: International, National and Regional Perspectives* (New York: Routledge, 1996), 181–206. He examines tensions between modernity and so-called Asian values, as well as Singapore's investment in infrastructure to facilitate synergy and social control.

[34] Kim Tan and Fernando, "Singapore," 128. They add a third category of "ambivalent nationalism" (129).

[35] Ibid., 128.

[36] Efforts to make the term more inclusive include: Pheng Cheah and Bruce Robbins (eds.), *Cosmopolitics: Thinking and Feeling beyond the Nation* (Minneapolis: University of Minnesota Press, 1998); Sheldon Pollock, Homi K. Bhabha, Carol A. Breckenridge, and Dipesh Chakrabarty. "Cosmopolitanisms." *Public Culture* 12.3 (fall 2000): 1–14; Eduardo Mendieta, "From Imperial to Dialogical Cosmopolitanism," *Ethics & Global Politics* 2. 3 (2009): 241–258; and Arjun Appadurai, "Cosmopolitanism from Below: Some Ethical Lessons from the Slums of Mumbai," *The Salon* 4 (2011): 32–43.

when *Be with Me* (Singapore 2005; dir. Eric Khoo) was rejected by Hollywood for its foreign-language Oscar category due to the large amount of English-language dialogue. The film was perhaps too cosmopolitan to be foreign. Singapore's "Speak Good English Movement" to counter the spread of Singlish and make the city friendlier to so-called cosmopolitan business might have worked against its effort at acquiring an Oscar.[37] The role of film commissions in guiding decisions that affect both culture and finance is significant. Established in 1998, the Singapore Film Commission (MediaCorp) and its Raintree Pictures employs a "'local' film paradigm" in supporting films with local talent, resources, stories, and shooting locations and a "'regional' film paradigm" in supporting co-productions with companies in Hong Kong, which are written and directed by non-Singaporeans and set in Hong Kong, Thailand, or Taiwan.[38]

Like Singapore, Dubai, and other port cities now part of the UAE were historically important entrepôts for maritime trade between China, Southeast Asia, South Asia, and Africa. Rather than top-down cosmopolitanism, multiculturalism unfolds in Mumbai-based collective CAMP's *From Gulf to Gulf to Gulf/Kutchi Vahan Pani Wala* (UAE–India–Yemen–Somalia–Qatar–Pakistan–Oman–Kuwait–Kenya–Iraq–Iran 2009–2013; dir. Shaina Anand and Ashok Sukumaran), conceived for the Sharjah Biennale as a collaboration with migrant sailors.[39] Dubai also features in middle-class South Asian female expatriate organization of the singing competition "Camp ka Champ" for South Asian male expatriates, who work as laborers, in (then) Dubai-based Lebanese filmmaker Mahmoud Kaboor's *Champ of the Camp* (UAE–Qatar–Lebanon 2013), which played at DIFF with an outdoor screening for South Asian bachelors. Such cosmopolitanisms, however, are not featured in tourism campaigns. They do enter into some of the short films in the EFC and Muhr Awards—and to a different extent appeared in Kuwaiti and Bahraini films of the 1970s and 1990s. At the same time that films *From Gulf to Gulf to Gulf* and *Champ of the Camp* challenge notions of *asala*

---

[37] Kim Tan and Fernando, "Singapore," 140.

[38] Ibid., 133.

[39] For a discussion of CAMP, see: Dale Hudson and Patricia R. Zimmermann, *Thinking through Digital Media: Transnational Environments and Locative Places* (New York: Palgrave Macmillan, 2015), 227–231.

and cosmopolitanism in tourism campaigns, they also reject discourses of victimization, which appear in the news and sometimes even in well-intended art projects.[40] Such films restore dignity and complexity to lives of migrant laborers without making excuses their treatment. Dialogue and song lyrics in both films are primarily in South Asian languages of Bengali, Bhojpuri (Indian) English, Hindi, Kutchi, and Urdu rather than Arabic.

Anglophone small nations based on local market size, such as Australia, Canada, and the United Kingdom, are also unable to compete with Hollywood on its own terms—that is, with commercially oriented English-language content akin to the *Transporter* franchise (France–USA 2002–2008) and its "refueled" lasted issue (France–China 2015) by EuropaCorp. Such places adopt strategies for niche markets, such as foregrounding national heritage, including colonial arrogance, or offering something unusual like "weird sex and snowshoes," to borrow the title of a book on Canadian cinema. The alternative model has been that of New Zealand, which courted Hollywood to shoot its *Lord of the Rings* franchise (2001–2003), leaving behind improved infrastructure, along with recognition as a new union-bypassing option to British Columbia and the Czech Republic for transnational Hollywood, if not international prestige for New Zealand's own filmmaking. Established in 1978, the New Zealand Film Commission (NZFC) readjusted its approach to target three types of filmmaking, much as Ireland has done: large-scale Hollywood productions that take advantage of massive tax incentives and render the country unrecognizable as the imaginary spaces of Middle Earth or Skull Island; medium-budget co-productions; and lower-budget films funded fully or primarily that focus on local stories, including those of indigenous nations such as the Maori.[41] Despite the emphasis on assisting international films with no connection to New Zealand, such

---

[40]An example is the "salary portraits" in *Skyscrapers and Shadows* (2010). Kristin Giordano and Andrew Gardner photographed South Asian, Southeast Asian, and African migrants on a Qatari beach, holding signs that indicated their monthly salaries in US dollars. Intended to evoke shock and outrage, the portraits inadvertently reproduce visual strategies in rank-based scientific classification that translated eugenics into colonial photography, as well as practices of classifying prisoners and the mentally ill. The project also included glass display boxes with items donated by migrant workers that enhanced the voyeuristic lens. These portions of the project were not included in most exhibitions.

[41]Petrie, "New Zealand," 161, 168–169.

as *King Kong* (New Zealand–USA–Germany 2005; dir. Peter Jackson) and *The Chronicle of Narnia: The Lion, the Witch, and the Wardrobe* (UK–USA 2005; dir. Andrew Adamson), Duncan Petrie argues that the NZFC "continues to be informed by a culturalist (or cultural nationalist) imperative, backing filmmaking talent driven by the desire to 'tell their own stories'."[42]

A comparable multimodal approach appears to be developing in the UAE, particularly in Abu Dhabi, where Image Nation publically voices its investment in supporting "local talent" while initially offering massive tax incentives to Hollywood and Bollywood. The UAE, however, occupies a different place in the world that Singapore and New Zealand. With a predominantly Muslim population and a predominantly Arab citizenry, UAE-based financial mechanisms also support Arab filmmakers to produce films, many of which continue from festivals to theatrical exhibition, VOD, and DVD. Rather than directly through the Abu Dhabi Film Commission (ADFC), which offers a 30% cash-rebate in addition to other benefits, or the Dubai Film and Television Commission, financial and creative support for these films is administered through funds such as SANAD in Abu Dhabi and Enjazz in Dubai. Many of these films would not otherwise have been realized. Funded in part by SANAD, Annemarie Jacir's *Lamma Shoftak/When I Saw You* (Jordan–Palestine–UAE–Greece 2012), for example, is set in a training camp for *fedayeen* before the events of Black September (1970–1971) that saw the PLO expelled from Jordan.[43] Comparably, Naji Abu Nowar's *Theeb* (Jordan–UAE–Qatar 2014) about the final days of the Ottoman Empire from the perspective of young male Bedouins received funding from SANAD, yet none from the Royal Film Commission in Jordan. To avoid political and artistic compromises demanded by many European and U.S. finding sources for films about Palestine, Susan Youssef's retelling of ninth-century *Layla Majnun* in contemporary Gaza and the West Bank, *Habibi Rasak Kharban/Darling, Something's Wrong with Your Head* (Netherlands–Palestine–USA–UAE 2010), also benefited from support from the DFM's Enjazz. Variations on co-production, then, play a more significant role in Emirati filmmaking than standard categories in film

---

[42] Ibid., 168.

[43] Dale Hudson, review of *Lamma Shoftak/When I Saw You* (Jordan-Palestine-UAE-Greece 2012; dir. Annemarie Jacir), *Jadaliyya* (22 March 2013): www.jadaliyya.com/pages/index/10743/when-i-saw-you.

and media studies has on offer. Small nations, then, can help other small nations (especially stateless nations) convey their perspectives in feature films for international audiences.

BETWEEN GRASSROOTS MOVEMENTS AND STATE COLLABORATIONS WITH CORPORATIONS

National consciousness is relatively recent in the UAE. The term "Emirati" to define identity, for example, only began to replace *muwatin* (citizen) in the 1980s and 1990s, as historian Matthew MacLean notes.[44] Since the 1990s, it has also become increasingly difficult for states to isolate so-called national cultures, which tend to fade and blend into transnational cultures in a more accelerated and decentralized manner than in the past. The Gulf emirates are particularly useful for understanding the interplay of national and transnational cultures in light of the transcultural networks that linked port cities and villages to the broader Indian Ocean World from China and Southeast Asia through South Asia and down through East Africa up to the Red Sea and over to the Mediterranean Sea for centuries and continue today.

Emirati filmmaking attempts to differentiate itself from conventions in popular Arabic-language films from Cairo and Tagalog-language films from Manila that screen commercially in the UAE, along with Hindi ones from Mumbai's Bollywood, Tamil-language films from Chennai's Kollywood, Telugu ones from Hyderabad's Tollywood, and Malayalam-language films from Kochi's and Trivandrum's Mollywood. In so doing, Emirati filmmaking risks being subsumed into Hollywood and European productions of Arab art cinema that often entails political and artistic compromises demanded by foreign/expatriate producers and financers for any number of reasons, including maximizing profit by universalizing stories to make them as either "relatable" or "exotic" to audiences with no actual interest in Emirati points of view. Funded by Image Nation Abu Dhabi, Al Janahi's second feature *Dhil al Bahr/Sea Shadow* (UAE 2011), Mostafa's second and third features *From A to B* (UAE 2014) and *The Worthy* (UAE 2016), and Saeed Saleen Al-Murry's second feature *Sayer Al Jannah/Going to Heaven* (UAE 2015) demonstrate

---

[44] Matthew MacLean, "Resident Expert: What Drives National Identity?" interview in *Salaam*, New York University Abu Dhabi (26 July 2015): http://nyuad.nyu.edu/en/news/research-innovation/2015/07/resident-expert--what-drives-national-identity-.html.

technical maturity in the sense of conventional narrative structures and high production values that appeal to European festival programmers. Their first features—Al Janahi's *Al Dayra/The Circle* (UAE–Kuwait 2009), Mostafa's *City of Life*, and Al-Murry's *Thawb al-Shams/Sun Dress* (UAE 2010)—have been unfairly evaluated by foreigners on technical merit rather than cultural relevance and the nuance of their stories, which reject foreign and resident expatriate stereotypes for Emiratis, as has Saleh Karama's *Henna* (UAE 2009). Set in Abu Dhabi, Humaid Al Suwaidi's *Abdulla* (UAE 2015) addresses differences in opinions amongst Emiratis on music and film—and even pokes fun at filmmakers who rely on foreign crews who do not understand Arabic.

Superficial evaluations by Hollywood- or European-trained critics and filmmakers, including Arab ones, recall early critiques of Nollywood by francophone West African and anglophone South African filmmakers, who felt threatened by the popular and financial success of Nollywood's purposeful disregard for narrative conventions and respect for production values. Although Nollywood has already eclipsed Hollywood to become the second-largest producer of films globally, Hollywood insiders have only recently begun to partner with Chinese and Indian productions—and have yet to align with Nigerian ones. Nollywood's production values have expanded from the "imperfect" images of early work, such as Chris Obi Rapu's *Living in Bondage* (Nigeria 1992), to the "world class" images of award-winning films, such as Kunle Afolayan's *The Figurine* (Nigeria 2009) and the US$2 million-dollar-budget *October 1* (Nigeria 2014) in the short span of twenty-five years. Nollywood's stories and storytelling, however, have not assimilated to dominant models on offer by Hollywood and Europe, which are often estranging to Nigerian and other African audiences due to the colonial underpinnings of their narrative forms and logic. Films are released in English, Yoruba, Hausa, Igbo, and Edo. Most of the films are currently produced by women, often critiquing patriarchal structures. Privately funded, Nollywood films engage ethnic, religious, and linguistic differences in Nigeria, and their appeal resides in their attention to local stories—including ones about social problems—and storytelling modes that audiences found not met in imported foreign films from Bollywood, Hong Kong, and Hollywood.[45] In this way, Nollywood offers a model

---

[45] Pierre Barrot, *Nollywood: The Video Phenomenon in Nigeria* (Bloomington: Indiana University Press, 2009).

for rejecting the exclusionary practices of so-called world-class standards in order to build audiences for films that are locally relevant and meaningful. Bypassing theatrical exhibition and moving from straight-to-video to online streaming via services like iROKOtv, Pana TV, and iBAKATV have opened Nollywood's market to the world. They find large audiences not only in Nigeria and the diaspora—from Lagos to London's Little Lagos—but also in the Caribbean, Latin America, North America, and throughout Africa, including South Africa, where they compete against an older and more established local film and television industry.

In addition to Nollywood, locating the production of Emirati filmmaking could entail drawing upon the South Korean model of transitioning from manufacturing cars to producing media as part of its post-1992 globalization (*segyehwa*) policies that generate profits but, more significantly, acknowledge media's cultural role in mobilizing national pride by promoting South Korean media as a global brand abroad and exercising the soft power that it entails, as well as in mitigating popular dissatisfaction with the increased structural inequalities under neoliberalism at home. Rather than Nollywood's grassroots organization that has now consolidated into a multisite industry, Hallyuwood ("wave" in Korean via Chinese with the suffix "wood") is a carefully calibrated collaboration between state and corporate agents. In addition to direct governmental collaboration with multinational conglomerates like Daewoo and Samsung, South Korea's industry was protected by quotas on foreign media.[46] The Hallyuwood model suggests possibilities for developing programs and policies in the UAE, where K-dramas (*hanguk deurama*) are so popular that they are televised in both dubbed and subtitled versions; moreover, flash mobs of choreographed dancing based on the music videos for K-pop hits have taken place in Dubai malls. Emirati filmmaker Majid Al Ansari found more inspiration from Hallyuwood than Hollywood for his debut feature *Zinzana/Rattle the Cage* (UAE–Jordan 2015), citing Park Chan-wook as a role model.

South Korea's commitment to making media on its own terms, rather than assimilating to Hollywood's terms, represents a model of developing filmmaking locally rather than "selling out" as an exotic backdrop for Hollywood- or European-produced or financed films. Such investments in local production might alter the terms by which the UAE is

---

[46]Roy Stafford, *The Global Film Book* (London: Routledge, 2014), 143–144.

discussed, not unlike ways that Al Jazeera altered mass media coverage of the MENA, particularly through its English-language Al Jazeera English. To cite another regional example, Turkish "new cinema" and soap operas (*televizyon dizileri*) depart from the melodramatic conventions of Yeşilçam, the popular genre films of the period from the 1950s to the 1970s often indebted to Hollywood genres, to change some of the terms of international discussions. Jack Shaheen advised in an interview with *Qatar Today* that young Arabs need to "do something," that is, they should not be silent or passive but should "break the appalling silence" that allows the Hollywood, European, and Israeli film industries to define the terms by which Arabs are represented cinematically.[47] Production alone, however, is inadequate. It needs to be combined with efforts to educate aspiring filmmakers on ways to translate Gulf perspectives and storytelling practices onto film and efforts to convene and sustain audiences.

Between Transnational Cinema and Indigenous Media

Although certain Arab distributors for art-house fare have proposed that the UAE should invest in fewer, high-quality films rather than supporting large numbers of "low-quality" films, there is much to be gained in facilitating the development of a critical masses of films with local perspectives regardless of their alleged quality. Indeed, Nollywood underscores as much from both a financial and a cultural point of view. Controlling the discourse involves both the production of more content with a local inflection and less concern for foreign standards that can undercut indigenous perspectives or render them illegible. Although indigenous media is often associated with disempowered and disenfranchised populations, particularly ones who have been dispossessed of territory and sovereignty, filmmaking in the Arab Gulf somewhat counter-intuitively shares much in common with indigenous media. DIFF functions—and ADFF functioned—like México's Festival Internacional de Cine en Morelia/Morelia Film Festival in terms of its dual

---

[47] "Arab Stereotypes: The Eternal Enemy" (interview with Jack Shaheen), *Qatar Today* (November 2013): 84–85. Shaheen is best known in this regard for his book *Reel Bad Arabs: How Hollywood Vilifies a People*, updated version (Olive Branch Press, 2009).

programming of indigenous media alongside art and commercial films. Since 2003, Morelia's festival operates primarily as a *cultural* event, rather than a *commercial* one like Cannes or Sundance. In many ways, the symbolic value of including disparate media under a single festival exceeds the financial value of branding insofar as it redresses some of the historical and cultural effects of the asymmetrical power relations within globalizing media ecologies. Indigenous filmmakers share the stage with commercial filmmakers. DIFF also includes several programs of festival screening dedicated to narrative and documentary filmmaking by Gulf filmmakers.

Emirati short films share indigenous media's rejection of the so-called rules of commercial cinema in order to tell stories that might not make sense in the style of Hollywood blockbusters or European art cinema. Whereas commercial film festivals like CIFF and cultural ones like JCC offer awards to so-called best filmmakers, actors, and technicians, indigenous media festivals often offer awards for social commitment, as Amalia Córdova notes.[48] Production values are not universal criteria for evaluating the significance of a film. Although most Emiratis have cultural, economic, and political power unimagined by most indigenous groups in Latin America, Asia Pacific, and elsewhere, short films by Emiratis, particularly students, work toward a comparable objective of sustaining cultural identity as a minority population. Indigenous media is often inaccessible to foreigners—and sometimes even withheld from exhibition to anyone outside the community. Unlike audiences for international features at ADFF and DIFF, audiences for Emirati shorts are predominantly Emirati. Post-screening discussion takes place in Arabic without translation into English, thereby claiming a space for Emiratis within the international film culture of festivals. These discussions also resist the self-authorized cosmopolitan privilege of certain expatriates as the uncontested arbiters of culture and knowledge through expectations that everything will be translated into English for them—and that they will see films with recognizable features such as classical narrative arcs and individual heroes patterned after Hollywood and European examples.

---

[48] Juan Francisco Salazar and Amalia Córdova, "Imperfect Media and the Politics of Indigenous Video in Latin America," in *Global Indigenous Media: Cultures, Poetics, and Politics*, eds. Wilson and Stewart (Durham: Duke University Press, 2008), 39–57.

The short films tend to focus on identity in flux—dialect, accent, cultural and environmental heritage, national dress, legends, advantages and disadvantages of being a minority in their home state, and other everyday experiences. Some address social problems—mixed parentage, migrant labor, and racism against darker-skinned Emiratis and South Asians. The EFC was open to all filmmakers from, or living in, the Arab Gulf to allow non-national local voices to participate in the discussion. The Muhr Awards are open to filmmakers "from across the Arab world, Asia and Africa." Short films often focus on cultural heritage, as in *Ana Arabi/I Am Arab* (UAE 2009; dir. Ahlam Al Bannai and Jumana Al Ghanem) on Arab identity, and *Lahjatna/Our Accent* (UAE 2011; dir. Mariam Al Nuaimi), on the damaging and alienating effects on Arabic language and Emirati accents by the multilingualism of everyday life in the UAE. *Al Kandorah* (UAE 2010; dir. Lamya Al Mualla and Maitha Al Haddad) examines feelings about the kandura; *Layers* (UAE 2011; dir. Manal Wicki) on the fashion of the abaya. Accent, language, and national dress (kanduras and abayas) are audible and visible markers of national identity and citizenship. They reify national identity above tribal identities, and they also tackle taboo subjects of ethnic identities, such as "intermarriages" with South Asians, Iranians, Europeans, and descendants of African slaves. Cultural connections to history and legend are often topics that work toward cultural preservation and renewal, such as the animated *Ostora/The Legend* (UAE 2012; dir. Hani Kichi) and *Um Duwais* (UAE 2012; dir. Sarah Zohair and Majida Al Safadi) on Emirati legends of the djinn—the latter taking a feminist perspective for the female figure of Umm Duwais, a beautiful djinn who seduces wayward men. Nayla Al Khaja's short films, particularly *Arabana* (UAE 2006), *Marra/Once* (UAE 2008), *Malal* (UAE 2010), and *Haywan/Animal* (USA 2016), advocate feminist perspectives on contemporary life in the Gulf. The short animation *Mad Camel* (UAE 2011; dir. Mohammad Fikree) offers a humorous perspective on camels in the desert that reject the orientalizing gaze of Hollywood, notably the ubiquitous establishing shots of camels running across highways for films set an urban Dubai that has been mysteriously distanced from its airport (Fig. 8.3).

Other films examine the concerns of young Emiratis, such as *Constructing Dreams/Ahlam that al-Insha'a* (UAE 2009; dir. Moath bin Hafaz) on the dreams of migrant construction workers, framing them as agents of their lives rather than victims of their circumstances, *Y.E.S. to School* (UAE 2012; dir. Thabit Al Mawaly) on student volunteers who

Fig. 8.3 Animated opening title for *The Gamboo3a Revolution* (2012). Image credit: Abdulrahman Al Madani, Saeed Al Emadi, and Saeed Salmin

help restore a school in the northern emirate of Ajman, and *Yoolad Helm fel Ainain/Dreams in Their Eyes* (UAE 2012; dir. Abeer Al Marzooqi, Ayesha Al Ameri, and Khawla Al Mamaari) about Palestinian refugees in Lebanon. Partly inspired by a character on *Sha3beyat Al Cartoon* (UAE 2006–present), an animated series that addresses social issues, the student film *Dhahirath al Qamboa'a/The Gamboo3a Revolution* (UAE 2012; dir. Abdulrahman Al Madani, Saeed Al Emadi, and Saeed Salmin) playfully documents feelings on the popular (and *indigenous*) trend of the "camel hump" under the shayla. The film explores a range of opinions on the trend, ranging from accusations that the practice is *haram* (forbidden) to praise for its inventiveness, to jokes that height-conscious young women place yogurt containers under their shaylas in addition to high heels under their abayas. The film unsettles both domestic and foreign assumptions about national dress. Female characters in the film question why there is controversy over female fashion trends when young men, who circulate publically with spiky hair and no ghutra, receive no comments about their physical appearance. Sahar Al Khatib and Shamma Bunawas's documentary *Ana Rajol/I'm A Man* (UAE 2006) examines expectations of masculinity for young Emirati men who take care of their skin and nails. Other films challenge

Fig. 8.4 Scene from *The Gamboo3a Revolution* (2012). Image credit: Abdulrahman Al Madani, Saeed Al Emadi, and Saeed Salmin

conservative perceptions of cultural tradition, such as Amal Al-Agroobi's *Nisf Emirati/Half Emirati* (UAE 2012) about living in the UAE with one foreign parent. The films critique—implicitly rather than explicitly—social norms and customs, modeling a productive nuance often absent in foreign journalism (Fig. 8.4).

Director of the *Grandmother's Farm* films, Ahmed Zain's short *Gheamt Shroog* (UAE 2010) narrates a story of a group of teenage boys who skip school to cause trouble in Abu Dhabi. They steal food from a South Asian restaurateur and gaze lasciviously at women on a beach. The film gently implicates the state's education policies and relaxed parental involvement in child-rearing, much like François Truffaut's *Les Quatre Cent Coups/The 400 Blows* (France 1959) did in Paris after the second World War. Short films by non-nationals also acknowledge the present-day globalized Gulf in narratives about a young Ethiopian woman's arrival for a domestic job in Al Ain in *The Journey* (UAE 2012; dir. Hana Makki), as she learns what she might expect about expatriate life from a South Asian taxi driver. More significantly, she receives the invaluable reminder that "every work is honor," something that is important to many UAE residents who must accept jobs below their education and experience to send remittances home or fund a future dream in a place devastated by domestic corruption or foreign exploitation. Rafed Al-Harthi and Ray Haddad's documentary *Itaa'm khams Miya/Feeding Five Hundred* (UAE 2013) investigates the South Asian expatriate Siddiq, who has gone into debt by feeding stray cats in Abu Dhabi for more than fifteen years, even forgoing trips home to see his wife and children. The student documentary *No More, the Return* (UAE–Russia 2014; dir. Ayaz Kamalov) explores the question of why and whether Emirati history is being forgotten against the newly inaugurated Qasr al Hosn Festival, which annually reintegrates the white fort of Sheikh Shakhbout bin Sultan Al Nahyan into living cultural heritage after having been underacknowledged for decades.

Although such films are not necessarily or primarily made with foreign audiences in mind, twofour54's Creative Lab produces short films based on ideas by aspiring young filmmakers, some of which have been selected to represent the UAE to foreign travelers as in-flight entertainment on Etihad Airways, as does the DFI on Qatar Airways. Among them, *The Long Way Down* (UAE 2012; dir. Yessar Howaidy) and *Visa Run* (UAE 2012; dir. Mounir Barakar) attempt to address negative British stereotypes of *all* Arabs as terrorists and the Gulf as a haven for terrorists, as well as negative Emirati stereotypes of *all* British expatriates as immoral, immodest, and ignorant of the colonial history that links Britain to the UAE. The synergy between twofour54 and Etihad offers a means of promoting Emirati filmmaking. If the airline offers "flying reimagined"—to borrow a recent campaign for its enhanced in-flight services—then its inflight entertainment E-BOX might reimagine ways that we can think of exhibiting Emirati filmmaking, that is, another niche market akin to narrowcasting on YouTube.

Less visible to airline passengers is the work of Nujoom Alghanem, whose documentary shorts and features offer nuanced and substantive insights into historical and contemporary aspects of Emirati culture. They draw upon her sense of sound, rhythm, and texture evident in her poetry, but they are deeply analytical and intellectual, drawing upon her sense of history and commitment to filmmaking. Her short documentary *Between Two Banks* (UAE 1999) examines Khor Dubai (Dubai Creek) through the disappearing occupation of rowing boatmen, inspired by Khamees Marzouq, the last remaining one in Dubai. In *Samma Qarribah/Nearby Sky* (UAE 2014), Alghanem documents Fatima Ali Alhemeli's struggle to become the first Emirati woman to enter her camel in the largely male-dominated auctions in Abu Dhabi. Alghanem's documentary practice often focuses in part on legendary figures from the living history of the northern Emirates, such as the traditional healer Hamma from Sharjah in *Hamama* (UAE 2010) and the singer Saif Alzibadi in Um Al Quwain in *Sawt Al Bahar/Sounds of the Sea* (UAE 2014), thus countering from the globalized images of modern Dubai as a stand-in for *all* of the UAE or of the dunes of the Empty Quarter as stand-ins for Saudi Arabia, Afghanistan, or the fictional planet Tatooine for Hollywood productions.

Her documentaries are not uncritical recovery and preservation of history, nor are they commodified by non-critical nostalgia or cosmopolitanism; instead, they are critical engagements with ongoing unsettled debates over identity and culture inflected by her frequent collaboration with poet and cultural historian Khaled Albudoor. Unlike the feature films produced or financed by twofour54, which focus on stories about young Emirati and other Arab men living in the UAE, Alghanem's films convey stories about women (and men) and their historical importance to Gulf cultures. As documentaries, her films appeal to anthropologists, historians, and sociologists. At the same time, the high production values and complex analysis in her films makes them appeal to cinéphiles with no prior interest in the UAE. Her films, however, are not presently available for purchase for home or school use, so they can only be seen at festivals and special screenings at cultural events.

Aspirations and Speculations

In light of the diversity in Emirati filmmaking and early stages of developing a sustainable exhibition platform for audiences living in the UAE and sustained support for cultural institutions, such as film journals, cinémathèques, and film education, the question of locating Emirati filmmaking became more precarious after the canceling of two festivals and one competition where Emirati films were screened publically and achievements were recognized with awards.[49] Egyptian film critic and programmer Joseph Fahim describes the situation as the movement of ADFF from the Abu Dhabi Tourism and Culture Authority (TCA),

---

[49]European cultural institutions often program Emirati shorts before their own feature films, such as the Goethe-Institut's Heritage Film Festival.

which itself replaced the Abu Dhabi Authority for Culture and Heritage (ADACH), to twofour54 under the MZA anticipated the shift in decision from "becoming the biggest festival in the region" to "allowing commerce to triumph over art development."[50] In his view, Abu Dhabi is moving from a counter-Hollywood model of cultivating cultural capital in the manner of states like France and South Korea to a Hollywood-complicit model of accumulating financial capital—even at the expense of contributing to negative stereotypes for the region.

Abu Dhabi's twofour54 and Dubai's Studio City cater to high-budget foreign productions that tend to offer ambivalent representations of the UAE, such as *Mission: Impossible—Ghost Protocol* (USA–UAE 2011; dir. Brad Bird) and *Furious 7* (USA–Japan 2015; dir. James Wan), which do not substantially differ from the anti-Gulf Arab condescension powered by outdated white feminist and queer pleasures evident in *Sex and the City 2* or from overtly nationalist Bollywood films like *Happy New Year* (India 2014; dir. Farah Khan) in which Dubai may as well be Goa. Free zones also cater to high-budget productions that outright erase the specificity of the UAE, as in *Star Wars: Episode VII—The Force Awakens* (USA 2015; dir. J.J. Abrams), *Star Trek Beyond* (USA 2016; dir. Justin Lin), and numerous Bollywood and other Indian films, including *Dabangg* (India 2010; dir. Abhinav Singh Kashyap). Although the films might not contribute to the cultural life of the UAE, apart from some pride—and may, in some cases, detract from it—investment in developing infrastructure for foreign film production does help diversify the UAE economy from dependency on a single commodity in the early 1970s towards sustainability in multiple sectors, thus contributing to national security. *Furious 7*, for example, produced USD 390 million in China alone, that is, more than the domestic market of Canada and the United States, where it produced USD 350 million.[51]

Although Hollywood films are highly profitable—and even popular—in the UAE, it is unclear that apprenticeships to Hollywood producers will contribute to preparing Emiratis to tell their own stories. Foreign

---

[50] Joseph Fahim, "What Happened to the Abu Dhabi Film Festival?," *Al Monitor* (May 2015): http://www.al-monitor.com/pulse/originals/2015/05/gulf-uae-abu-dhabi-film-festival-cancelled-adff-dfi-cinema.html#.

[51] These figures are quoted on *The Numbers: Where Data and the Movie Business Meet* (no date): http://www.the-numbers.com/movie/Furious-7.

features produced by twofour54 are nonetheless diverse and include ones that tell stories unlikely to be financed by Hollywood and Europe, such as *Amreeka* (USA–Canada 2009; dir. Cherien Dabis) and *Zinzana*, yet also orientalist films like *The Best Exotic Marigold Hotel* (UK–USA–UAE 2011; dir. John Madden), its sequel *The Second Best Exotic Marigold Hotel* (UK–USA 2015; dir. John Madden), the racially insensitive *The Help* (USA–India–UAE 2011; dir. Tate Taylor) with its nostalgia for the pre-Civil Rights United States. It also supports films that challenge misperceptions on Islam, helping finance Karen Johar's *My Name Is Khan* (India 2010), which depicts post-9/11 Islamophobia against South Asian Muslims in the United States, as does the DFI financing of Mira Nair's *The Reluctant Fundamentalist* (USA–UK–Qatar 2013).

Although Hollywood and European industry professional and technicians often disparaged EFC and Muhr Awards films for "lacking stories" or "technical knowhow," these assessments seem naïve and self-promoting at times. Alia Yunis points out that Emirati filmmakers display an awareness of both "their privilege and the limited production values of their work" in which "plot, pacing and story take a backseat to creating a setting that favors the sea, sun and virtues of purity and innocence," often through the bond of friendship between two males or critical nostalgia for a pre-oil era.[52] Audiences acculturated to the predictability of Hollywood's formulaic three-act narrative structures might find Emirati features frustrating, but, as Yunis points out, such formulas are "not part of Bedouin storytelling, which is anecdotal and/or poetry based," evident in less emphasis on dialogue to support plot and themes than facial expression and emotional landscape.[53] In this regard, they share much with Bollywood, Kollywood, and Nollywood. Yunis suggests that increased comfort by Emirati filmmakers with self-critique could facilitate the development of Emirati filmmaking that would challenge Hollywood hegemony in the local exhibition market. In this regard, the loss of ADFF, GFF, and EFC diminishes the presence of a healthy film cultures where aspiring filmmakers can observe as established filmmakers from the Maghreb, Mashriq, South Asia, and Africa *critique* their

---

[52] Alia Yunis, "Film as National Building: The UAE Goes into the Movie Business," *CINEJ Cinema Journal* 3.2 (2014): 57–59.

[53] Yunis, "Film as National Building," 68.

own cultures—and sometimes their own states—from positions of *patriotism* rather than derision. Whereas Hollywood limits its investment to allegedly universal stories about middle-class white people and so-called global production values, filmmakers from regions around UAE would like to see less corruption in Egypt, for example, fewer fundamentalisms appropriating Islam in Pakistan, Syria, and Tunisia or Hinduism in India, and less sectarian suspicion in Lebanon or normalization of Israeli occupation of Palestine.

It remains to be seen whether the cancellation of ADFF and EFC will follow the precedent in neighboring Qatar of the cancellation of DTFF after four editions in 2012 to make space for two smaller—and less Hollywood-oriented—festivals. The Ajyal Youth Film Festival emphasizes community-based programming to build community across generations, which marked its fourth edition in November 2016, and the Qumra Film Festival offers first- and second-time filmmakers educational and financial support. These festivals mobilize different strategies towards the development of Qatari film culture outside the shadow of the well-intentioned, if sometimes culturally naïve, tutelage of a foreign film festival, such as Tribeca. In particular, the DFI has moved from programs that produce short films for students and other nonprofessional filmmakers to programs that educate students on media literacy, so that they can one day make their own films and convey different perspectives on both Qatar and the world. DIFF has enhanced its programming of Emirati feature-length and short films since the demise of ADFF, EFC, and GFF, suggesting that it might coalesce into vibrant location for Emirati filmmaking.

Due to its small yet highly diverse population, Emirati filmmaking must address multiple niche audiences rather than the so-called universalized ones of Hollywood. To support aspiring and established Emirati filmmakers, a vibrant film culture supported by regular film screenings, critical journals, and film education that is not only technical, but conceptual, historical, and theoretical, is necessary. Film production curricula based on analogue (celluloid) models are increasingly irrelevant, even in the United States. Presently, most of what is written about films is limited to newspaper and magazine journalism, which at best creates awareness of films but at worst rephrases the content of press releases. By supporting a film journal and cinémathèque with regular programming throughout the year, twofour54 and other UAE state agencies could provide a more integrated approach to its publicized goal of "growing local talent and nurturing the local film community."[54] Critical engagement with history and culture through the medium of film could help alter debates more productively than technical training or tutelage in Hollywood film conventions and practices. If Emirati filmmaking is to be located, then the question of locating it remains speculative, that is, locating it on the existing maps of "world cinema" challenges us to rethink the comfortable habits of defining cultures by nation-states or geopolitical regions and evaluating so-called technical imperfections as a consequence of scarce financial resources. There remains much work to be done by academics. As with Nollywood in Africa and Hallyuwood in East Asia, Emirati filmmaking could change the terms by which we conceive and evaluate Arab, Middle Eastern, and MENA filmmaking in ways that we cannot presently anticipate.

Acknowledgements This essay benefits from conversations with friends and colleagues, including Mohannad Al Bakri, Adel Al Jabri, Intishal Al Timimi, Awam Amkpa, Nezar Andary, Saglar Bougdaeva, Özge Calafato, Raman Chawla, Nadia Farès, Butheina Kazim, Mohammad Khawaja, Sheetal Majithia, Matthew MacLean, Cristina Mouallem, Sana Odeh, Gwenn Okruhlik, Kellen Quinn, E. Nina Rothe, Ella Shohat, Robert Stam, Robert Young, and Alia Yunis, as well as the support of Virginia Danielson, Renji Jacobs, Nicholas Martin, Rosel Erese, and Justin Parrot at the NYUAD Library, along with student research assistants Rand Abdulrahman, Amani Alsaied, Rabha Ashry, Hasan Nabulsi, and Sala Shaker, of Reindert Falkenburg, Philip Kennedy, Nils Lewis, and Nahed Ahmed at the NYUAD Institute, and of Nele Lenze, Charlotte Schriwer, Zubaidah binte Abdul Jalil, and everyone at the Middle East Institute at National University of Singapore. Any errors, however, are my own.

---

[54] "Mawaheb Overview," *Image Nation* website (2015): http://imagenationabudhabi.com/en/mawaheb/overview-mawaheb/.

CHAPTER 9

Protest Poetry On- and Offline: Trans-regional Interactions in the Arabian Gulf: An Example from Bahrain

Nele Lenze

INTRODUCTION

Cultural production formed an essential part of the recent uprisings across the Arab world, including electronic writing in a variety of platforms. In the age of new media, the distribution of literary production has changed and now offers a wide spectrum for the transmission of stories. Arab countries in the Gulf such as Oman, the United Arab Emirates (UAE), Saudi Arabia, Qatar, Bahrain, or Kuwait now have an active scene of authors who create literature, on a variety of available media platforms, particularly online. Online literature has emerged in the form of short stories posted on blogs, in forums, and online publishing houses, generating much commentary. Videos of recitation of poetry circulate on YouTube. Twitter and Facebook also serve as platforms for distribution. These methods of online distribution all contribute to the proliferation of digital literature in the Gulf.

N. Lenze (✉)
Middle East Institute, National University of Singapore,
Singapore, Singapore

© The Author(s) 2017
N. Lenze et al. (eds.), *Media in the Middle East*,
DOI 10.1007/978-3-319-65771-4_9

Like music and visual art, online literary texts serve as important continuations of traditional culture such as poetry and new media. More and more writers combine traditional forms of story transmission or classical poetry with YouTube videos, images, gifs or animation on blogs.[1]

Furthermore, online literature has found its way into mainstream media and is discussed in a variety of national newspapers, on TV, and on the radio, which in turn contributes to a new awareness of literary writing and production, as well as of the increase in literary production. In addition, writing online opens up possibilities to publish with less intervention from the censors in contrast to more traditional forms such as print media. In many countries, the internet has been an important platform for disseminating cultural production and news, even before the dramatic events of 2011.[2] Especially in those Gulf countries where the rate of internet penetration is high and high-speed access is readily available, literary and visual output has been distributed since the early 2000s. For example, in 2015 in Bahrain, the UAE and Qatar, the penetration rate was around 94%, compared to 65% in Saudi Arabia.[3]

In this chapter, I will consider a poem that was recited in Bahrain—and which went viral—as an example of the role of poetry recitation as a form of protest both on- and offline. Building on this, other means of dissemination of online literature will be explored to show connections and differences in a context of global and regional interactions online. Looking at the phenomenon of art as political dissent gives insights into a blossoming political culture that is strongly embedded in regional traditions. These recitations receive attention also from a global community through their distribution on the internet.

I will reflect on political dissent as a major part of cultural production and distribution online, reflecting on two aspects of this phenomenon. On the one hand, political and cultural activists are distributing their work more or less uncensored. On the other, governments establish or support counter-platforms for cultural dissemination in order to exert control over cultural production online. Ways of cultural dissemination in open platform and on platforms supported by governments will be part of the discussion of outreach and local audiences.

CULTURAL EXPRESSION AND CONTEXTUALIZATION: POETRY IN PRE-AND POST-PROTEST BAHRAIN

Historically, poetry has been a part of the literary tradition in Bahrain. Since the beginning of the twentieth century, written poetry has begun to proliferate in the country. Early modern Bahraini poetry can be traced back to Shaykh Ibrahim ibn Muhammad al-Khalifa (1850–1933), but the first and more influential romantic poet from Bahrain was Shaykh Muhammad ibn 'Isa al-Khalifa (1876–1964), whose poetry had a nationalistic character. Another prominent poet to mention is 'Abd al-Rahman Raf'iya (*1939), who was one of the first poets to be critical of social circumstances in Bahrain and who also wrote poetry in colloquial dialects. Inspired by him, or following his example, an increasing number of Bahrainis began to compose poetry and in 1969 the Bahrain Writers' Association was established. By the end of the 1970s, female poets such as Fawzia al-Sindi, Nabila Zubari, and Fathia Ajlan began to be recognised as poets, and in the 1990s, a new generation of poets, including Layla al-Sayed, Ali al-Jalawi, Hessa Buanain, Fatima al-Taytun and Karim Radhi, emerged as prominent writers. Many of them now live in exile because their work is considered to be politically controversial by the Bahraini authorities.[4]

Recent recitations of poetry stand in a long tradition of poetry recitations that have their roots in pre-Islamic times.[5] Poets such as Imru' al-Qays (early sixth century), al-Khansa, Abu Nuwas and many more are representatives of early Arabic poetry from the region. The historical antecedents of more recent Arabic protest poetry are well demonstrated in the work of the Palestinian poet Mahmud Darwish. Darwish is the most important representative of protest poetry in the twentieth century, whose work has been referenced and recited by people all over the Arab world. He subsequently gained worldwide recognition through the translations of his work into other languages.[6] More recently in Tunisia, where poetry has also played an important role during the uprisings, other protest poets became widely popular. Poets such as Belgachen Ya'qubi and Lazhar Dahwi continue to influence the cultural sphere of protest culture, and the works of the famous Tunisian poet Abu'l-Qasim al-Shabi (1909–1934) witnessed a resurgence during the uprisings.[7] These are examples from outside the Gulf countries and refer to poetry written in Arabic. They are mentioned here because they set the phenomenon of protest poetry in a wider frame.

Within the huge variety of cultural expression that emerged during the Arab Uprisings, poetry, music, graffiti, film, and other forms of art have been used to convey political messages to a wider audience. In the Middle East, poetry has been performed for centuries to express political views and other sociopolitically-oriented messages.

In the online sphere it is important to note that poetry had been published and disseminated for many years, even before the start of the uprisings of 2011. Already in the early 2000s, with the start of wider accessibility of the media, cultural production online has increased significantly, particularly with the popularity of Web 2.0 tools. These emerged in the mid-2000s, and have made more poetry accessible online, not only in Bahrain but all over the Arab world.

A brief overview of the political situation in Bahrain is indispensable to achieving an understanding of the importance of the poetry that will be discussed in this chapter. Omar Al-Shehabi offers a more detailed overview on political movements in Bahrain.[8] Since 2011, Bahrain's protest have received more attention in the media. It has experienced constant political protests in that year, which have been mostly answered by police and military force (or violence) not only by local forces, but also with the engagement of the Saudi Arabian and Emirati military. These protests were initiated because the Shi'i population demanded equal treatment and an end of systematic discrimination.[9] Demands differ as a variety of political groups are actively resisting. On the one hand, there are demands for the country to be political reformed into a democratic constitutional monarchy. On the other hand, regime change is an explicit aim.[10] The initial demands later evolved into calls for political freedom as well as for an end to the monarchy, specifically the rule of King Hamad b. 'Isa Al Khalifa. They culminated in the mass protests of February 17, 2011, the so-called 'Bloody Thursday', a result of a major protest that took place at the Pearl Roundabout (Dawwār al-Lu'lu') in Manama, the capital of Bahrain. Four people were killed and about 300 were injured that night.[11] By February 2015, almost one hundred people had lost their lives in ongoing protests and hundreds have been arrested and imprisoned—and continue to be imprisoned—for expressing anti-government sentiments.[12]

In Bahrain, poetry by both women and men holds an important place in the 2011 protests on Dawwār al-Lu'lu', as well as in other locations.

One of the best-known Bahraini recent poets is 'Ayat al-Qormazi who recited her own political poems on public squares in Manama. 'Ayat al-Qormezi's poetry is not only important for expressing public offline dissent in Bahrain, but as a result of her activism, a multitude of other artists have also contributed to the movement.

In the following section, I will briefly consider the poem by 'Ayat al-Qormezi that was performed at the Dawwār al-Lu'lu' in March 2011.[13] I will not provide a literary analysis of the poem; instead I will discuss it in the context of ensuing online interactions and political dissent.

'Ayat al-Qormezi's Poetry Recitation

For this chapter, the untitled poem recited by 'Ayat al-Qormezi [14] on March 25, 2011, stands as one example among the wide variety of political poetry in the Arab World. For different countries and regions as well as political events, poetry serves as a form of protest. In the context of the demonstrations in Bahrain in 2011, I chose this poem because it received attention both locally and abroad.

'Ayat al-Qormezi, at the time a 19-year-old student, performed an untitled poem depicting a conversation between Satan and King Hamad Bin Khalifa, as a form of protest during the early days of the Bahraini uprising. She performed the poem at the Dawwār al-Lu'lu' in front of about 300 people in a recital that lasted approximately ten minutes.

Perhaps the strongest attack on the ruler can be found in the following excerpt of the poem:

(...)

Hamad Says

> Hold on my brother Satan,
> I have not yet finished filling my stomach
> with their blood
> I have not yet finished filling my stomach
> with their blood
> I have not yet naturalized the rest of my family, friends and their
> women
> I have not yet instructed all my fellow thugs
> To become birth-giving machines where mother and father work
> together while my other thugs collide with them too
> I have not yet instructed all my fellow thugs

To become birth-giving machines where mother and father work
together while my other thugs collide with them too
I have not yet finished forcing every candle of dreams (youth) on
this motherland
To each traffic light he stands
Begging each passerby
"Please buy water bottles from me"
While nobody responds to his call
I have not yet finished torturing every turbaned man in this land
Every youth and child
Nor have I yet finished stomping upon the followed of youth inside
my prisons
I have not yet finished opening a million routs to humiliation
Nor have I yet finished putting this entire nation into the state of
lamentation
Not yet O Satan has the number of youths with martyrdom upon
their chest heightened
With no job, nor occupation held
Forget them, they deserve it
Hamad says to forget you, you deserve it! What do you say?
Down with Hamad
Not yet O Satan has the number of youths with martyrdom upon
their chest heightened
With no job, nor occupation held
I have not yet finished paying each south Asian on this precious land
To hold our flag up (at pro-government rallies) shouting
in a poor Arabic accent Long lives the father of Salman
I have not yet finished sucking blood from flat to flat with the bur-
den of bills
Meanwhile the thugs have lands and houses
But not to worry those affected don't exceed 120 in number
I don't anyone will be able to hear their cries
Sarcasm Hamad hasn't yet received the new figures of Bahrain
TV. He still thinks we at Pearl Square are still 120 and doesn't know
that we have actually increased to 320

(…)[15]

In order to get an understanding of the political dimensions of the
complete poem, a brief summary follows:

In her poem al-Qurmazi voices a common criticism, stating that the
violence of King Hamad's against his own people is beyond even Satan's

comprehension. She raises issues of corruption, media manipulation, and the problem of mobilizing Shi'i and Sunni groups against each other.

As can be seen in the video uploaded to YouTube, during the recitation, the audience joins into chant some of the lines of her poem in order to show their agreement. "Down with Hamad" was one of the most-repeated phrases.

The next part of the poem gives Satan's reply. Satan calls King Hamad overconfident and reminds him of the high numbers of protestors that have crowded Bahrain's streets. He makes it clear that King Hamad, with his brutal treatment of the protestors, has actually become worse than Satan. A repetition of the line 'Sunnis and Shi'is are brothers' follows this statement. During the performance, the audience confirms this by repeating 'Sunnis and Shi'is are brothers and we should never sell this nation'. Al-Qormezi continues her poem with a passage acknowledging the martyrs that have sacrificed their lives during the uprising. It concludes with Satan's final suggestion to King Hamad to gather his 'trash of a useless regime' because the nation is 'out of his league'.

After the poetry reading al-Qormezi was arrested and imprisoned.[16] Her identity was exposed through a Facebook group that was established to denounce political activists and expose their workplace and their names.[17] According to a number of sources, during the nine days of her imprisonment, she was tortured and threatened in multiple ways.[18]

As poetry performance and recitation has a long tradition in the region, it is a particularly appropriate tool to attract and engage an audience. Reaching out to a wide group of people that feel connected not only to the content but also to the form of disseminating oppositional opinion helps to form a closer bond. This is one reason why al-Qormezi's performance had such a strong impact and led to harsh personal consequences such as public humiliation and imprisonment.

Colloquial poetry has always created a close connection to a live audience.[19] Oral poetry has a long historical and cultural tradition in the Gulf; it has the ability to move the audience's emotions and to create a more personal connection with a story or narrative account. As we can see from the outstanding popularity of Mahmud Darwish's poetry, this genre of literary expression can help to create a unified identity for people who are united behind the same cause. The use of colloquial language is not only inherent to this form of protest poetry, but also has a commonality within the regionalisms of the online sphere.[20]

While literary expression has appeared in the physical public spaces in the Middle East, such as print media, with the spread of internet access, a larger output of literary works is now available online. This is mostly because of the possibility of publishing a text instantly, and is clearly demonstrated in the case of al-Qormezi's poetry recitations, which were filmed and then uploaded to YouTube where they have subsequently reached more than 100,000 viewers since they were first posted in 2012.

With the uploading of the video, not only local audiences became aware of the performance, but it also reached an international audience which was able to take notice of the events as they unfolded in the country. As the videos increased in popularity, they began to appear with English subtitles in order to make the delivery accessible to an international public. Al-Qormezi's recitation also gained a considerable amount of attention because of her arrest and imprisonment by the authorities shortly after her recital.[21] As a result of these events, the poet b0camse a national figure.

POLITICAL DISSENT, CULTURAL PRODUCTION, AND STATE COUNTER-ACTIONS

When examining political dissent and cultural production in the Gulf, two streams of state responses can be observed. On the one hand, protest poetry continues to be performed and produced and its creators get arrested and imprisoned, unless they are already living in exile. On the other hand, authorities have started co-opting art as a form of political expression by creating physical and virtual platforms for 'clean' poetry that is not targeted against the state. These literary works are not protest poetry, but they still a form of dissemination of political views. Government institutions or institutions connected to the government have tried to offer platforms that encourage internet users to share cultural products. For example, in Kuwait the online publishing house Nashiri (www.nashiri.net) distributes a huge variety of locally produced literary texts, but clearly states that everything published needs to be in accordance with the moral understanding and law of Kuwait.[22] In order to regulate poetic and other cultural expressions, Bahrain's regime established an official poetry festival in 2012 where state-approved poets and performers could present lyrical texts.[23]

Means of self-expression are limited because of government restrictions. Hence the opportunities that open up with participatory culture online are of great importance in the context of authoritarian regimes, as they help to exchange and develop ideas in less restricted or censored spaces than would be possible offline.[24] Of course, there are also *dawawin* and *majaalis*[25] and book clubs where people can discuss sensitive issues in private with an invited audience. These are private spaces that encourage both debate and exchange. In contrast to the internet they are not accessible to a general audience and are not open to the public.

The online sphere can also serve as a less censored place for publication. As we have seen in instances of political activism across the world, participants tend to be more engaged online than in a physical location due to the comparatively minimal effort and commitment required. This form of online activism is generally known as 'slacktivism'.[26]

During the recent uprisings in the Arab World, it became obvious that actual physical participation is the key to initiating political change and speaking up against the authorities. al-Qurmazi virtual space is merely a tool for dissemination and organization, as the internet shutdown in Egypt has shown, people still mobilize without the need for social media tools.

There are certain benefits to the general public when it comes to the distribution of cultural goods on the internet. Online, it is easier to reach a wider—and sometimes even a global—audience. Identity can also be superficially anonymized in order to avoid societal punishment. However, electronic surveillance tools can help to identify most political activists, so that virtual space is not necessarily a safer place in itself than physical space. In addition to that, it clearly shows the authorities what part of society disagrees with the political agenda of the government and gives an overall picture of current moods and trends.

While there are many differences (related to speed of publication, editing process, etc.) between publishing online and publishing in print, virtual and non-virtual spaces also share a number of similarities. One of them is that both spaces can easily be destroyed. A virtual place can be shut down or censored and thereby made inaccessible; similarly, a physical space such as Dawwār al-Lu'lu' can be torn down and transformed into something new which bears no resemblance to its symbolic past. However, in order for activists to reach people on the ground as well as the authorities, performances or mass gatherings are necessary to create awareness of discontent. Certainly, more literary and other cultural production from the Gulf countries can be found online than in any physical space, merely because a virtual space creates the illusion of being a more protected environment as well as of having relatively low barriers of distribution. This means low barriers in terms of censorship, but also because users self-publish, which allows them to skip the procedures of getting texts approved by editors and publishers.

There are plenty of reasons for not allowing a publication to be accessible, the most common explanation being because of its deviation from generally accepted values and norms. One common criticism of poets raised by authorities across the Arab World is that they might spread secular thoughts or even blasphemous views through their works. Shaykh Yusuf al-Qaradawi,[27] for example, accused Tunisian poet Awlad Ahmad of atheism, while in Saudi Arabia, the poet Rushdi al-Dawsari was arrested because his poem allegedly contained 'socratic symbols'.[28]

Internationally known incidents in Saudi Arabia have been reported where poets and writers have been arrested for publishing online material that the authorities deem to be controversial. One such case is that of Habib al-Maatiq, a poet who was sentenced to several years' imprisonment for working on the website of the al-Fajr Cultural Network. The website reported repeatedly on protests in the Eastern provinces of Saudi Arabia. Other examples include the arrest of Saudi novelist Turki al-Hamad for being suspected of tweeting critical thoughts on Islam, and the Palestinian poet Ashraf Fayadh, who was arrested for non-proven allegations of spreading atheism on Twitter in 2013 and 2014, and is currently facing a sentence of 800 lashes and eight years in prison.

Ways of Cultural Dissemination Online: From Open Forms of Distribution to Institutionalized Platforms

In addition to the wealth of examples of poetry appearing on online platforms such as YouTube, there is also a continuously increasing amount of short stories, visual novels, and poetry that is being presented online in forums, on blogs, or on personal websites. Publications can be disseminated on Facebook, Twitter and on message boards. Disseminating cultural products via these tools is relatively unrestricted because it does not need to be in accordance with moral values and censorship filters enforced by some autocratic countries, with only selective self-censorship needing to be applied.

Online writers can now publish either on their own on blogs or on other Web 2.0 platforms, meaning they have more freedom when it comes to language and content. In forums, for example, language is often very colloquial and it seems that as a result of the vast amount of stories being published, monitoring is fairly limited. On blogs writers publish either under their own name or using a pseudonym; here, they are very much in charge of their own product, design, and output. However, it is also easier to track their activities, if the content they publish is unacceptable to authorities. If caught, poets and other artists that work on political themes are regularly tortured or imprisoned for their works.

For more institutionalized platforms of publication, a number of outlets can serve as examples. Bahrain, the UAE, and Kuwait encourage their youth to publish in a controlled infrastructure for cultural production online. Platforms such as the Kuwaiti e-publisher Dar al-Nashiri, mentioned previously and Jihat al-Shi'r facilitate the distribution of poetry and literature to an Arabic-speaking audience. Dar al-Nashiri is not a state-run enterprise but it enables poets and writers to disseminate their work in a surrounding that works well in accordance with the law.

Commonly, e-publishing houses distribute articles, stories, or novels on their websites and may also include podcasts and video programs. These products can either be read online or downloaded in a format that is readable on computers or e-readers. The literary texts are published there for the first time. Texts on e-publishing websites are commonly edited, in contrast to those on forums or blogs. Publishing texts through Dar al-Nashiri is different from the more private method of publishing on a personal blog or from distributing texts in forums. Firstly, authors at Dar al-Nashiri publish under their real names, and with a short biography of the writer. Secondly all stories are published in Modern Standard Arabic and must not violate morals or the law.[29] Dar al-Nashiri is well established within its cultural environment in Kuwait, having been featured in local newspapers, as well as having won the "Internet Contest Award 2005", sponsored by Shaykh Salim al-Ali al-Sabah of Kuwait.[30] The enforced guidelines make Dar al-Nashiri seem a rather formal way of online distribution, as writers are more limited in their production than they are through independent publishing in forums and blogs. On the other hand, distributing with Dar al-Nashiri implies that an audience is already established and users do not need to encourage readers to visit their websites.

Another more institutionalized form of publishing can be found in the UAE. This year, the Abu Dhabi Authority for Culture & Heritage started a series of publications by young Emirati authors through a "Digital Publishing Corner". Together with Apple, the 'My Library' application was launched at the Abu Dhabi book fair. This is a project that makes available publications in the Emirati National Library, including the Qalam project which encourages young Emirati writers to publish digitally as well as in print. Through this partnership, these applications are now available on iPhone and the iPad.[31]

According to interviews I conducted in Oman in 2009/10 and through an online survey in the UAE, Kuwait, and Saudi Arabia, authors and poets seem to disseminate works on both institutionalized and independent publishing spaces. Sometimes they also publish in state-run newspapers as an additional outlet to their private publications.[32] Both independent and institutionalized platforms try to reach a wider audience and interact with readers as well as other artists. When going deeper into the subject, it is interesting to ask how the different platforms of publishing affect the content and form of the literary work. Within the findings of my field research in the Gulf, it appears that self-censorship is one of the outcomes of publishing in more controlled environments.

OUTREACH AND LOCAL AUDIENCES

Similar platforms to those mentioned above that disseminate political opinions online, either from an activist's perspective or from a regulated perspective, can be found in many countries of the world. Being locally and globally reachable is a major benefit of digital publications for all writers. For example, the physical place where al-Qurmazi's poetry performance took place, the Pearl Roundabout/Dawwār al-Lu'lu', no longer exists, as it was torn down by the authorities to prevent further protests.[33] The removal of the physical place of protest seems like a desperate attempt to create silence, naively suggesting that removing the physical place of opposition would somehow prevent the opposition from being active. As the protests continue in Bahrain, it is clear that despite the physical removal of Dawwār al-Lu'lu', opposition movements continue to exist. When physical spaces become inaccessible, the virtual space gains more importance. This is significant, because it suggests that instant audience outreach can shift to a virtual space. On the other hand, as an example of the opposite development, when the internet is shut down, more protestors might find their way to the streets, as witnessed in Egypt. This might be a very specific case but it serves here to show that mobilization is still very much related to cause rather than to a particular medium. In addition to mobilization as a benefit of the internet, archiving activism online, for example on YouTube, is important. For example, Twitter archives have been important for later work on the early days of the Egyptian uprisings. "Tahrir Documents" is a website that engages in an ongoing effort to archive and translate activist papers from the 2011 uprising and there are many other similar platforms.[34]

The audience of these cultural products is mostly local, or at least regional, rather than global. Poetry is, first and foremost, performed and composed for an audience that is familiar with a certain dialect and cultural heritage. Online, use of a regional language is intended to reach a regional audience, which may seem counter-intuitive when talking about a global medium. The same is true for short stories in forums as well as on blogs. A regional use of language means that in the different countries of the Arab World writers may use dialect in their writing instead of Modern Standard Arabic, which unites traditional media all over the Arab-speaking countries. Regional dialects (more so Gulf dialects than wider-known dialects such as Egyptian or Lebanese which are promoted through TV shows and series) are not familiar to every Arabic speaker and might thus limit the audience that is receiving and reading as well as interacting with published texts.

Local production of online cultural content empowers writers and activists and also helps like-minded people find a common point of identity. This is important, as people with the same interest have the possibility of connecting with each other. This is especially helpful if those involved do not know each other beforehand or do not know that there are others who have the same mindset—ideological, creative, or otherwise. Local literature can spread within the region if the same language is spoken; it also has the possibility of reaching a global audience when translation is available. Global interactions are mostly made through performances of political dissent.

The internet in the Gulf opens up a variety of methods for distributing cultural production to the rest of the world. YouTube videos of musicians, activists, or comedians can be easily disseminated and might find an audience wider than just fans from the region. The same is true for audio files on Soundcloud or texts and imagery such as memes, photos and comics on microblogging platforms and blogs. Digital artist 'Abdullah al-Mutayri from Kuwait emphasizes that communication strategies online are stretched far in the Gulf. This enables people to keep a strong focus on the local or regional while simultaneously forming a connection to the global an aspect highlighted by the examples provided in this chapter.[35]

CONCLUSION

Bahrain, as an example of a country with only limited freedom of expression, is a relevant example in the Gulf demonstrating the restrictive conditions that political poets are subjected to. The case of al-Qormezi is one recent representation of protest poetry that has to be seen in a wider context of historical political and poetic expression all over the Arab World. Newer forms of dissemination online of literature and poetry are in forums, on blogs, on Instagram and YouTube publishing while traditionally content would be shared in newspapers, books, and orally. Depending on the intentions of the writers, different platforms can be chosen to distribute works. The usage of institutionalized and less controlled platforms is of great importance for spreading political messages through cultural means. While the internet offers opportunities for producing less controlled publications that artists and activists can use, more institutionalized platforms help to convey messages in accordance with guidelines laid out by authorities. It is also apparent that institutionalized and privately run cultural production spaces reach out to a wider audience through multiple approaches. One of these is to encourage more participation through organizing competitions and offering prizes. More institutionalized platforms might be more prestigious due to handing out of prizes or offering printed versions of the writings. Online media help to promote local and regional messages, which is necessary especially when physical spaces are inaccessible. Independent platforms need more engagement from the writers when it comes to promoting their works and finding an audience, but they also offer more freedom when it comes to content, language and styles.

To conclude, one may suggest that live performance and recitation on the street is a necessary component of creating protest cultures to enable them to reach a local audience, and to encourage movements on the ground. This form of expression reaches the audience immediately and involves them in the enactment. In addition, online media is a highly effective tool for the instant sharing of common ideas and cultural products. It holds fewer barriers than publishing in print or organizing a live recitation, which offers more immediate physical risk. However, the political consequences in terms of publishing through either of these spaces, online or offline, remain much the same.

NOTES

1. The Jordanian writer Mohamad Sanajleh produced the novel "shāt" (chat), which is integrated in a flash animation and hosted on the website of the "Arab E-Writers Union". Chat is an interactive novel that leads the user through its story by encouraging him to click on each new text bit, offering extra text pieces in pop-up windows that simulate IM conversations, http://www.arab-ewriters.com/chat.
2. Pan-Arab organizations such as the Arab E-Writers Union were founded earlier (2005) but also in forums in the Gulf short stories and poetry was published in the early 2000s.
3. This means the majority of the population has access to the internet which makes it a less elitist medium in the Gulf than in other countries where only a more wealthy and/or more educated part of the population is able to go online. "Middle East Internet Users, Population and Facebook Statistics 2015," Internet World Stats. Accessed February 20, 2016, http://www.internetworldstats.com/stats5.htm.
4. Hameed al Qaed, *Pearl, Dreams of Shell.* Colorado: Howling Dog Press, 2007.
5. Suzanne Pinckney Stetkevych, ed., *Early Islamic Poetry and Poetics.* Oxford: Ashgate Variorum, 2009, xvii.
6. In the late 1970s and 1980s in English, French and German and following that in many other languages.
7. Mohamed-Salah Omri, "A Revolution of Dignity and Poetry," *Boundary 2*, no. 39 (2012).
8. Omar Al-Shehabi. "Political Movements in Bahrain Across the Long Twentieth Century (1900–2015)." *Oxford Handbook of Contemporary Middle-Eastern and North African History.* Amal Ghazal and Jens Hanssen (eds). April 2017, http://www.oxfordhandbooks.com/view/10.1093/oxfordhb/9780199672530.001.0001/oxfordhb-9780199672530-e-27?mediaType=Article.
9. Kristian Coates, "Bahrain's Uncertain Future," *Foreign Policy*, November 23, 2011. Accessed March 11, 2012, http://foreignpolicy.com/2011/11/23/bahrains–uncertain–future/.

10. Omar Al-Shehabi, "Political Movements in Bahrain Across the Long Twentieth Century (1900–2015)." *Oxford Handbook of Contemporary Middle-Eastern and North African History*. Amal Ghazal and Jens Hanssen (eds). April 2017. p. 16, http://www.oxfordhandbooks.com/view/10.1093/oxfordhb/9780199672530.001.0001/oxfordhb-9780199672530-e-27?mediaType=Article.

11. "Bahrain Protests: Police Break Up Pearl Square Crowd," *BBC News*, February 17, 2011. Accessed April 15, 2011, http://www.bbc.com/news/world-middle-east-12490286.

12. "Individuals Killed By Government's Excessive Use of Force Since 14 February 2011," Bahrain Center for Human Rights, updated 6 February 2015. Accessed February 23, 2016, http://bahrainrights.org/en/node/3864.

13. Her performances are documented here: "2012 يناير الثورة شاعرة قصدية ائر للحرية الحر مهرجان مزي لقرا آيات 6 YouTube, January 16, 2016. Accessed February 23, 2016, https://www.com/watch?v=alx2Kn5mJdw.

14. The poem is untitled but commonly known as the poem of the heroine 'Ayat al-Qurmazi (شعر البطلة آيات القرمزي) The complete poem can be found here: "حركة ميه سلا الا ي جعفر" Mzmzmz. Accessed February 23, 2016, http://mzmzmz.nforum.biz/t1872–topic.

15. The video of the original performance can be found here: "Ayat al-Qurmazi—A Poem Worth a Year of Brutal Torture and Imprisonment," YouTube, June 15, 2011. Accessed February 20, 2016, https://www.youtube.com/watch?v=mcCEk9s82ac.

16. Patrick Cockburn, "Locked Up for Reading a Poem," *Independent*, June 2, 2011. Accessed February 23, 2016, http://www.independent.co.uk/news/world/middle-east/locked-up-for-reading-a-poem-2292032.html.

17. Marc Owen Jones, "Social Media, Surveillance, and Spying in the Bahrain Uprising," in *Social Media in the Arab World: Communication and Public Opinion in the Gulf State,* eds Barrie Gunter, Mokhtar Elareshi, Khalid Al-Jaber. London: I.B. Tauris, 2016, p. 189.

18. Nahrain Al-Mousawi, "A Poetry of Resistance: The Disappearance of Ayat al-Qormezi in Bahrain's Hidden Story," *Jadaliyya*, June 14, 2011. Accessed February 23, 2016, http://www.jadaliyya.com/pages/index/1883/a-poetry-of-resistance_the-disappearance-of-ayat-a.

19. Read more on that in "Colloquial Arabic Poetry, Politics, and the Press in Modern Egypt" by Marilyn Booth, Published online: January 1, 2009, http://dx.doi.org/10.1017/S0020743800021966 and Noha Radwan, *Egyptian Colloquial Poetry in the Modern Arabic Canon: New Readings of Shi'r al-'Amiyya*. New York: Palgrave Macmillan, 2012.

20. That means that despite the internet being a worldwide phenomenon and information being globally accessible, users tend to access more regional

or local websites than international ones as a result of language barriers and stronger interests in regional news.

21. Richard Spencer, "Bahraini woman poet tells of torture while in custody," *The Telegraph*, July 14, 2011. Accessed February 20, 2016, http://www.telegraph.co.uk/news/worldnews/middleeast/bahrain/8638396/Bahraini-woman-poet-tells-of-torture-while-in-custody.html.

22. Rules for publishing are posted on the website, "كيف تصبح كاتبا في ناشري؟" Nashiri. Accessed February 23, 2016, http://nashiri.net/join.html.

23. "باقات من الشعر الملوّن في مهرجان "الشعر ألوان الحياة" بمتحف موقع قلعة البحرين" Al Ayam. Accessed February 23, 2016, http://bit.ly/1OrEcmm.

24. A deeper discussion of this topic can be found in *The Participatory Condition in the Digital Age*, eds Darin Barney, Gabriella Coleman, Christine Ross, Jonathan Sterne, and Tamar Tembeck. Minneapolis: University of Minnesota Press, 2016. And also Henry Jenkins, *Confronting the Challenges of Participatory Culture: Media Education for the 21st Century*. Cambridge, MA: MIT Press, 2009.

25. These are private venues where men gather or congregate, discussing topics of relevance.

26. The *Oxford English Dictionary* defines the term as "working to achieve political or social change by using the Internet to carry out actions that are thought to require little effort or time." "Slacktivism," Oxford Dictionaries. Accessed February 23, 2016, http://www.oxforddictionaries.com/definition/learner/slacktivism.

27. Al-Qaradawi is an Egyptian Islamic theologian with strong ties to the Muslim Brotherhood who has published over 120 books.

28. Iman al-Qahtani, "Saudi poet busted for "sorcery" poems," *Al Arabiya*, November 9, 2008. Accessed February 23, 2016, http://www.alarabiya.net/articles/2008/11/09/59794.html.

29. Rules for publishing are posted on the website: "كيف تصبح كاتبا في ناشري؟" Nashiri.

30. More on this on the personal website of Ḥayāt al-Yāqūt http: "الأدب!"...اكاديميةنور اموكب" Hayat. Accessed February 23, 2016, www.hayatt.net.

31. "The Abu Dhabi Authority for Culture & Heritage announces the activities of the 21st Session of the Abu Dhabi International Book Fair," Abu Dhabi International Book Fair. Accessed February 23, 2016, http://www.adbookfair.com/the-abu-dhabi-authority-for-culture-heritage-announces-the-activities-of-the-21st-session-of-the-abu-dhabi-international-book-fair/.

32. More on that in the thesis: Nele Lenze, "Telling stories online in the Gulf: prolegomena to the study of an emerging form of Arabic literary expression" (Ph.D. diss., University of Oslo, 2012).

33. "Bahrain Tears Down Protest Symbol," *Al Jazeera*, March 18, 2011. Accessed February 23, 2016, http://www.aljazeera.com/news/middlee ast/2011/03/201131823554586194.html.
34. "Tahrir Documents". Accessed 19 September 2016, http://www.tahrir-documents.org/about/.
35. Abdullah al-Mutairi, interview by Emily Wang, *Electra Street*, November 2014. Accessed February 23, 2016, http://electrastreet.net/2014/11/interview-with-abdullah-al-mutairi/.

BIBLIOGRAPHY

Booth, Marilyn. "Colloquial Arabic Poetry, Politics, and the Press in Modern Egypt." 1 January 2009. http://dx.doi.org/10.1017/S0020743800021966.

Dean, Jodi. "Why the Net is Not a Public Sphere." *Constellations* 10 (2003): 95–112.

Jones, Marc Owen "Social Media, Surveillance, and Spying in the Bahrain Uprising." In *Social Media in the Arab World. Communication and Public Opinion in the Gulf States.* Barrie Gunter, Mokhtar Elareshi, Khalid Al-Jaber eds. London: I.B. Tauris, 2016) p. 189.

Omri, Mohamed-Salah. "A Revolution of Dignity and Poetry," *Boundary* vol. 2, 39 (2012).

Radwan, Noha. *Egyptian Colloquial Poetry in the Modern Arabic Canon.* Palgrave Macmillan, 2012.

Stetkevych, Suzanne Pinckney, ed. *Early Islamic Poetry and Poetics.* Oxford: Ashgate Variorum, 2009.

Online sources

"كيف تصبح كاتبا في ناشري ؟" Nashiri. Accessed February 23, 2016, http://nashiri.net/join.html.

"باقات من الشعر الملوّن في مهرجان الشعر ألوان الحياة" بمتحف موقع قلعة البحرين". Al Ayam. Accessed February 23, 2016, http://alay.am/rkH1uV.

"Bahrain Protests: Police Break Up Pearl Square Crowd." BBC News. February 17, 2011. Accessed April 15, 2011, http://www.bbc.com/news/world-middle-east-12490286.

"Bahrain tears down protest symbol." *Al Jazeera*, March 18, 2011. Accessed February 23, 2016, http://www.aljazeera.com/news/middlee ast/2011/03/201131823554586194.html.

"Individuals Killed By Government's Excessive Use of Force Since 14 February 2011." Bahrain Center for Human Rights, updated 6 February 2015. Accessed February 23, 2016, http://bahrainrights.org/en/node/3864.

"Middle East Internet Users, Population and Facebook Statistics 2015." *Internet World Stats*. Accessed February 20, 2016, http://www.internetworldstats.com/stats5.htm.

Abu Dhabi International Book Fair, Accessed February 23, 2016, http://www.adbookfair.com/the-abu-dhabi-authority-for-culture-heritage-announces-the-activities-of-the-21st-session-of-the-abu-dhabi-international-book-fair/.

al Qurmazi, Ayat. (شعر البطلة آيات القرمزي) The complete poem can be found here: "جعفر حركة ميه سل الا ي" Mzmzmz. Accessed February 23, 2016, http://mzmzmz.nforum.biz/t1872-topic.

Al-Mousawi, Nahrain. "A Poetry of Resistance: The Disappearance of Ayat al-Qormezi in Bahrain's Hidden Story." *Jadaliyya*, June 14, 2011. Accessed February 23, 2016, http://www.jadaliyya.com/pages/index/1883/a-poetry-of-resistance_the-disappearance-of-ayat-a.

al-Qahtani, Iman. "Saudi Poet Busted for "Sorcery" Poems." *Al Arabiya*, November 9, 2008. Accessed February 23, 2016, http://www.alarabiya.net/articles/2008/11/09/59794.html.

Al-Shehabi, Omar. "Political Movements in Bahrain Across the Long Twentieth Century (1900–2015)." *Oxford Handbook of Contemporary Middle-Eastern and North African History*. Amal Ghazal and Jens Hanssen (eds). April 2017. http://www.oxfordhandbooks.com/view/10.1093/oxfordhb/9780199672530.001.0001/oxfordhb-9780199672530-e-27?mediaType=Article.

Coates, Kristian. "Bahrain's Uncertain Future." *Foreign Policy*, November 23, 2011. Accessed March 11, 2012, http://foreignpolicy.com/2011/11/23/bahrains-uncertain-future/.

Cockburn, Patrick. "Locked up for reading a poem." *Independent*, June 2, 2011. Accessed February 23, 2016, http://www.independent.co.uk/news/world/middle-east/locked-up-for-reading-a-poem-2292032.html.

Lenze, Nele: "Telling Stories Online in the Gulf: Prolegomena to the Study of an Emerging Form of Arabic Literary Expression" (PhD diss., University of Oslo, 2012). https://www.duo.uio.no/bitstream/handle/10852/34188/Telling-stories-online-in-the-Gulf-Nele-Lenze.pdf?sequence=1.

Oxford Dictionaries. Accessed February 23, 2016, http://www.oxforddictionaries.com/definition/learner/slacktivism.

Sanajleh, Mohamad. "shāt" (chat), http://www.arab-ewriters.com/chat.

Spencer, Richard. "Bahraini Woman Poet Tells of Torture While in Custody." *The Telegraph*, July 14, 2011. Accessed February 20, 2016, http://www.telegraph.co.uk/news/worldnews/middleeast/bahrain/8638396/Bahraini-woman-poet-tells-of-torture-while-in-custody.html.

Tahrir Documents. Accessed 19 September 2016. http://www.tahrirdocuments.org/about/.

Wang, Emily. "Interview with Abdullah al-Mutairi." *Electra Street*. Accessed February 23, 2016, http://electrastreet.net/2014/11/interview-with-abdullah-al-mutairi/.

Videos

"ائر للحرية الحر مهرجان مزي لقرا آيات الثورة شاعرة قصدية6ينية 2012" YouTube, January 16, 2016. Accessed February 23, 2016, https://www.youtube.com/watch?v=alx2Kn5mJdw.
"Ayat Al-Qormezi—A Poem Worth a Year of Brutal Torture and Imprisonment." YouTube, June 15, 2011. Accessed February 20, 2016, https://www.youtube.com/watch?v=mcCEk9s82ac.

CHAPTER 10

Arabic in a Time of Revolution: Sociolinguistic Notes from Egypt

Ivan Panovic

Looking back at what is often referred to as the Egyptian Revolution of 2011 and trying to assess its legacy in today's Egypt, one may be tempted to conclude that very little has changed in Egyptian society in a way that could be described as 'revolutionary', let alone 'for the better'. Around January 25, 2016, many opinion pieces were published to mark the fifth anniversary of the uprising which had put an end to Hosni Mubarak's three-decade rule in only eighteen days. Repeatedly, these articles invoked feelings of disillusion and very little hope. And a year later, one only needs to read the chapter on Egypt in the Human Rights Watch World Report 2017[1] to conclude that, when it comes to ruthlessness and authoritarianism, the current president of Egypt, Abdel Fatah el-Sisi, has already put Mubarak to shame.

While, at first sight, this conclusion may hold true in the political and socio-economic spheres, significant changes have been taking place

I. Panovic (✉)
Linguistics and Multilingual Studies, School of Humanities,
Nanyang Technological University, Singapore, Republic of Singapore

© The Author(s) 2017
N. Lenze et al. (eds.), *Media in the Middle East*,
DOI 10.1007/978-3-319-65771-4_10

in the sociocultural domain for quite some time now. The most important among them, I argue, is the transformation of the Egyptian linguascape. In this chapter, I discuss contemporary literacy practices against the background of some recurrent ideological debates in the Arabic-speaking world. Rather than focusing exclusively on media, which, as will become evident below, I do take into consideration, here I describe the ongoing reconfiguration of the linguistic repertoires that many Egyptians had been creatively using in various vernacular literacy events and in different domains since long before the uprising of 2011. These repertoires are still used, and will continue to be used in ever more diverse and diversifying ways. In other words, I describe one revolution in Egypt (and, arguably, in the entire Arab world) that will not be countered—the sociolinguistic one.

ARABIC AND DEMOCRACY

In an article published in *The Guardian* on June 14, 2003, Niloofar Haeri commented on the linguistic situation in the Arab World and concluded:

> Today many in the Arab world are talking about the lack of democracy in their region. But there is little debate about a linguistic situation that makes it hard for political pluralism to flourish. No one except the Arabs themselves can bring democracy to their societies. And for that to happen, there is an urgent need for a language that facilitates open debate and questioning—not least about language itself. But the minority of Arabs who are proficient in classical Arabic continue to claim that everyone understands the language and so there are no problems.
>
> An inclusive and accessible language is essential to freedom of speech. Otherwise, we continue to spin.

(Haeri 2003a)

The entire article is the gist of a broader argument which Haeri pursued in her book *Sacred Language, Ordinary People* (2003b), and was based on her ethnographic research that explored the nexus of language ideologies, culture and everyday life in contemporary Egypt. The main research questions were driven by the fact that in Egypt, just like in any other Arab country, the official language is (what Haeri labels) 'Classical Arabic' (as in 'the language of the Qur'an'), a variety that is no one's 'mother tongue' and can only be acquired through formal schooling. At the same time, what people throughout the Arab world do acquire as their 'mother tongues' are regional vernacular varieties that differ, often considerably, from Classical Arabic, but are not given any kind of statutory official recognition. Furthermore, argues Haeri, due to its strong links and associations with the Holy Qur'an and Islam, Classical Arabic is considered 'sacred' by the majority of Muslims, Arabs and non-Arabs alike. This situation, in turn, presents a serious challenge to any attempt at 'modernizing' the language so that it can cope with the demands of the contemporary age. From the article, we also learn that when British journalists, subeditors and writers are asked about language and who or what defines 'correct usage', most of them 'respond that "time" is the ultimate authority. Once a usage becomes prevalent, it must be, and is, accepted as the correct one'. This attitude to English, which Haeri finds 'quite democratic', contrasts with her findings from Egypt where the subeditors and writers whom she had interviewed during her fieldwork responded to the same question by saying that the ultimate authority for Classical Arabic is the Qur'an, a holy book most Muslims believe to be 'the word of God'.

Haeri does recognize that Arabic has indeed changed over the course of its long history. Certain grammatical rules have become simpler compared to those we find in classical literary texts, and new words have entered the lexical stock of the language while many others have become obsolete. All this, however, is not enough to consider it 'modern' which is why Haeri maintains the designation 'classical' when writing about what in Arabic linguistics and sociolinguistics at least, is usually referred to as 'Modern Standard Arabic'.[2] Haeri builds her argument against the 'modern' status of this variety by drawing on the notions of *ownership* and *custodianship*:

> A mother tongue is something we own; we are its masters, so to speak. A language that neither we nor anyone else speaks as a mother tongue, a language, furthermore, that is considered sacred by its users, does not have owners—only custodians. Arabs are the custodians of their official language but not its owners.
>
> [...] Only when custodians become owners of a language can they really turn it into something modern.
>
> (Haeri 2003a)

In brief, 'Classical Arabic' is not modern, and the fact that it is maintained as the official language in the Arab countries while regional varieties are denied such recognition, creates a sociopolitical condition that is not conducive to 'freedom of speech' and is, by implication, incompatible with democracy.

Predictably enough, Haeri's views did not resonate well with many Arab intellectuals who criticized her 'for a number of reasons, all of which are ideological' (Bassiouney 2014: 300). Controversial as it turned out to be, however, Haeri's argument is rather compelling. And she is not a lone voice in advocating that any attempt at analyzing and understanding the political conditions in the Arab world must also take into serious consideration the sociolinguistic situation in the region. Rather similarly, in his book *Why Are The Arabs Not Free?*, Moustapha Safouan (2007) discusses 'the politics of writing' and the relationship between writing and power in the Arab world. He even goes a step further than Haeri. If there is anything Haeri may have left implicit in her book, Safouan spells it out in his. In a nutshell—and here I reduce his rich, erudite and gripping argumentation to its most provocative and radical propositions: Arab despotism is directly predicated on the linguistic situation. Arab rulers are politically invested in maintaining the linguistic status quo, which hinders the spread of literacy as a necessary precondition for democracy. Ordinary people are alienated from the written word as it is written in a language they do not master. Therefore, they are kept away from, and outside of, active participatory political life. The only way to escape this dire predicament is to do away with the current status of 'Classical Arabic'. Regional vernaculars should be officially recognized and used as full-fledged, spoken *and written*, languages in all domains of life, including those from which they have been legally or ideologically excluded, such as education. The well-known historical scenario in which the Romance languages emancipated themselves from Latin is offered as an emancipatory model for regional Arabics, and, by extension, Arabs themselves. This is probably where, for many a Muslim, Safouan's ideas are likely to come across as drastic and disturbing: as in the case of the Bible, whose translations into vernaculars in Europe prompted a language shift away from Latin, Safouan's scenario calls for translations of the Qur'an into Arabic vernaculars. For many Arabs and Muslims, this is unthinkable. While Safouan's book deserves an article–long, close reading against the backdrop of the criticism that has been directed at it,[3] this, admittedly sketchy, summary of his main arguments provides another example of the standpoint that postulates a strong link between democracy (or lack thereof) and the linguistic situation in the Arab world.

Sociolinguists have a word for such a linguistic situation—*diglossia*. As formulated by Charles Ferguson in 1959, diglossia refers to the coexistence of two varieties of the same language within a community, whereby these two are acquired in two different ways—one natively, the other one learned in school. Moreover, they are said to be functionally distributed and used in different domains—the native one being regularly spoken by everybody in the community but rarely written, the learned one being spoken only in certain formal contexts but maintained as the primary medium of writing and formal education.

For more than half a century, scholars have been revisiting Ferguson's definition. Their attempts to revise, reformulate or simply refute it have turned the notion of diglossia into one of the hot buttons of modern sociolinguistics. That debate, however, is beyond the scope of this chapter. Suffice it to say that most sociolinguists nowadays would agree that, in the case of Arabic, the term 'designate[s] a specific kind of linguistic *continuum*, between the local vernacular at the one pole and at the other a high standard norm not used by anyone as mother tongue' (Mejdell 2002: 317 n.1, my emphasis). In other words, it does not necessarily imply some kind of a sharp, either-or, binary opposition of the two. In fact, as I demonstrate below, the contemporary sociolinguistic reality is far more complex than any notion of *di*–glossia can account for, regardless of how broadly we may define the term, as long as it is premised on the assumption that actual language practices should be understood exclusively with reference to the dynamics between *two* varieties only. But the oppositional duality which is inherent to the concept of diglossia and exemplified in both Haeri's and Safouan's depictions, must not be discarded either because it lies at the core of the hegemonic language ideology in Arab societies. As a matter of fact, it is exactly this (perception of) dichotomy that animates, more than anything else, Arabic speakers' metalinguistic discourses, especially among those, and they are many, who take upon themselves the role of defenders of standard Arabic against what they regard as an encroachment of the vernaculars upon the domains they believe should be reserved for the standard.[4] Regardless of their social status, educational background, gender, age, religious affiliation, political allegiances, linguistic repertoires, and, importantly enough, their level of proficiency in standard Arabic, for the great majority of

Arabic speakers, diglossia is a key reference point in almost any discussion about language whether they interpret it as a social problem that should be solved, or as a cultural specificity that, even if difficult, is there to stay. This ideology of diglossia, more so than its linguistic manifestations, is what conditions a sociocultural climate in which any call to 'elevate' the vernaculars and eventually replace standard Arabic can easily be met with resistance and hostility, even when framed as a call for democracy and freedom of speech.[5]

LANGUAGE AGAINST THE REGIME

Let me now turn to the recent historical period which is often referred to as the 'Arab Spring', the period when 'the Arabs themselves' (or at least some of them) tried to 'bring democracy to their society'. What was happening during those days from a sociolinguistic point of view? What was the protesters' linguistic weapon of choice? Did they find 'an inclusive and accessible language' which, according to Haeri, 'is essential to freedom of speech'? Did they actually want and need only one? Or, did they variably claim ownership over different linguistic and semiotic resources which they drew on creatively and strategically? Finally, has the 'Arab Spring' brought about change in the direction of a more democratic 'politics of writing' (*sensu* Safouan), or had the relationship between writing and power already been destabilized in such a way that newly emerging sociolinguistic conditions could have paved the way for the 'Arab Spring'?

I approach these questions by focusing on literacy practices of the Egyptian uprising of 2011, that is, I look at the uprising through some of its written manifestations. The main aim, however, is not to provide a comprehensive and detailed account, which would be an impossible task for a book chapter, but to utilize revolutionary literacy practices as a reference point in a broader discussion of the contemporary Egyptian *linguascape*, the term I use here, echoing Sender Dovchin (2017), to refer to fluid linguistic and semiotic resources, as well as the complex, locally meaningful, everyday language practices in which these resources are employed. My theoretical standpoint is informed by 'the new literacy studies', an approach to writing that breaks away from the literacy–illiteracy dichotomy by studying literacy as a social practice (Barton 2007; Barton and Papen 2010; Street 1984, among others). In that tradition, literacy is no longer understood as something present or absent. Instead of referring to the ability to read and write, the term becomes pluralized (*literacies* or *literacy practices*) so as to encompass a variety of the locally meaningful, culturally constructed and socially contextualized practices involved in the everyday acts of reading and writing.

> A focus on language practices moves the focus from language as an autonomous system that preexists its use, and competence as an internal capacity that accounts for language production, towards an understanding of language as a product of the embodied social practices that bring it about. [...] To talk of language practices, therefore, is to move away from the attempts to capture language as a system, and instead to investigate the doing of language as social activity, regulated as much by social contexts as by underlying systems.
>
> (Pennycook 2010: 9)[6]

This is an important corrective to the rigid separation between 'the standard Arabic' and 'the vernacular Arabic(s)' which is so often recycled and reinforced in the ideologically charged pro-standard (or standard-defending) discourse, but equally so in the pro-vernacular (vernacular-emancipating) one, as long as the implicit or explicit linguopolitical agenda of the latter envisions radical measures that would ultimately abolish the current standard. One problem with such an approach is that narratives which are grounded in the conviction that standardization and official recognition of the vernacular will somehow solve all language–related problems, construct the 'native speaker' as the main protagonist, or, in this case, the beneficiary of a radical language reform. The native speaker is depicted as a disenfranchised 'owner' of a vernacular (that is, his or her officially unrecognized 'mother tongue') who needs to be saved and liberated. The very notion of 'native speaker', however, has by now been seriously questioned in applied linguistics and by many scholars who work on World Englishes or language contact (Davies 2003). Indeed, standard Arabic has no 'native speakers', but it may very well have its 'native users', a category put forward by Dilworth Parkinson (1991) to refer to native speakers of regional Arabic varieties who, by virtue of being exposed to the standard in their daily lives, develop 'native intuitions' regarding its use.[7] Therefore, a radical emancipatory scenario which places concern for the native speaker at the center of its reformist endeavor may be well-founded and convincing when pointing to the many social and educational problems that emerge as a result of ill-defined, outdated, or even non–existent language policies—problems that certainly need to be addressed and dealt with, but such a scenario may very well neglect what the native speakers actually do in many 'spaces of sociolinguistic freedom'—a term I use to refer to the contexts and domains of language use in which the speakers' or writers' choices are not constrained.[8] What we encounter in those spaces is in fact a multiplicity of linguistic and semiotic resources and language practices, their creative and often playful employment, and the increased complexification, rather than the reduction, erasure of difference, unification or homogenization, which the processes of codification and standardization are meant to achieve.

> Once we accept that language is a social practice, it becomes clear that it is not language form that governs the speakers of the language but rather the speakers that negotiate what possible language forms they want to use for what purpose. From this point of view, Canagarajah (2008) suggests, if we want to retain a notion such as competence, it refers not so much to the mastery of a grammar or sociolinguistic system, as to the strategic capacity to use diverse semiotic items across integrated media and modalities.
>
> (Pennycook 2010: 129)

In this light, and by drawing on the premise that 'language emerges from social practice rather than being mobilized for social practices to happen' (Pennycook 2010: 133), I understand the uprising as a range of 'embodied social practices' which in turn 'bring about' language practices. The uprising and language are understood to be mutually constitutive. Having outlined the theoretical framework within which language is understood as a social and local practice, in the following section I take up some examples of writing as it was practiced as part of the uprising.

WRITING AGAINST THE REGIME

Literacy practices were constitutive of the uprising in multiple ways. It is by now widely known that social media, such as Facebook and Twitter, were used extensively to schedule demonstrations, coordinate activities among protesters, discuss the latest developments on the ground, spread rumor and information, share jokes and memes, and comment on the events as they unfolded.[9] During the demonstrations, especially in Tahrir

Square, 'demonstrators verbalized their revolt on signs, placards and banners' (Cameron and Panović 2014: 140). As Karima Khalil puts it,

> [...] feelings of pride in being Egyptian and of a wondrous empowerment granted by the square's communal spirit [...] inspired an astonishing and spontaneous explosion of creativity in the square. [...] Thousands, voiceless for so long, *chose to express their feelings in writing.* Signs made of paper, cardboard, fabric, bandages, and even shoes declared a multitude of eloquent messages.

> (Khalil 2011: 14, my emphasis)

Tahrir Square (in English, Liberation Square) holds a special place in the hearts of those who participated in the demonstrations. Likewise, for those who followed the uprising through mediated representations on satellite channels or the internet, it is probably the first thing that comes to mind whenever those momentous eighteen days that led to Mubarak's resignation are invoked. Yet, historiographically speaking, the fact that Tahrir became a metonym for the uprising is, of course, reductionist, myopic and unfair. Not only does it represent an act of erasure of the protests that were contemporaneously taking place in other parts of Egypt, it is also oblivious to the security breakdown and all the hardships and dangers that were engulfing the city and the country from right outside the invisible borders of Tahrir's Utopia. Another inaccuracy happens when the words such as 'unrest', 'uprising' or 'revolution' are used to refer only to those eighteen days. Even though most of my examples below go back to that period too, I should emphasize that the state of unrest in Egypt has not yet come to an end. It is, nevertheless, understandable how and why Tahrir Square came to be the symbol of the revolution. A spectacular and carnivalesque atmosphere would prevail in it as long as the protesters kept it 'occupied' during their peaceful demonstrations (except when they were attacked by security forces or thugs on camels, as was the case on February 2). That atmosphere served as a strong and empowering source of inspiration for the protesters throughout Egypt: and for those outside Egypt it became a global icon and exemplar of people power in 2011. What is often talked about as 'the spirit of Tahrir' was first and foremost a matter of language, a linguistic intervention: defiant chants, revolutionary songs, poetry, jokes, endless discussions, and, as Khalil captures it in the quotation above, a myriad of written messages resulting from creative multimodal engagements with language varieties, scripts, writing styles, materials, tools and formats.[10] Having emerged as the embodiment of defiance, this materialized revolutionary language transformed the linguistic landscape of Liberation Square and translated the square into a symbol of liberation.

In an article which is to my knowledge the most comprehensive treatment of this temporary revolutionary linguistic landscaping of Tahrir Square, Mariam Aboelezz (2014) provides a geosemiotic reading of a large corpus of protest messages and signs, thus following in the footsteps of Ron and Suzie Scollon (2003), who emphasize the importance of the spatial situatedness of signs and discourses in the material world. Paying attention to both the 'geographical and social context' of Tahrir Square, Aboelezz studies 'the relationship between the discourse of the protest messages on the one hand, and the space of Tahrir Square on the other' and devises 'six conceptual frames for the space of Tahrir Square within which the relationship between discourse and space can be meaningfully discussed' (2014: 16). In addition to being interpreted as successively: (1) a 'symbolic space' (in the sense highlighted in the previous paragraph but in greater detail), Tahrir was also inscribed by the revolutionary signs; as (2) a 'central space', a meeting point toward which the protesters from Cairo and other parts of the country would gravitate due to its central location; (3) a 'spiritual space', where protesters prayed and which many of them discursively framed by displaying messages with spiritual and religious content; (4) a 'playful counter-space', or an unregulated site of transgression, festivity, playfulness and humor[11]; (5) an '"Arab" space', in which some messages spoke or referred to the rest of the Arab World; and as (6) a 'glocal space', in which messages pregnant with culturally specific meanings and local references were displayed and carried around side by side with those more 'outward' looking signs which engaged with 'global' themes: and sometimes, those 'global' and 'local' references would be fused within a single sign.

It wasn't all about text, of course. As already mentioned, by manipulating various semiotic resources and modes of expression, such as cartoons, images, photos, colors, letter sizes, representations of the Egyptian flag and/or the coat of arms, ways of writing,[12] as well as surfaces on which these messages were inscribed, protesters engaged in sophisticated acts of multimodal meaning–making. Also, it wasn't just about the physical location of the signs in the material world of the square, but equally about their location in relation to the protesters' bodies. Some demonstrators effectively utilized their faces and hands as writing surfaces (e.g. Khalil 2011: 52–53), some others strategically chose specific body parts on which to display messages written on different surfaces.[13] Such discursive elaboration of the protester's corporeal topography asks us to expand the notion of '*geo*semiotics' so as to include 'somatic' as well. It is, therefore, important to recognize that protest is a social and linguistic *performance*. Accordingly, the revolutionary messages (as well as writing practices which brought them into being) should also be understood as resources protesters used to stylize their revolutionary personae.[14]

Language-wise, the great majority of these signs were written in Arabic, some in standard Arabic, some in Egyptian Arabic, and some in an admixture of the two. While it is impossible, as well as futile, to talk about strict patterns of distribution, certain correlations have been noted to the effect that standard Arabic prevailed in religious messages (this always being the case when they contained verses from the Qur'an), while Egyptian Arabic dominated in humorous discourse (Aboelezz 2014; Zack 2012). Despite these findings, there is an ideologically significant pattern among some Arab scholars and intellectuals to distort the sociolinguistic account of the uprising. This specific discursive strategy of erasure of the vernacular (even though it flies in the face of the facts) is exemplified in the following lines written by El Mustapha Lahlali:

What is striking about the Egyptian revolution is the rare use of the Egyptian dialect. This is very revealing indeed. It indicates that the revolution is led by those in the middle-class, who master both Modern Standard Arabic (MSA) and English. The rare use of the dialect could be attributed to the fact that Egyptians have used MSA in order to communicate their action to the wider Arab population.

[and again, in the conclusion:]

MSA remains the most widely used language in these slogans. Some slogans, however, have been written in English. This is a good indicator of how actively the Egyptian middle-class participated in the revolution. Perhaps contrary to expectations, the Egyptian dialect did not feature prominently in the slogans. Only a few slogans were written in the Egyptian dialect, a fact that tends to support the view that the Egyptian revolution was led by the young, educated middle-class. Nevertheless, the absence of dialect in the revolution could be attributed to the desire of Egyptian protesters to communicate their action to the wider Arab public.

Again, the issue of the Arabic language as a rallying point across the Arab world has been brought to the fore here.

(Lahlali 2014)

In the quotation above, an ideological fantasy is passed off as a socio-linguistic fact, and followed by an unsubstantiated pseudo–sociological speculation about the class background and linguistic competences of those who supposedly 'led' the revolution. The author sets out to analyze 'the discourse of Egyptian slogans', but we are not told what exactly is meant by the word 'slogan'. Judging by the occasional appearance of the adjective 'written' (as in the quotation above), it seems that by 'slogans' he refers to signs, rather than chants. Be it as it may, Lahlali claims that 'the Egyptian dialect did not feature prominently in the slogans', but nothing could be further from the truth. The widespread use of the Egyptian Arabic (in both signs and chants) has by now been extensively documented (Aboelezz 2012, 2014; Baker 2016; Khalil 2011; Mehrez 2012; Zack 2012)[15] In his article, Lahlali presents 29 examples, of which only the last two are in Egyptian Arabic, the rest being in standard Arabic. This small data set, unfortunately, tells us very little about what was happening on the ground. The author informs us that '[t]he data was collected between January and March 2011, from different media sources, notably Social Media, al-Jazeera, al-Arabiya and BBC Arabic'. The data are skewed and this strong bias toward standard Arabic can be explained in two ways. Either the author opted for a cherry–picking approach, or the large media outlets he mentions as sources (al-Jazeera, al-Arabiya and BBC Arabic) had done that for him by 'sanitizing' and 'standardizing' the actual language practices of the Egyptian protest.[16] If the latter had been the case, the author would have had an interesting topic to write about, especially since his article was published in *Arab Media & Society*. Instead, the current article can only be read as an ideologically motivated desire to give standard Arabic a 'role' bigger than the one it had.

In her discussion of 'language as a social variable in Egypt directly before, during, and after the January 25, 2011 Revolution', Reem Bassiouney (2014: 326–331) provides another example of this discursive strategy by referring to a text published in *al-Ahram* on March 26, 2011.[17] The article was written by Farouk Shousha (فاروق شوشة), an Egyptian poet and former secretary-general of the Arabic Language

Academy in Cairo. Again, by ignoring the reality and erasing the Egyptian Arabic from the demonstrations, Shousha writes a panegyric to 'the youth of the revolution', claiming that throughout the uprising they exclusively used standard Arabic. It is true that the famous chant of the Egyptian protests, as well as the entire 'Arab Spring'—'The people want to bring down the regime' (إسقاط النظام الشعب يريد)—was in standard Arabic.[18] And so were some other chants that resonated in Tahrir and other sites of protest throughout Egypt. But Shousha somehow manages to hear everything that was chanted in Tahrir as standard Arabic. His main argument is that Mubarak's regime was responsible for the overall linguistic decadence and language corruption. It was the regime who pushed Egyptians away from standard Arabic and made them use the vernacular. In their struggle for democracy and through their demand to bring the regime down, which they articulated in the 'correct language', not only did the Egyptians liberate themselves from that corrupt regime in eighteen days only, but, in the process, they also liberated themselves from the corrupt vernacular (their 'mother tongue'?) and miraculously re-appropriated the standard from which the regime had been keeping them alienated for a long time. So, just as in Safouan's scenario, in Shousha's too language is the main emancipator of the masses and their empowering vehicle toward a state of democracy and freedom. For Safouan, that language is vernacular Arabic, for Shousha, it is the standard. And somewhere in between these two imaginary uniformities, we find a variety of linguistic practices and literacies which are anything but uniform.

One Language to Rule Them All?

One thing Lahlali reports about correctly regarding the protest signs in Tahrir is that some of them were written in English. English was occasionally used by itself, in which case the targeted audience of such a sign could be said to be (both local and) global, but often it was mixed with Arabic/s, in which case the targeted reader of the sign is a bilingual who knows both Arabic and English (Aboelezz 2014: 617–618). Several commentators also take note of a special category of multilingual signs—those that featured foreign languages and scripts (including Egyptian hieroglyphics), often in combination with Arabic, all variations on the theme 'if you can't understand us/Arabic, maybe you'll understand this' (Cameron and Panović 2014: 140), or 'out in any language' (Aboelezz 2012). These signs are interesting as examples of language creativity and wit, but, overall, they are not representative of 'ordinary' contemporary literacy resources or practices in Egypt. The uprising should be understood as an extraordinary social practice, or a political and cultural performance, which, following the approach adopted in this chapter, brings about extraordinary language practices. This is not to say that all revolutionary literacy practices were extraordinary or unique, or that only extraordinary circumstances provide a fertile ground for linguistic creativity. On the contrary, my main argument here is that what we witnessed in Tahrir were scaled-up manifestations of literacies that had been around for quite some time. They just became more visible; and those that stood out in some way, such as the multilingual writing practices, should be seen as a creative diacritic to the culturally established repertoires, not as their expansion.

So, what are those by now relatively established linguistic and semiotic resources, and how can we describe literacy practices within the contemporary Egyptian linguascape? I argue that the great majority of contemporary written artifacts in Egypt, from tweets to ads to books, result from variable manipulations and recombinations of three linguistic varieties and two scripts. The varieties are standard Arabic, Egyptian colloquial Arabic and English. The scripts are the Arabic script and the Roman script. While it may seem odd at first to include English, its social significance is reflected in the fact that in the current economic constellation, some level of proficiency in English is a prerequisite for most well-paid jobs in Egypt. Being the language of instruction in the private educational sector which is not affordable to the majority of the population, English is a major vehicle of social stratification and class reproduction. It should also be stressed that these three 'varieties' are not understood here as fixed and bound systems of elements and rules. Each name is a theoretical abstraction meant to represent simultaneously activated cognitive, psycholinguistic and sociolinguistic processes through which the speaker/writer/reader recognizes, understands and classifies concrete instantiations of speech/writing, ascribes to them social meanings and evaluations, and ultimately groups them together as 'standard Arabic', 'Egyptian Arabic' or 'English' despite the variability among utterances or texts.[19] Another sociolinguistic caveat is in order: each of these three designations stands for a range of culturally recognizable repertoires on which the speaker/writer draws as a communicatively competent member of his or her speech community when indexing different stances and/or performing various identity positions. Same goes for the scripts. They are understood as two repertories of conventional graphic symbols, but how they will actually be put to work, i.e., how the words will be spelled, depends on what orthographic conventions are applied by the writer. These conventions may range from highly established and codified ('standard') to non-codified but conventionalized ('non-standard') to highly idiosyncratic ('individual' but nevertheless culturally recognizable and interpretable by the readers). What this means is that writers make complex word-to-word decisions about what (and how) they want to 'say' in writing and make appropriate choices by drawing on the repertoires they have access to.

Within the nexus of these five linguosemiotic repertoires, there are potentially six combinations: Arabic-scripted standard Arabic, Arabic-scripted Egyptian Arabic, Arabic-scripted English, Roman-scripted standard Arabic, Roman-scripted Egyptian Arabic, and Roman-scripted English. Again, these six combinations are general approximations. The writer, for example, may decide to insert an Arabic letter in the middle of a word written in Roman script (taẓrir). These 'eccentric' cases of *script-fusing* (Panović 2017) stand out, however, and achieve a 'special effect' precisely because they cross over the conventionally accepted categories of the repertoires I describe here.

In practice, however, the use of Roman script to write standard Arabic seems to be socially and culturally dispreferred and it is very rarely encountered in written data.[20] Consequently, the resulting system contains five categories of language+script combinations, though it must be noted that Arabic-scripted English represents a marginal category, employed only occasionally and, again, usually creatively—for 'special effects'. Depending on the writer's choices, these five combinations can be further mixed and combined within a stretch of text. Table 10.1 summarizes and schematizes these resources:

Table 10.2 exemplifies each category with a tweet from my Twitter data set collected in the period between January 15 and April 30, 2011.

Table 10.3 draws on the same data set but provides three examples of 'mixed tweets', that is, *some* of the ways in which different individuals combine/mix different categories. Tweets are particularly interesting because they demonstrate that even within the 140–character constraint, users can engage in diverse and creative literacy practices, mixing across two or more resource categories. Due to space limitations, however, I leave a sociolinguistic interpretation of these choices for another publication.

Table 10.1   Resources in contemporary writing practices in Egypt

	ar (Arabic script)	rom (Roman script)
SA	arSA	romSA (?)
EA	arEA	romEA
ENG	arENG	romENG®

SA—Standard Arabic, EA—Egyptian Arabic, ENG—English, ®—rarely used, (?)—extremely rarely found in the data

Table 10.2   Egyptian tweets exemplifying the script-variety recombinations presented in Table 10.1

	Arabic script	Roman script
SA	رسالة الى الشباب : أنتم صناع التغيير. قوتكم فى عددكم وفى شجاعتكم و فى وضوح رؤيتكم وفى وحدة صفكم التفوا جميعا حول الهدف الأسمى. الحق معنا A message to the youth: You are the creators of change. Your strength is in your number, in your courage, in your clear vision and in your unity. Gather, all of you, around the highest cause. We are right	(?)
EA	هوا الدكتور كاتب لظباط اسكندريه علي قتل مواطن كل اسبوعين؟ ايه الخره دا؟ Has the doctor prescribed to the police officers in Alexandria to kill a citizen every fortnight? What kind of shit is that?	Msh shart tmoot fe 7arb 3shan teb2a shahid, ettamen, Ay wa7ed yemoot ba3d el sawra yeb2a shahid It's not necessary for you to die in a war to become a martyr, rest assured, anyone who dies after the revolution becomes a martyr
ENG	لول .. ذات واز هيلاريوس... D : <lwl thāt wāz hylāryws>*	#Egypt officials confirmed that #cairo-explosion is just a sonic boom from an overflying aircraft. We're safe!

*The text enclosed between angled brackets represents the letters of the Roman alphabet that are close equivalents of the corresponding graphemes in the Arabic alphabet

This proposed model, as illustrated on a small sample of Twitter data, claims to be able to account for the great majority of resources used in contemporary literacy practices in Egypt. It does not claim that every literate Egyptian has access to and draws on all these categories. Some individuals may draw on all of them, others only on some. The model

Table 10.3 Mixing of literary resources within single tweets

---

1 The challenge facing us now in Egypt is the gap between the "Great isn't good enough" generation & "ليس بالإمكان أفضل مما كان" generation.
gloss:
ليس بالإمكان أفضل مما كان—it can never be better than it used to be
resources:
romENG, arSA
(insertion of Arabic-scripted standard Arabic into a tweet in English)

2 (B reacts to A's tweet)
A: I had a fight with flool in #Tahrir. she2 ye2ref. old people should be at their retirement houses and shut the fuck up
B: @A yep the extreme majority of the flool I hv met r old ppl with a nasty loud voice:(m3rfsh byn2oohm kda wla eh
glosses:
flool—the remnants of the old regime
she2 ye2ref—disgusting
m3rfsh byn2oohm kda wla eh—I don't know if they are picking them like that or what
resources:
romENG, romEA
(code-switching between Roman-scripted English and Roman-scripted Egyptian Arabic)

3 وإنه ليحز في نفسي أن أرى من أبناء قومي من مثل هذا الشاب. الإعلام المصري مش عايز حملة تطهير ده عايز حملة تطعيم ضد الغباء

translation:
"It hurts my soul to see that a young man like this one belongs to the sons of my people. The Egyptian media doesn't need a cleansing campaign, it needs an anti-stupidity vaccination"
resources:
arSA, arEA
(code-switching from standard Arabic in the first sentence to Egyptian Arabic in the second).

---

is flexible, though, since it allows for the inclusion or exclusion of additional categories and combinations as these are encountered in the data. It can also be easily adapted and modified to other Arabic-speaking contexts by identifying the relevant distribution of varieties and scripts used in a particular community. In this case, by identifying the productive categories, I do not make any claims about their 'representativeness'. I am perfectly aware of the fact that the Arabic-scripted standard Arabic dominates the official and institutional textual production. But in the case of vernacular literacy practices, we need more categories to work with.

As far as these language+script combinations are concerned, Egyptian Arabic is the most 'flexible' variety, equally at home when written in Arabic or Roman script.[21] Nevertheless, the latter (often referred to as *Franco* by young Egyptians) represents a marked variety and is characterized by a high degree of variability. Having emerged for the purposes of digital communication at the time when Arabic script was not supported, its continuing use even today is often criticized, especially within the trope of the decline of Arabic. But, it is here to stay.

> Today Arabic script is well supported by digital technology, but Romanized Arabic has not disappeared. It is still used in CMC by many, mostly younger, Arabs, but it has also become a sort of alternative transcription system that can be found alongside Arabic script on music CDs or film posters (Yaghan 2008: 46). What began as a *technologically imposed* rather than entirely voluntary practice (romanizing Arabic to make it usable on computers and mobile phones) is now being voluntarily maintained as a part of (youth) culture. It has come to be seen as an additional linguistic/semiotic resource which writers can exploit for various purposes.

> (Cameron and Panović 2014: 54, emphasis in the original)[22]

Unlike Franco, which is a relatively recent and therefore contested category, Egyptian Arabic written in Arabic script has a long history. Still, when discussing the language use during the protests, some authors seem to be surprised by the visibility of Egyptian Arabic in that context. So, for example, Mariam Aboelezz, whose work otherwise demonstrates a very nuanced and theoretically informed understanding of the changing character of writing practices in the Egyptian sociolinguistic setting, seems quite content with Ferguson's description written nearly sixty years ago when she makes the following comment regarding the use of written Egyptian Arabic about protest messages in Tahrir Square:

> As *a text book case of classical diglossia*, two varieties of Arabic are in everyday use in Egypt (Ferguson 1959). Given this classical written/spoken divide it is *striking* that Egyptian Arabic should feature so heavily in the written protest messages – more or less on par with Standard Arabic.

> (Aboelezz 2014: 6161, my emphasis)[23]

This visibility of Egyptian Arabic during the uprising may become less 'striking' once *vernacularity* (understood here as the increase and spread

of vernacular literacies) and its sites of expression are properly historicized and placed in a cross–cultural perspective.[24] That is not to say that
linguistic strategies employed in the acts of writing during the uprising
were not interesting. They certainly were, but their significance is not so
much in their supposed novelty or visibility as much it is in their transformative potential to further sociolinguistic change in Egypt by advanc-
ing vernacularization that had already been underway.

More than ten years ago, Madiha Doss identified a significant increase
in the use of Egyptian Arabic, either exclusively or in an admixture with
standard, in three major spheres of writing—literary writing, non-liter-
ary writing and online writing (what she calls 'cyberspeech') (2006: 54),
and the history of 'written Egyptian vernacular' is much longer, spanning six centuries, as documented in a recently published anthology
(Doss and Davies 2013).[25] Similarly, having analyzed a corpus of texts,
Gabriel Rosenbaum established that 'conventions for [Egyptian Arabic]
orthography are now beginning to crystallize' (2004: 320). Previously,
he discussed an emerging alternating style in Egyptian prose that seemed
to have been breaking the hitherto acceptable literary norm of employing Egyptian Arabic in writing the dialogue in plays or novels, in that
Egyptian Arabic is now increasingly encountered in the narrative as well
(Rosenbaum 2000). Manfred Woidich (2010) traces the emancipation of
Egyptian Arabic over the last century and a half and demonstrates how
from its earlier locatedness and function within the text to represent the
spoken word (dialogue, or a first–person narrative), Egyptian Arabic has
gone through a stage when a number of authors started employing it for
the third-person narration, and finally reached a stage in which it is also
used for expository writing. Through such an elaboration of function,
Woidich argues, Egyptian Arabic has become an 'Ausbaudialekt', so what
it lacks to become a 'standard' would be official recognition, codification, and institutional support.

Ziad Fahmy (2011) gives an excellent historical account of the construction, negotiation and spread of collective Egyptian identity and dissemination of Egyptian nationalism among 'ordinary' Egyptians in the
late nineteenth and early twentieth centuries. His work is based on colloquial Egyptian sources, including many textual ones, which were mostly
neglected in previously written historiographies that tended to focus
on the 'intellectual origins' of Egyptian nationalism. In their respective

discussions of the growth and development of the Egyptian 'dialect literature', both Davies (2006) and Woidich (2010) also identify the late nineteenth century (around 1870) as the period when prose writing in the colloquial becomes a societally visible, even if marginal, cultural practice 'through the conduit of the magazine and newspaper, new vehicles for colloquial literature that were to play an essential role in its development through the first decades of the following century' (Davies 2006: 598). Inevitably marginalized and traditionally denounced as 'vulgar' by the elite, writing in the colloquial, already tamed in the 1930s and 1940s, became virtually extinct by the beginning of the second half of the twentieth century (Fahmy 2011). It was the Nasserist ideology of pan–Arabism and strong faith in the power of education, which was seen as capable of bridging the gap between the two varieties, that gave the final blow to the production and dissemination of colloquial texts. From the 1990s onwards, however, there has been an increase and, in the history of social and cultural experience of diglossia unparalleled spread of Egyptian Arabic in publicly disseminated and consumed writing. The main contributing factors, as identified by Doss (2006: 67), are: 'decentralization of printing and a more inclusive cultural and social position which entails a change of attitude towards the different language registers'.

Today, the main sites of vernacularization in Egypt are the internet, advertising and (mostly smaller, experimental) publishing. Given the exceptionality of the days in Tahrir, and since until those days the only places where most people could verbalize their dissent were the virtual places of the internet and social media, it is not striking at all that, as they left Facebook to take to streets, people brought with them their most powerful weapon against the regime—language.

This overview puts the ongoing vernacularization into historical perspective. It is clear by now that vernacularization is not new. It has only accelerated in recent years due to the spread of the internet and Web 2.0 whereby new technologically mediated, unregulated spaces have emerged and the increasing number of people can engage in literacy practices away from prescriptivist control. This is not something new either; in fact, the developments in Egypt correspond to what we know from studies in many other places around the world (Androutsopoulos 2011): whether diglossic or not, many communities are experiencing the simultaneity of vernacularization and de-standardization (or, depending on the perspective, post-standardization). What makes Egypt (and the

Arab world)[26] interesting is the fact that the 'status' of standard Arabic had always been undermined, long before the vernacularization took off at its current pace. Namely, as noted by Mejdell (2008a), 'the relative lack of polyfunctionality, *i.e.* by not covering most spoken styles and registers', standard Arabic is already a different kind of 'standard language' compared with standard languages in some European countries. From that perspective, writing has been ideologically constructed as the main domain of the standard (Ferguson 1959), and the main manifestation of vernacularization then is the 'spread' of vernacular into that domain. Talking about a 'spread', however, is unproductively metaphorical since it emulates the discourse of the defenders of the standard, who themselves entertain metaphors of encroachment or attack. It is therefore more accurate to talk about changing writing practices and attitudes (Doss 2006; Kindt et al. 2016), and, keeping in mind its historical continuity, the acceleration (or scaling up) of vernacularization. Simply put, more and more people are now finding ways and venues to write about what they want in whatever 'varieties' they see as worth writing. People will continue to tweet, write blogs, compose poetry, publish books, or try to enlarge Wikipedia in their mother tongue (Panović 2010), and along the way they will be pushing the ongoing sociolinguistic change forward. This process is unstoppable and irreversible.

Let me now revisit the questions I raised early on in this article. In their quest for democracy in 2011, Egyptian protesters did not embrace only one variety, be it standard or colloquial. Neither do we have any indication they may have wanted a single variety for everything. Instead, the extraordinary events of the uprising brought to the fore language practices that had already been a part of the Egyptian linguascape, thus making them more visible to those who were not (or refused to be) aware of them. In the context of the demonstrations in Tahrir Square, these practices could be described as 'metrolingual'. According to Emi Otsuji and Alastair Pennycook, *metrolingualism* refers to 'creative linguistic practices across borders of culture, history and politics, [metrolingualism is] a product of modern and often urban interaction, describing the ways in which people of different and mixed backgrounds use, play with and negotiate identities through language' (2010: 240).

Regarding the relationship between writing and power, that relationship had already been destabilized, and newly emerging sociolinguistic conditions could indeed have paved the way for the 'Arab Spring', though one needs to be cautious when making such claims.[27] Without assuming causation, I argue that in Egypt, at least, there is an interplay between sociolinguistic change and political change. I do not wish to suggest that Egyptian Arabic is somehow more democratic than the standard, or that it is a better vehicle for articulating dissent.[28] But by subverting the authority of the standard language, vernacularization does create conditions for increased participation. It pluralizes discourses and gives a voice to those who may feel uncomfortable writing in standard Arabic. Vernacularization, therefore, creates conditions for debate, critique, collaboration and political mobilization. But what is still observable across diverse literacy practices is that in many of them standard Arabic still plays a role even though 'writing' has long ceased to be its exclusive domain. Therefore, it is about time sociolinguists of writing practices in Egypt stopped recycling Ferguson's description of a bygone era as something against which the present should appear to be 'surprising'. Knowing what we know about the workings of vernacularization, both across time and across cultures, we have no reason to believe that, had there been Facebook in 1950s, or in any century before, those literate among the ordinary Egyptians and Arabs would have been updating their statuses in nothing but Classical Arabic.

From Tahrir Square via Square One to Where…?

I opened this chapter with a brief, gloomy reference to the lamentable political, social and economic conditions in today's Egypt. Yet the careful reader could have spotted my deliberate use of a modal verb—'this conclusion *may* hold true in the political and socio-economic spheres…'. The reason is that, amidst all too many pessimistic accounts that were published around the fifth anniversary of the uprising, a remarkable book came out offering a different perspective. Combining his firsthand experience of the unrest, which at the time he used to report on for *The Guardian*, with extensive research on the conditions that had led to the revolution, Jack Shenker (2016) provides a rich, layered and engaging account of the uprising. It is microscopically attentive to the details of the daily, local struggles, survival strategies and acts of resistance of the disenfranchised ordinary people across the country; and it is compellingly broad and deeply historicized when interpreting the political and economic context within which those struggles should be understood. While in academic and journalistic circles the jury may still be out when it comes to deciding if what has been happening in Egypt since

January 2011 could be described as a 'revolution' at all, for Shenker such a dilemma does not exist. Not only was it a revolution, as his argument runs boldly throughout the book, but it still is a revolution. He does recognize the revolution's abruptly halted and unfinished character, as well as the repressiveness of the current regime, but he nevertheless charts the trajectories of a turmoil that is yet to happen. He traces its seemingly small but ongoing manifestations and instantiations of its transformative potential in seemingly disparate and fragmented sites of revolt, ranging from self-organized activities of workers to those of street artists, writers and musicians. Some may find his optimism unwarranted. But I find Shenker's focus on what I would label here as the vernacularity of the Egyptian revolution appealing. He insists on putting things into a historical perspective. He understands the revolution to be an ongoing, fragmented and layered process. Dominant discourses about the revolution are saturated with binary oppositions, so an alternative explanation should take them into serious consideration, yet position itself outside those dualisms. Finally, careful attention should be paid to seemingly irrelevant, marginal and marginalized, informal and non–institutionalized practices that bring about small incremental changes which over time may build up to something important.

It is clear by now that my reading of Shenker's book reflects my approach to the sociolinguistic change in Egypt. This change, too, is incremental and fragmented; it is not coordinated in any way and it will continue to unfold in a social climate which becomes ideologically polarized every time questions about language are raised. While it is tempting to celebrate this diversity, multiplicity, fragmentariness and complexity of literacy practices of those who can read and write, many real-life problems related to language-issues still persist. And future language policy makers and planners in Egypt will need to address them. As Pennycook (2010: 132) suggests,

> Language policy can become a very different project from its current orientation towards choosing between languages to be used in particular domains, or debating whether one language threatens another. If language policy could focus on translingual language practices rather than language entities, far more progress might be made in domains such as language education.

Indeed, those future language policymakers of Egypt will perhaps want to start by identifying what the locally meaningful language practices are and how those can inform decision-making, especially when it comes to one of the most burning issues—education. Given that English has become an important asset for social upward mobility, perhaps they will want to find ways how to 'distribute' it to those in need. Perhaps they will accept the fact that Egyptian Arabic has long become a second standard in the country, albeit unofficial. Finally, perhaps they will want to assess the value which the current standard has on the Egyptian linguistic market (Haeri 1997), and start putting an effort into reinventing it beyond its symbolic value into an asset people would be motivated to acquire.

For the time being, radical solutions in either direction would be very remote from ways in which people negotiate and integrate various linguistic and symbolic resources in their acts of reading and writing. But what the future holds for the standard Arabic is hard to guess.

I have already noted (and illustrated with the examples from my Twitter data) that computer-mediated communication in general, and social media in particular, are among the main domains of the vernacularization of writing. But I wish to bring this chapter to an end with two photographs which illustrate how some of the 'new literacies' of Egypt discussed here are increasingly being enregisered (Agha 2003, 2005) and commodified (Heller 2010). The first photo (Fig. 10.1) is of my coffee cup which I bought in a shop in Cairo in January 2016. It is my morning reminder of the years I spent in Cairo, of the moments of excitement and hopefulness I shared with my friends there during the uprising, and of that sense of disappointment I get when I go back to visit. Written in English, albeit in Arabic script, it simply says:

شيت هابنز <šīt hābnz>—Shit happens.

The second photo (Fig. 10.2) features a t-shirt from the same shop. As if to send a subtle and appropriate political and prophetic message, it displays a line from the well-known song 'The Flower of Cities' (زهرة المدائن) by the famous Lebanese singer Fairouz (فيروز)—'The glaring anger is arriving' (*Ar.* الغضب الساطع آتٍ /al-ġaḍab-u al-sāṭiᶜ-u āt-in/) Composed to commemorate the displacement of Palestinians after Israel's victory in the 1967 Six-Day War, the song is dedicated to Jerusalem. It is written and performed in standard Arabic. It would be hard to find many Egyptians or Arabs, regardless of their linguistic allegiances, with whom this song would not strike a chord… What struck a chord with me when I spotted the t-shirt was how creatively

Fig. 10.1 Shit happens (Arabic-scripted English)

the designers exploited the multimodal, cross-lingual, (near-) homophone potential of the @-sign /at/, and incorporated it (instead of the word ت / āt/) into the 'classical' rendering of the sentence in which even the vowel signs and nunnation (تٍ/āt-in/) have been duly marked—a feature rarely found in printed Arabic texts, except in the text of the Qur'an, some classical literary works, textbooks for kids, and here and there in contemporary texts, when the author wants to disambiguate a word. What the creative designers of this t-shirt came up with speaks for itself—a classic in Classical with a modern twist! Maybe under the custodianship of the younger generations, we will finally see the 'Classical Arabic' being inflected so as to become modern.

Fig. 10.2   الغضَبُ الساطِعُ آتٍ@ ('The glaring anger is arriving')

NOTES

1. See "Egypt: Events of 2016," Human Rights Watch World Report (www.hrw. org/world-report/2017/country-chapters/egypt), as well as the Amnesty International Annual Report for 2016/2017 (https://www.amnesty.org/en/countries/middle-east-and-north-africa/egypt/report-egypt/)—both sites last accessed on April 11, 2017.
2. Actually, there are many labels in circulation, varying from publication to publication and from one author to another. It is not uncommon for

an author to adopt and use the 'native' terminology—some kind of spelling variation of the words (*al-*)*fuṣḥā*, for the 'standard' (*Ar:*—اللغة العربية الفصحى — *lit.* 'the most eloquent Arabic') and (*al-*) *ʿāmmiyya* (العامية, 'the common/colloquial/vernacular') in case of Egyptian or other regional varieties spoken in the Mashreq (the eastern part of the Arab world), or (*al-*)*dārija* (الدارجة) for the varieties of the Maghreb (the Arab west). As I have experienced on several occasions when I talked about my research, the use of these native categories, which I usually prefer, can sometimes be challenged by native Arabic speakers, some of whom feel that the term *Fusha* (fus·ha) in particular refers to the 'classical Arabic', which they find to be an inaccurate designation for the currently wide-spread form of the standard. At the same time, there is no widely accepted Arabic term corresponding to the term 'Modern Standard Arabic' (MSA). Not without hesitation, throughout this paper I use the designation 'standard' (for MSA/*fuṣḥā*) and 'vernacular/colloquial' or 'Egyptian Arabic' (for *ʿāmmiyya*).

3. See, for example, El-Youssef (2007), Lahlali (2010), and Suleiman (2011: 111–121).

4. Gunvor Mejdell (2008b) charts the contemporary language debate and social practice in Egypt by providing numerous examples from Egyptian printed media. For a similar overview regarding the Arab world in general, see Mirko Colleoni's account of Al Jazeera TV programs that featured debates about language-related issues (2014). Across several episodes, the guests were mostly from the defenders' camp, yet on two occasions, one of the participants in the duels (with two different guests) was Rafiq Ruhana, a Lebanese poet, teacher and apparently strong proponent of the claim that Lebanese is a distinct language. Throughout the shows, the prominent topics were the ones we usually encounter in this kind of debate: diglossia, the spread of foreign languages to the detriment of standard Arabic; the spread of vernaculars, again, to the detriment of the standard; the decline of educational sector in which Arabic is the medium of instruction compared to the growing importance of English (or other foreign languages) in education and society as a whole; the negative influence of mass media on young generations' linguistic competencies in standard Arabic,... By and large, Niloofar Haeri's conclusion quoted above, how 'the minority of Arabs who are proficient in classical Arabic continue to claim that everyone understands the language and so there are no problems' (2003a) seems somewhat inaccurate. On the contrary, complaints about the decline of Arabic are abundant in public discourse. To her credit, however, Haeri is aware of this fact and discusses it in more detail in her other works (1997, 2003b). For a historical overview of these recurrent ideological debates, see Suleiman (2003, 2006).

5. See also Suleiman (2011: 29–31).

6. For an overview of the two theoretical perspectives (language-as-system *vs.* language-as-practice) and major epistemological and methodological implications of this conceptual distinction, see Wright (2015).

7. For a discussion of pedagogical implications of this notion of a 'native user' of Arabic (and a range of competencies this user has, or is supposed to have) with respect to teaching of Arabic as a foreign/second language, see Wahba (2013).

8. See, for example, Deumert (2014) and Sebba (2007: 24–57).

9. This does not imply that the internet was 'crucial' in the Egyptian revolution. In fact, I distance myself from unsubstantiated celebratory uses of descriptors such as the 'Internet Revolution'. But I do maintain that the use of social media is a significant characteristic of social life in Egypt today. Miriam Aouragh and Anne Alexander (2011), for example, provide a balanced and insightful discussion of the role of the internet and social media in the Egyptian uprising.

10. Elliot Colla (2012) captured this power of 'the poetry of revolt' early on, in his essay that first appeared online in *Jadaliyya* during the first week of the uprising (http://www.jadaliyya.com/pages/index/506/the-poetry-of-revolt, last accessed on April 11, 2017).

11. Liesbeth Zack (2012) discusses 'the use of humour on the signs and banners seen during the demonstrations in Tahrir Square' and classifies the jokes into several categories: (1) 'Kentucky-jokes', through which the protesters sarcastically re–appropriated and thus rejected the rumors coming from the pro-regime circles and media that they are foreign agents to whom KFC meals are distributed; (2) '(variations on) existing (Egyptian) proverbs'; (3) 'variations on the theme "Leave, I want to have a shower"'; (4) 'explaining their point in another language'; (5) 'professionals offering their services' (e.g. a dentist to 'extract Mubarak'); (6) 'references to cows' ('because of [Mubarak's] resemblance to the cow on the box of *La Vache qui Rit*-cheese wedges. At the same time, the cow is a symbol of foolishness.' 720); and (7) 'various'.

12. While the majority of signs were hand-written, some were word-processed on computers and printed out.

13. One among many dramatic examples is the photograph of four brothers who stood in Tahrir with their mouths taped shut with the message 'no talk until he leaves' (لا كلام قبل الرحيل). Originally, they were six. Two brothers had been killed in Tahrir (Khalil 2011: 80–81).

14. For discussion of 'style' in sociolinguistics, see Coupland (2007).

15. For chants, see also the Facebook group 'Slogans of the Egyptian Revolution (شعارات الثورة المصرية)', (https://goo.gl/ygT8Yh)—last accessed on April 11, 2017.

16. This second scenario though, does not explain how the data that were reportedly also collected from 'Social Media' exhibits such a marked bias.

17. Here, I refer to the online edition of the article "لغة شباب الثورة" ("The language of the youth of the revolution") (http://www.ahram.org.eg/archive/The-Writers/News/69442.aspx, last accessed on April 11, 2017). Bassiouney, however, states the date of its publication as 'March 27' (Bassiouney 2014: 326).

18. The chant was apparently first heard during the uprising in Tunisia. It was readily adopted by the Egyptian protesters only to spread throughout the Arab world wherever the subsequent demonstrations took place.

19. The term 'writer' here is to be understood as the text producer.

20. It is, on the other hand, the preferred practice among the Arabists and other scholars when they (need to) transcribe or transliterate Arabic.

21. The Roman alphabet is often supplemented by numerals to write Arabic letters that have no Roman equivalents (e.g. 2—ء, 3—ع, 5—خ, 7—ح, etc.).

22. See also Aboelezz (2009).

23. Similarly, in her account of 'the evolution of the Arabic language through online writing,' Saussan Khalil (2012), goes as far as to describe it as 'the explosion of 2011' even though in her discussion she mentions several earlier examples of writing in Egyptian Arabic.

24. Jannis Androutsopoulos (2010: 206) distinguishes two senses of vernacularity, both of which are important for my argument here: 'The first is offered by the notion of vernacular literacies, classically defined as literacy practices that are not part of educational or professional institutions but are relatively free from institutional control, rooted in everyday practice, serving everyday purposes, and drawing on vernacular knowledge. [...] Secondly, in a sense familiar to sociolinguists, 'vernacular' refers to local varieties of language, those that are the first to be acquired: the most local and informal, uncodified, and often classified as non-standard.'

25. In fact, as is the case with much of contemporary vernacular writing, quite a few of these texts could be categorized as 'mixed' rather than written exclusively in Egyptian Arabic.

26. What I describe here pertains to Egypt. For an account of changing writing practices in Morocco, see Elinson (2013). For an overview of the dynamics between orality and culture, and examples of vernacular writing in other parts of the Arab world, see Holes (2013).

27. While the Arabic-speaking world is often discussed as a single sociolinguistic setting, especially when it comes to diglossia, and even though similar ongoing sociolinguistic changes regarding vernacularization are happening in other parts of the Arab world, their pace and trajectories vary across different Arab countries—they are historically situated and dependent upon the concrete social, cultural, demographic, economic

and political conditions. In other words, while I do claim that vernacular literacy practices are becoming an increasingly prominent feature of
contemporary social life throughout the Arab world, this does not imply
that identical sociocultural or political ramifications of this development
are expected in every Arab country.

28. However, Zeinab Ibrahim (2010), discusses the stylistic role of Egyptian
    Arabic in the opposition press, whose occurrence is most prominent in
    headlines and direct quotations. She elaborates on contextual factors
    and social meanings of code switching in written texts, highlighting the
    purpose of establishing 'solidarity with the reader' as one of the main
    motives for resorting to vernacular. Similarly, in her analysis of 'bivalent
    strategy' in mixed style texts in one opposition newspaper, *al-Dustūr*,
    Mejdell comments: 'One may say that al-Dustūr challenged the regime
    and the establishment—through both political and linguistic acts of defi-
    ance' (2014: 273).

REFERENCES

Aboelezz, Mariam. "'Out' in Any Language!" *The Linguist* 51, No. 1 (2012): 14–15.

Aboelezz, Mariam. "The Geosemiotics of Tahrir Square: A Study of the Relationship between Discourse and Space." *Journal of Language and Politics* 13, No. 4 (2014): 599–622.

Agha, Asif. "The Social Life of Cultural Value." *Language & Communication* 23 No. 3–4, (2003): 231–273.

Agha, Asif. "Voice, Footing, Enregisterment." *Journal of Linguistic Anthropology* 15, No. 1 (2005): 38–59.

Androutsopoulos, Jannis. "Localizing the Global on the Participatory Web." In *The Handbook of Language and Globalization*, edited by N. Coupland, 203–231. Oxford: Blackwell Publishing, 2010.

Androutsopoulos, Jannis. "Language Change and Digital Media: A Review of Conceptions and Evidence." In *Standard Languages and Language Standards in a Changing Europe*, edited by T. Kristiansen and N. Coupland, 145–159. Oslo: Novus Press, 2011.

Aouragh, Miryam and Anner Alexander. "The Egyptian Experience: Sense and Nonsense of the Internet Revolution." *International Journal of Communication* 5 (2011): 1344–1358.

Baker, Mona, ed. *Translating Dissent: Voices from and with the Egyptian Revolution*. Abingdon and New York: Routledge, 2016.

Barton, David. *Literacy: An Introduction to the Ecology of Written Language*. 2nd ed. Oxford: Blackwell Publishing, 2007.

Barton, David and Uta Papen, eds. *The Anthropology of Writing: Understanding Textually-Mediated Worlds*. New York: Continuum, 2010.

Bassiouney, Reem. *Language and Identity in Modern Egypt*. Edinburgh: Edinburgh University Press, 2014.

Cameron, Deborah and Ivan Panović. *Working with Written Discourse*. London: Sage, 2014.

Colla, Elliott. "The Poetry of Revolt." In *The Journey to Tahrir: revolution, protest, and social change in Egypt*, edited by J. Sowers and C. Toensing, 47–52. London and New York: Verso, 2012.

Colleoni, Mirko. "Diglossia and the Influence of Foreign Languages as Debated in Arabic Al Jazeera TV Programmes." In *Alf laḥǧa wa Laḥǧa: Proceedings of the 9th AIDA Conference*, edited by O. Durand, A.D. Langone, and G. Mion, 123–139. Vienna: LIT Verlag, 2014.

Coupland, Nikolas. *Style: Language, Variation and Identity*. Cambridge: Cambridge University Press, 2007.

Davies, Alan. *The Native Speaker: Myth and Reality*. Clevedon: Multilingual Matters, 2003.

Davies, Humphrey. "Dialect Literature." In *Encyclopedia of Arabic Language and Linguistics*, edited by K. Versteegh, M. Eid, A. Elgibali, M. Woidich, and A. Zaborski, 597–604. Leiden and Boston, 2006.

Deumert, Ana. *Sociolinguistics and Mobile Communication*. Edinburgh: Edinburgh University Press, 2014.

Doss, Madiha. "Cultural Dynamics and Linguistic Practice in Contemporary Egypt." In *Cultural Dynamics in Contemporary Egypt (Cairo Papers in Social Science)*, vol. 27, edited by M. Abdelrahman, I.A. Hamdy, M.S. Rouchdy, and R. Saad, 51–68. Cairo: The American University in Cairo Press, 2006.

Doss, Madiha and Humphrey Davies, eds. *Written Egyptian Arabic: Selected Texts, 1401–2009*. Cairo: Al-Hay'a al-Misriyya al-'Amma lil-Kitab, 2013. (Original in Arabic).

Dovchin, Sender. "The Ordinariness of Youth Linguascapes in Mongolia." *International Journal of Multilingualism* 14, No. 2, 2017: 144–159.

El-Youssef, Samir. "The Talking Cure." *New Statesman*, October 18, 2007. Retrieved (http://www.newstatesman.com/books/2007/10/arab-safouan-standard-free).

Elinson, Alexander E. "Dārija and Changing Writing Practices in Morocco." *International Journal of Middle East Studies* 45, No. 4 (2013): 715–730.

Fahmy, Ziad. *Ordinary Egyptians: Creating the Modern Nation through Popular Culture*. Stanford: Stanford University Press, 2011.

Ferguson, Charles. "Diglossia." *Word* 15 (1959): 325–340.

Haeri, Niloofar. "The Reproduction of Symbolic Capital: Language, State, and Class in Egypt." *Current Anthropology* 38, No. 5 (1997): 795–816.

Haeri, Niloofar. "Arabs Need to Find Their Tongue." *The Guardian*, June 14, 2003a. Retrieved (http://www.theguardian.com/comment/story/0,,977260,00.html).

Haeri, Niloofar. *Sacred Language, Ordinary People: Dilemmas of Culture and Politics in Egypt*. Basingstoke: Palgrave Macmillan, 2003b.

Heller, Monica. "The Commodification of Language." *Annual Review of Anthropology* 39 (2010): 101–114.

Holes, Clive. "Orality, Culture, and Language." In *The Oxford Handbook of Arabic Linguistics*, edited by J. Owens, 281–299. Oxford: Oxford University Press, 2013.

Ibrahim, Zeinab. "Cases of Written Code Switching in Egyptian Opposition Newspapers." In *Arabic and the Media: Linguistic Analyses and Applications*, edited by R. Bassiouney, 23–46. Leiden: Brill, 2010.

Khalil, Karima, ed. *Messages from Tahrir: Signs from Egypt's Revolution*. Cairo: The American University in Cairo Press, 2011.

Khalil, Saussan. "The Evolution of the Arabic Language through Online Writing: The Explosion of 2011." in *BRISMES 2012 Graduate Conference Papers: Change and Continuity in the Arab World*, 2012. Retrieved (http://www.isn.ethz.ch/Digital-Library/Publications/Detail/?ots591=0c54e3b3-1e9c-be1e-2c24-a6a8c7060233&lng=en&id=151357).

Kindt, Kristian Takvam, Jacob Høigilt, and Tewodros Aragie Kebede. "Writing Change: Diglossia and Popular Writing Practices in Egypt." *Arabica* 63, No. 3–4 (2016): 324–376.

Lahlali, El Mustapha. "The Discourse of Egyptian Slogans: From 'Long Live Sir' to 'Down with the Dictator.'" *Arab Media & Society* 19(Fall 2014). Retrieved (http://www.arabmediasociety.com/?article=850).

Lahlali, Mustapha. "Book Review: Moustapha Safouan, Why Are the Arabs Not Free?—The Politics of Writing. Oxford: Wiley-Blackwell, 2007. 128 Pp." *Discourse & Society* 21 No. 2, (2010): 240–241.

Mehrez, Samia, ed. *Translating Egypt's Revolution: The Language of Tahrir*. Cairo: The American University in Cairo Press, 2012.

Mejdell, Gunvor. "Features of Luġa Wusṭā: Mixed Discourse in Spoken Arabic in Egypt." In *Aspects of the Dialects of Arabic Today: Proceedings of the 4th Conference of the International Arabic Dialectology Association (AIDA), Marrakesh, April 1–4, 2000. In honour of Professor David Cohen*, edited by A. Youssi, F. Benjelloun, M. Dahbi, and Z. Iraqui-Sinaceur, 317–328. Rabat: Amapatril, 2002.

Mejdell, Gunvor. "Is Modern Fuṣḥā a 'Standard' Language?" In *Linguistics in an Age of Globalization: Perspectives on Arabic Language and Teaching*, edited by Z. Ibrahim and S.A.M. Makhlouf, 41–52. Cairo: The American University in Cairo Press, 2008a.

Mejdell, Gunvor. "What Is Happening to Lughatunā L-Gamīla?: Recent Media Representations and Social Practice in Egypt." *Journal of Arabic and Islamic Studies* 8, (2008b): 108–124.

Mejdell, Gunvor. "Strategic Bivalency in 'Written Mixed Style'?: A Reading of Ibrahim Isa in Al Dustur." In *Alf lahğa wa Lahğa: Proceedings of the 9th AIDA Conference*, edited by O. Durand, A.D. Langone, and G. Mion, 273–278. Vienna: LIT Verlag, 2014.

Otsuji, Emi and Alastair Pennycook. "Metrolingualism: Fixity, Fluidity and Language in Flux." *International Journal of Multilingualism* 7, No. 3 (2010): 240–254.

Panović, Ivan. "The Beginnings of Wikipedia Masry." *al-Logha* 8 (2010): 93–127.

Panović, Ivan. "'You Don't Have Enough Letters to Make This Noise': Arabic Speakers' Creative Engagements with the Roman Script." *Language Sciences*, 2017.

Parkinson, Dilworth. "Searching for Modern Fuṣḥā: Real-Life Formal Arabic." *Al-'Arabiyya: Journal of the American Association of Teachers of Arabic* 24 (1991): 31–64.

Pennycook, Alastair. *Language as a Local Practice*. Abingdon and New York: Routledge, 2010.

Rosenbaum, Gabriel M. "'Fuṣḥāmmiyya': Alternating Style in Egyptian Prose." *Zeitschrift für arabische Linguistik* 38 (2000): 68–87.

Rosenbaum, Gabriel M. "Egyptian Arabic as a Written Language." *Jerusalem Studies in Arabic and Islam* 29 (2004): 281–340.

Safouan, Moustapha. *Why Are The Arabs Not Free?: The Politics of Writing*. Oxford: Wiley-Blackwell, 2007.

Scollon, Ron and Suzie Wong Scollon. *Discourses in Place: Language in the Material World*. London and New York: Routledge, 2003.

Sebba, Mark. *Spelling and Society: The Culture and Politics of Orthography around the World*. Cambridge: Cambridge University Press, 2007.

Shenker, Jack. *The Egyptians: A Radical Story*. London: Allen Lane, 2016.

Street, Brian. *Literacy in Theory and Practice*. Cambridge: Cambridge University Press, 1984.

Suleiman, Yasir. *The Arabic Language and National Identity: A Study in Ideology*. Edinburgh: Edinburgh University Press, 2003.

Suleiman, Yasir. "Charting the Nation: Arabic and the Politics of Identity." *Annual Review of Applied Linguistics* 26 (2006): 125–148.

Suleiman, Yasir. *Arabic, Self and Identity: A Study in Conflict and Displacement*. Oxford: Oxford University Press, 2011.

Wahba, Kassem M. "Arabic Language Use and the Educated Language User." In *Handbook for the Arabic Language Teaching Professionals in the 21st Century*, edited by K.M. Wahba, Z.A. Taha, and L. Englan, 139–155. Abingdon and New York: Routledge, 2013.

Woidich, Manfred. "Von Der Wörtlichen Rede Zur Sprachprosa: Zur Entwicklung Der Ägyptisch-Arabischen Dialektliteratur." In *Dialektliteratur heute – regional und international. Forschungskolloquium am Interdisziplinären Zentrum für Dialektforschung an der Friedrich-Alexander-Universität Erlangen-Nürnberg, 19.11.2009–20.11.2009*, edited by H.H. Munske, 63–94. Erlangen: Friedrich-Alexander-Universität Erlangen-Nürnberg, 2010. Retrieved (https://opus4.kobv.de/opus4-fau/files/1499/04_Woidich_Aegyptisch_Arabische_Dialektliteratur.pdf).

Wright, Sue. "What Is Language?: A Response to Philippe van Parijs." *Critical Review of International Social and Political Philosophy* 18, No. 2, (2015): 113–130.

Yaghan, Mohammad. "'Arabizi': a Contemporary Style of Arabic Slang." *Design Issues* 24, No. 2 (2008): 39–52.

Zack, Liesbeth. "'Leave, I Want to Have a Shower!': The Use of Humour on the Signs and Banners Seen during the Demonstrations in Tahrir Square." In *Between West and East: Festschrift for Wim Honselaar on the occasion of his 65th birthday*, edited by R. Genis, E. de Haard, J. Kalsbeek, E. Keizer, and J. Steltman, 711–729. Amsterdam: Pegasus, 2012.

INDEX

A

Abdel Fatah el-Sisi, 223
Abdel Fattah Al-Sisi, 76
Abu Dhabi, 85, 165, 167, 169,
    170, 173, 174, 181, 188–190,
    196–199, 219
Abu Dhabi Authority for Culture and
    Heritage, 199, 214, 219
Abu Dhabi book fair, 171, 214
Abu Dhabi Film Festival (ADFF), ix,
    165, 169–172, 177, 192, 193,
    198, 200, 201, 219
Abu Dhabi Media Zone Authority,
    171, 172, 199
Abu Dhabi Vision 2030, 169
Activism, xix, xx, xxv, xxvi, 7, 8, 11–13,
    47–49, 55, 62, 96, 207, 211
Activists, xviii, xx, xxiv, xxv, xxvi–xxviii,
    4, 5, 8, 10–12, 14, 40, 49, 62,
    90, 66, 67, 90, 91, 94–97, 99,
    101, 102, 175, 204, 209, 211,
    214–216
Afghanistan, 112, 198
Aflamnah, 173
Ahmet Davutoğlu, 148, 149
Ajyal Youth Film Festival, 169, 201

AKP, 147, 149
Aleppo, 92, 93, 101, 153
Algerian TV, 81
Al Hayat Media Center, 111, 127
Al Jazeera, 4, 40, 75, 76, 94, 109, 127,
    130, 169, 192, 220, 234, 249
Al Kataib Foundation, 111
Alliance Française, 170
Al-Qaʻida, 107–111, 126, 127
Alserkal Avenue, 169, 170, 174
Al-Shabaab, 107, 110–114, 116, 122,
    123, 127
Alternative public sphere, xxvii, 21,
    24, 36, 38
American University, x, 54, 58, 79, 83
Amman, 56, 83–85
Ammar 404, xviii
Anatolia, 151–153
Android, 113
Ankara, 149, 150, 156–158, 160
Anti-terror campaigns, 108, 109
Arab broadcasting industry, xxviii, 72,
    73, 82, 83
Arab Christian, 153
Arab despotism, 226
Arab Emirates, 48

© The Editor(s) (if applicable) and The Author(s) 2017
N. Lenze et al. (eds.), *Media in the Middle East*,
DOI 10.1007/978-3-319-65771-4

Arab feminist, 52
Arab Gulf, 165, 176, 178, 180, 185, 192, 194
Arab history, 71
Arabian Peninsula, 111, 167, 177
Arabic media, 71
Arabic publications, 71
Arabic vernaculars, 226
Arab media, 13, 14, 16, 72, 82–85, 155, 157, 166, 234
Arabsat, 74
Arab Spring, xxvi, xxvii, 3–12, 16, 17, 29, 65, 183, 228, 235, 243
Arab Uprisings, xv, xvi, xxvi, xxvii, 12, 16, 17, 47, 49, 55, 60, 64, 206
Arab women, 12, 15–17, 45, 47–50, 56, 58, 60, 62–64
Arab world, xv, xxv, xxvi, 4, 6, 9, 11, 12, 25, 51, 52, 55, 62, 63, 66, 71–75, 78, 81, 84, 89, 145, 147, 150–155, 158, 161, 173, 194, 203, 205–207, 211, 212, 215, 216, 224–227, 232, 234, 243, 249, 251, 252
ART, 36, 72, 77, 80, 85
Art Jameel, 169
Asia, xxvi, 40, 84, 108, 177, 193, 194, 202
Ask.fm, 112
Assad, xxviii, 97–99, 102
  Bashar el-Assad, 156
  Bassel al-Assad, 91
Associated Press, 118
AUK, 58, 64
Australia, 108, 187
'Ayat al-Qormezi, 207, 218

B
Baath, 91
Bahraini, 12, 165, 186, 205, 207, 219

Bahrain, xxix, 7, 8, 12, 52, 53, 165, 172, 175, 186, 203–210, 213, 214, 216–220
Balkans, 148, 150, 154
Bangalore, 74
Bashar al-Assad, 91, 92, 97, 98, 100, 101, 103, 160
Bashar el-Assad, 156
Bassel al-Assad, 91
Bataclan, 121
BBC, 39, 82, 118, 130–132, 135, 218, 234
Beirut, 71, 102, 160, 181
Ben Ali, xvi, xx–xxiii, xxvi, 83, 89
  Zine al Abidine Ben Ali, xv
Bin Laden, 109
Blogger, xv, xviii–xxi, xxiii, 5, 27, 28
Blogs, xvii–xix, 5, 29, 203, 204, 212, 213, 215, 216, 243
Boko Haram, 107, 110, 127, 128, 136
Bollywood, 74, 167, 172, 176, 178, 188–190, 199, 200
Bosphorus, 155, 158

C
Cairo, xxviii, 51, 59, 71, 76, 79, 80, 83, 110, 156, 160, 168, 184, 189, 232, 235, 246
Caucasus, 148
CCTV, 82, 121–123, 134, 135
Central Asia, 148, 154
Charlie Hebdo, 128, 130
China, 74, 82, 98, 175, 186, 189, 199
Christian, 153
Cinématographiques de Carthage, 168
Citizen journalism, xxvi, 4, 9, 10, 14–16
Citizenship, 14–16, 54, 175, 194
Civil moment, 37

Civil movement, 36
Civil society, xxiii, 9, 24
Civil war, 6, 51, 168
Classical Arabic, 146, 155, 224–226, 244, 247, 249
CNN, 82, 85, 109, 117, 132
Code of Ethics, 119
Colonialism, 166, 179, 182
Cowen, Tyler, 72, 83
Creative Culture Catalyst, 178
Creative Documentary Platform, 173
Creative Lab, 197
Cross–cultural perspective, 241
Cultural imperialism, 160, 169, 180
Cultural production, xxvi, xxviii, 108, 109, 121, 125, 128, 129, 168, 178, 203, 204, 206, 210, 211, 213, 215, 216
Cyberactivism, xxvii, 3, 4, 6, 7, 10, 14–17
Cyberactivists, xv, xvi, xix, 98, 99, 102
Cyber-realism, 12, 13
Cyberspace, 10, 47, 50, 63, 64
Cyberspeech, 241
Cyberwar, 10
Czech Republic, 187

D
Daesh, 180
Damascus, 92, 93, 99–102, 153, 156
Davutoğlu, 146, 148–150
Dawwār al-Lu'lu', 206, 207, 211, 214
Demonstrations, xviii–xxiii, 47, 59, 94, 96, 207, 230, 231, 235, 243, 250, 251
Deraa, 94, 101
Diaspora, 4, 8, 11–13, 30, 31, 37, 170, 191
Digital age, 13–16, 45, 47, 56, 62, 219

Digital content, 90
Digital global communication net-works, 108
Digital Media, xxvii, 114, 96
Digital Media City (DMC), 73, 74, 78, 79, 81–83, 85
Doha, 160, 165, 167, 169, 174
Doha Tribeca Film Festival, 169
Dubai, xxvii, 74, 75, 78–83, 85, 157, 165, 167, 169–174, 178, 182, 186, 188, 191, 194, 197–199
Dubai International Film Festival (DIFF), 169, 170, 173, 177, 186, 192, 193, 201
Dubai Knowledge Village, 79
Dubai Media City, xxviii, 73, 74, 78, 79, 81–85

E
East Africa, 176, 182–184, 189
Ebola, 118
Egypt, xxvi–xxx, 5, 6, 8, 10–12, 15–17, 48, 53, 59, 73, 75–79, 84, 89, 96, 146, 151, 153, 155, 156, 159, 173, 177, 178, 183, 201, 211, 215, 218, 223–225, 231, 234–236, 238–242, 244, 245, 246, 249–251
Egyptian, x, xv, xxviii, xxx, 5, 8, 11, 12, 14–16, 73, 76–80, 82–86, 94, 146, 155, 156, 160, 167, 173, 176, 198, 215, 219, 223, 224, 228, 231–246, 249–252
Egyptian Arabic, 80, 233–242, 244, 246, 249, 251, 252
Egyptian revolution, 5, 8, 14, 16, 223, 233, 245, 250
Egyptians, xxx, 8, 11, 80, 224, 233, 235, 240, 241, 244, 246
Electronic repression, 90, 91, 93

Electronic war, xxviii
Eltahawy, Mona, 60, 64, 65
Emirates Film Competition (EFC),
    167, 170, 172, 177, 186, 194,
    200, 201
Emirati, 60, 166–168, 170–176,
    181, 183, 189, 190, 193–195,
    197–200, 201, 206, 214
Emirati Cinema Campaign, 170
Emirati filmmaking, xxix, 166, 169, 170,
    173, 175, 177–179, 183, 184, 188,
    189, 191, 197, 198, 200–202
EMPC, xxviii, 73, 76–86
Encryption, 112
Erdoğan, 156, 157
Europe, xxvi, 66, 71, 72, 108, 148,
    150, 175, 178, 190, 200, 226

F
Facebook, xv, xvii, xx, xxiii, xxiv,
    xxvi, 4, 5, 7, 22, 24, 27, 29–33,
    35–37, 39, 40, 47, 55, 59, 62,
    65, 66, 89, 94, 95, 98, 110, 112,
    114, 130, 136, 203, 209, 212,
    217, 221, 230, 242, 244, 250
Fairouz, 246
Falsification, 10
Fatwa, fatwas, 58, 59, 108, 160
Femen, 62
Film cultures, 166, 167, 169, 170,
    177, 193, 200, 201
Film Institute, 83, 169
Film journal, 167, 198, 201
Freedom of speech, xvi–xix, xxix, 224,
    226, 228
Free Students, 94

G
3G, 38, 113
Gangnam Style, 37

Gender Gap, 48, 51–53, 55, 63, 65
Ghonim, Walid, 90
Global icon, 231
Globalization, 22, 37, 38, 42, 72, 73,
    75, 107, 109, 111, 169, 178,
    185, 191
Globalized neoliberalism, 166
Global trends, 72, 74
Goethe-Institut, 170, 198
Google, 113, 131
Google Play, 113
GoPro, 123, 135
Grand Theft Auto, 125
Green Movement in Iran, 49
Guggenheim, 169, 175
Gulf, 7, 48, 57, 157, 165, 170, 172,
    174–186, 189, 192, 193, 194,
    196–198, 203–205, 209, 210,
    212, 214–219
Gulf Film Festival, 167, 172, 177,
    200, 201

H
Habib Bourguiba, xvii
Hack, 10
Hallyuwood, xxix, 177, 191, 202
Hezbollah, 124, 180
Hijab, 32, 34–36, 40, 56, 179
Hijaz, 153
Hindi, 178, 183, 187, 189
Hollywood, 74, 76, 120, 125, 126,
    172, 173, 177, 178, 180, 181,
    186–194, 198, 199, 201, 202
Homonationalism, 181
Hosni Mubarak, 223
Human Rights Watch, 223, 248

I
Image Nation Abu Dhabi, 173, 189
India, 74, 82, 175, 199–201

Indignant Movement, xxii
Instagram, 30, 35, 112, 216
Instant messaging, 30
Intelligence Services, 90, 92, 96, 97
Interpol, 116
Iqraa TV, 110
Iran, xxv, xxvii, xxx, 21, 22, 24, 25,
    28–30, 34, 35, 37–40, 98, 173,
    181, 184
Iranian, 22–25, 27, 30–33, 35–40, 95,
    99, 175, 176, 183, 194
Iranian Green Movement, xxiv, 30
Iraq, 52, 53, 111–113, 130, 159, 183
ISIS, xxiii, 60, 63, 111, 125–127,
    130, 131, 135, 136
Islam, 58–62, 62, 65, 152, 153, 172,
    179, 200, 201, 212, 225
Islamic Revolution, xxvii, 23, 36
Islamic State, 28, 38, 51, 107, 110–113,
    117, 124–128, 135, 136
Islamophobia, 183, 200
Islamophobic, 181
Italy, 77
iTunes, 170

J
Jeddah, 77
Jerusalem, 153, 246
Jihad, 62, 66, 108, 130, 131, 136,
    152
Jordan, xxviii, 48, 53, 56, 73, 75,
    77–81, 85, 86, 173, 176, 183,
    188
Jordan Media City (JMC), xxviii, 73,
    77, 78, 80–83, 85, 86
Jordan Production Company, 73
Journalists, xv, xx–xxii, 4–6, 9, 11, 47,
    71, 113, 114, 119, 128, 225
Justice and Development Party, 147,
    149
JustPast.it, 112

K
K24 TV, 115
Kafala, 175
K-drama, 177, 178, 191
Kenya, 111, 115, 119, 132–135
Khaja's Scene Film Club, 170
Khaleeji, 165, 168, 172, 181
Kollywood, 189, 200
Kuwait, xxvii, xxx, 47–56, 58, 64,
    165, 170, 172, 175, 186, 190,
    203, 210, 213, 214, 216

L
LBGTQ, 176
Lebanese, 186, 215, 246, 249
Lebanon, 52, 53, 124, 151, 159, 195,
    201
Liberation Square, 231, 232
Linguascape, xxx, 224, 228, 236, 243
Little Lagos, 191
London, 71, 116, 129, 133–135, 218
Louvre, 169

M
MAD Solutions, 173
Mahmud Ahmadinejad, 23
Mahmud Darwish, 205, 209
Malayalam, 183, 189
Mariam al Mansour, 60
Mazzika TV, 80
Media, xv, xvi, xx–xxiv, xxv–xxx,
    4–13, 22–25, 28, 29, 35–38,
    47, 57, 59, 62, 64, 71–79,
    81–83, 203, 204, 206, 209, 210,
    216, 217, 219, 224, 230, 234,
    249, 250
Media cities, xxviii, 72–79, 81–85
Media ecologies, 193
Media networks, xv, xxviii, 37, 108,
    110, 120, 121, 125, 128

Media Production, xxix, 71, 73, 111, 125, 127, 174
Media Revolution, 38
Media Speed Company, 74
Mediterranean Sea, 167, 189
Melody, 80
MENA, 48, 168, 171, 177, 179, 184, 192, 202
#ItsMensTurn, 35
Mernissi, Fatima, 52, 60
Metropolitan Museum of New York, 169
Middle East Broadcasting Center (MBC), 72, 80–82, 86, 151
Middle East Studies Association, 16, 17, 21, 170
Militarism, 120
Mobilization, xix, xxii, 4–6, 11, 13, 14, 62, 215, 244
Mobilizing, xviii, xx, 62, 191, 209
Modernities, 166, 178, 179
Modern Standard Arabic, 176, 213, 215, 225, 233, 249
Mohamed Bouazizi, xvi, xviii–xx
Mollywood, 189
Morocco, 48, 53, 74, 84, 151, 176, 181, 251
Mubarak, 8, 76, 89, 156, 223, 231, 235, 250
Mujahideen, 113, 123
Mukhabarat, 92, 95
Musalsa, 145
Musalsalat, 145, 146
Museum of Islamic Art, 169
Muslim, 52, 55, 56, 58–60, 62, 149, 151–154, 160, 226
Muslim Brotherhood, 76, 219
Mustafa Kemal Atatürk, 147
My Stealthy Freedom, 31, 33–36

N
Nairobi, 111, 113, 114, 121, 131, 134
Nasserist, 242

National Disaster Operations Centre, 115
Networking, 4, 5, 8, 11, 13, 64, 110, 112
New media, xxvii, 4, 6, 7, 10, 13, 15–17, 21–23, 25, 28–30, 35, 37, 38, 47–49, 52, 56, 60, 62–64, 73, 74, 79, 112, 203, 204
New Zealand, 177, 184, 185, 187, 188
The New York Times, 118, 129, 136
Nigeria, 177, 178, 190
Niqab, 56
Nobel prize, 12
North Africa, xv, 60, 62

O
Occupy Movement, xxii
Oman, 48, 53, 73, 203, 214
Online Activism, xv–xix, xxii–xxiv, xxvi, 8, 211
Online mobilization, xvii
Online sphere, 206, 209, 211
Opinion prisoners, xviii
Orbit, 72, 83
Ottoman Empire, 147–149, 152–154

P
Pakistan, 75, 82, 112
Palestine, 48, 49, 56, 153, 154
Paris, 71, 119, 121, 123, 129, 133–135
Pearl Roundabout, 206, 214
Platform, xvii, xxix, 24, 35, 36, 204
Poetry, xxix, 197, 200, 203–207, 209, 210, 212–218, 231, 243, 250
Political change, xxvi, 3, 7, 14, 63, 211, 244
Protest, xv, xix, xx, xxiv, xxviii, xxix, 12, 204–207, 209, 210, 214, 216, 232–235, 240

Q
Qatar, 48, 53, 151, 159, 203, 204
Qumra Film Festival, 169, 201
Qur'an, 50, 55, 86, 224–226, 233, 247

R
Raha Moharrak, 62
Ramada, 145
Ramadan, 54
Reality TV, 127
Recep Tayyip Erdoğan, 147
Red Sea, 167, 189
2.0 Revolution, xv, xxvi, 15
Revolution, xvi, xix, xxii, xxiv, 5, 89,
    94, 97, 100, 12, 217, 224, 231,
    233–235, 244, 245, 250, 251
Riyadh, 57, 74
Rome, 71

S
Satellite TV, xxv, xxvii, 49, 71, 74, 84
Saudi Arabia, xxvii, 6, 48, 51, 53, 62,
    74, 77, 82, 84, 203, 204, 212, 214
Saudi Arabian, 151
Saudi Broadcasting Center (SBC), 80,
    86
Second Life, 178
Self-expression, 4, 5, 14, 211
September 11, 84, 107, 117, 126,
    132, 136
Sharjah Biennale, 169, 186
Shaykh Yusuf al-Qaradawi, 212
Shi'i, 206, 209
Sidi Bouzid, xx, xxi
Silicon Valley, 74
Silk Road, 153
Singapore, 21, 100, 177, 184–186, 188
Skype, xxi, 89, 95
Slacktivism, 7, 211, 219
SNS, 22, 29, 30, 35, 37, 38

Soap operas, xxix, 25, 145, 146,
    150–152, 154–161
Social media, xv, xvi, xx–xxiv, xxvi–
    xxviii, 4, 5, 7–13, 22–24, 28–32,
    34, 36–38, 40, 89–91, 94, 97,
    99, 211, 218, 230, 234, 242,
    246, 250, 251
Social networking, 64
Social networks, xvii, xix, xxiii, 24, 27,
    29, 36, 38, 55
Sociolinguistic, xxx, 224, 226–228,
    230, 233, 234, 236, 237, 240,
    241, 243–245, 251
Soft power, xxix, 130, 146, 149, 150,
    191
Somalia, 112, 113, 115, 131
South Africa, 190, 191
South Asia, 182, 184, 186, 189, 200
South Korea, 177, 191, 199
Story-telling, 190, 192, 200
Studios, 76, 77, 79
Suicide bombers, 116
Suleiman the Magnificent, 152, 153, 157
The Sultan's Harem, 156
Sunni, 7, 60, 160, 209
Syria, xxiv, xxviii, xxx, 4, 6, 7, 15–17,
    90–97, 99–103, 112, 123, 130,
    135, 146, 147, 151, 153, 156,
    159, 160
Syrian, xxiv, 8, 10, 12, 13, 89, 90–94,
    97–103, 118, 146, 155, 156,
    160, 161
Syrian Computer Company, 91
Syrian Electronic Army, 10, 98, 102,
    103, 118
Syrian opposition, 8, 12, 13
Syrian revolution, xxiv, 160

T
Tahrir Square, 5, 60, 231, 232, 240,
    243, 250

Taliban, 107, 111, 128, 131
Tehran, 22, 23
Telegram, 30, 31
Telenovelas, 146, 155
Televangelist, 110
Television series, 145, 150
Terror, 128, 130, 132–136
    terrorism, xxviii, 98, 107, 108, 117,
        119, 122, 125, 126, 128, 129
    terrorists, xxiii, xxviii, 108, 109,
        111, 113–115, 118, 120, 122,
        124, 125, 127–129, 197
Terrorism, xxviii, 109, 118, 120, 121,
    129–136
Terrorists, xxiii, xxviii, 108–115,
    118–120, 122, 124, 125,
    127–129, 184, 197
Tollywood, 189
Tor, 97
Tourism and Culture Authority, 177,
    198
Traditional media, xxiv, xxvii, xxx,
    109, 113, 118, 215
Tumblr, 112
Tunisia, xv–xxiv, xxvi, xxx, 5, 7, 10,
    12, 48, 52, 53, 62, 74, 84, 89,
    94, 96, 176, 201, 205, 212, 251
Tunisian Revolution, xv, xvi, xxii, xxiv,
    xxvi
Turkey, xxv, xxvii, xxix, xxx, 48, 99,
    146–154, 156–161, 177
    Turkish, xxix, 49, 146, 147, 150, 151
    Turkish Republic, 147
Turkish, xxix, 147, 150, 151, 158,
    160, 161, 146–148, 150–152,
    154–161
Turkish Republic, 147
Twitter, xv, xvii, xx, xxviii, 4, 5, 7, 22,
    24, 29, 30, 37, 39, 40, 47, 65,
    89, 94, 97, 98, 110, 112–118,

    125, 128, 130–133, 136, 203,
        212, 215, 230, 237, 238, 246
Twitter Revolution, xv, 29
Twofour54, 85, 171, 197–201
Tyler, Amina, 62

U
UK, 31, 52, 74, 172, 188, 200
United Arab Emirates (UAE), xxix,
    xxx, 48, 53, 73, 75, 77–79,
    157, 165–167, 169, 170, 172,
    173, 175–179, 181–184, 186,
    188–192, 194–201, 203, 204,
    213, 214
United States (US), 7, 52, 108, 111,
    112, 117, 118, 125, 126, 130,
    131, 154, 175, 178, 180–182,
    185, 187, 190, 199–201
Uprising, xvi, xix, xxvi, xxviii, 4, 6, 7,
    12, 37, 62, 66, 90, 93, 94, 96,
    98, 203, 205–207, 209, 215,
    218, 223, 224, 228, 230, 231,
    233, 235, 236, 240, 241, 243,
    244, 246, 250, 251
Urdu, 178, 183, 187
U.S. State Department, 112, 125

V
Vernacularization, 241–244, 246, 251
Viber, 30, 40, 112
Virtual Terrorist Attacks, 116
VPN, 39, 97

W
Wadjda, 50, 51, 65
Warehouse 421, 169
Web 2.0, 39, 206, 213, 242

Western culture, 23, 37, 126
Westgate Mall, 111, 113–116, 118,
    121–123, 132, 134
WhatsApp, 30, 112
wi-fi, 113
Wikipedia, 117, 243
Williams, Pharrell, 22
Women's empowerment, 45, 48–53,
    55, 58, 62, 63
World Cup, 174
World Economic Forum, 48, 65
World Trade Center, 119

Y
Yemen, 6, 12, 53, 153
YouTube, xxix, 6, 7, 22, 93, 94, 117,
    130, 136, 170, 178, 197, 203,
    204, 209, 210, 212, 215, 216, 218

Z
Zayed University Middle East Film
    Festival, 171

CPI Antony Rowe
Chippenham, UK
2017-12-06 15:14